MW00772839

BLACK MALE TEACHERS: DIVERSIFYING THE UNITED STATES' TEACHER WORKFORCE

ADVANCES IN RACE AND ETHNICITY IN EDUCATION

Series Editor: Chance W. Lewis and
James L. Moore III

ADVANCES IN RACE AND ETHNICITY IN
EDUCATION   VOLUME 1

BLACK MALE TEACHERS: DIVERSIFYING THE UNITED STATES' TEACHER WORKFORCE

EDITED BY

CHANCE W. LEWIS

The University of North Carolina at Charlotte, NC, USA

IVORY A. TOLDSON

Howard University, Washington, DC, USA

United Kingdom – North America – Japan
India – Malaysia – China

Emerald Group Publishing Limited
Howard House, Wagon Lane, Bingley BD16 1WA, UK

First edition 2013

British Library Cataloguing in Publication Data
A catalogue record for this book is available from the British Library

ISBN: 978-1-78190-621-7
ISSN: 2051-2317 (Series)

ISOQAR certified
Management System,
awarded to Emerald
for adherence to
Environmental
standard
ISO 14001:2004.

Certificate Number 1985
ISO 14001

INVESTOR IN PEOPLE

CONTENTS

LIST OF CONTRIBUTORS

Chike Akua	Howard University, Washington, DC, USA
Jamil Alhassan	Creative Arts Morgan Village Academy High School, Camden, NJ, USA
Margarita Bianco	University of Colorado Denver, Denver, CO, USA
Gloria S. Boutte	University of South Carolina, Columbia, SC, USA
Ed Brockenbrough	University of Rochester, Rochester, NY, USA
Lawrence M. Clark	University of Maryland, College Park, MD, USA
Erin Croke	The City University of New York, New York, NY, USA
Candice Crowell	University of Georgia, Athens, GA, USA
Travis Dale	The City University of New York, New York, NY, USA
Julius Davis	Bowie State University, Bowie, MD, USA
William Ebenstein	The City University of New York, New York, NY, USA
Leslie T. Fenwick	Howard University, Washington, DC, USA
Lamont A. Flowers	Clemson University, Clemson, SC, USA
Toya Jones Frank	University of Maryland, College Park, MD, USA

Tambra O. Jackson	University of South Carolina. Columbia, SC, USA
Khary Golden	LEAP Academy University Charter School, Camden, NJ, USA
Camesha Hill-Carter	Southeast Missouri State University, Cape Girardeau, MO, USA
Nancy Leech	University of Colorado Denver, Denver, CO, USA
Chance W. Lewis	University of North Carolina at Charlotte, Charlotte, NC, USA
Randy R. Miller Sr.	LEAP Academy University Charter School, Camden, NJ, USA
James L. Moore III	The Ohio State University, Columbus, OH, USA
Curtis L. Morris	Education Consultant, Memphis, TN, USA
Vivian Gunn Morris	University of Memphis, Memphis, TN, USA
Justin Newell	LEAP Academy University Charter School, Camden, NJ, USA
Shafeeq Rashid	Georgia Military College, Milledgeville, GA, USA
Dawn Nicole Hicks Tafari	University of North Carolina at Greensboro, Greensboro, NC, USA
Ivory A. Toldson	Howard University, Washington, DC, USA
Kara Mitchell Viesca	University of Colorado Denver, Denver, CO, USA
Chezare A. Warren	University of Pennsylvania, Philadelphia, PA, USA
Brandy S. Wilson	Appalachian State University, Boone, NC, USA
Kamilah M. Woodson	Howard University, Washington, DC, USA

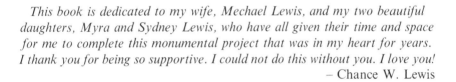

This book is dedicated to my wife, Mechael Lewis, and my two beautiful daughters, Myra and Sydney Lewis, who have all given their time and space for me to complete this monumental project that was in my heart for years. I thank you for being so supportive. I could not do this without you. I love you!
– Chance W. Lewis

Thank you to my family, friends, and colleagues who gave me early support and encouragement for this project. This book is dedicated to my wife, Marshella, for her undying support, patience, and critiquing, and my daughter, Makena, for inspiring me to aim higher. Thanks to my first teachers: my mother, Johnita Scott, and my father Ivory L. Toldson.
– Ivory A. Toldson

BLACK MALE TEACHERS: DIVERSIFYING THE UNITED STATES' TEACHER WORKFORCE

Black Male Teachers: Diversifying the United States' Teacher Workforce, is the first book in the series, Advances in Race and Ethnicity in Education. The book represents a collective effort between research scholars, policy experts, and in-service Black Male Teachers. Through this book, we affirm the values of teacher preparation that we introduced in our call for chapters. *Black Male Teachers* is a book to provide Black male teachers with the resources to advance in the profession, teacher education programs with needed training materials to accommodate Black male students, and school district administrators with information to help recruit and retain Black male teachers. Each chapter features policy and practice recommendations and a case example to spur action and increase opportunities for discussion.

The unique role of Black male teachers in American society is a subject of interest, debate, and speculation. Most researchers and other observers agree that the dearth of Black male teachers contributes to systemic issues in schools, such as cultural bias and stereotype threat, which directly or indirectly diminish the performance of Black students.

The U.S. Census estimates that 118,124 teachers in the United States are Black men, making them 1.8 percent of the active teaching force. Teachers comprise the largest professional occupation in the United States; accounting for the most professional employees among college-educated White women, Black women, and Black men. Despite the large number of teachers relative to other professions held by college educated Black men, they represent less than 2 percent of the teaching force, of a student body that is 7 percent Black male. By comparison, White female teachers comprise 63 percent of the teaching force, of a student body that is 27 percent White female. Considering the entire student body, the United States has one White female teacher for every 15 students and one Black male teacher for every 534 students.

Males of all races are underrepresented in the U.S. teaching force. The percent of White male P-12 students is twice the percent of White male teachers; the percent of Black male students is more than three times the percent of Black male teachers; and the percent of Hispanic male students is almost seven times the percent of Hispanic male teachers. The over-representation of White female teachers may mitigate some issues associated with the lower number of White male teachers, because they have cultural alignment with White males. However, irrespective of gender, Black and Hispanic teachers are underrepresented in the U.S. teaching force. Nationally, Black and Hispanic boys spend the majority of their school experiences under cross-gender and cross-cultural supervision.

Several reasons account for the dearth of Black male teachers. First, Black males are less likely to graduate from college. In the U.S. population, 16 percent of Black males and 19 percent of Black females have completed college. Second, Black males are less likely to major in education. In 2009, 7,603 Black males and 25,725 Black females graduated from college with a degree in education. Third, Black males who graduate with a degree in education are less likely to become a teacher. Only 23 percent of Black men with a degree in education become a P-12 teacher, compared to 27 percent for White men, 41 percent for Black women, and 42 percent for White women. Interestingly, Black men are more likely than any other race gender group to become educational administrators. Almost 7 percent of Black males with a degree in education become educational administrators, compared to 5 percent for Black females and White males, and only 2.8 percent for White females. "Managers" was one of the top five occupations for Black and White males with a degree in education.

The disproportionate number of Black students who are suspended, placed in special education, and do not graduate with their cohort suggest problems related to equity and inclusion in U.S. educational systems. One obvious solution to underachievement among Black students is to diversify the teaching force. Tripling the number of Black male teachers and maintaining the number of Black female teachers would make Black teachers representative of the Black student body, but more action is required to remove deep and persistent barriers for Black students.

Recently, because of an edict from U.S. Secretary of Education Arne Duncan, the media began to romanticize the idea of having more Black male teachers. For example, CNN.com posed the question, "Is placing Black men in the classroom the answer to solving some of the problems in the Black community such as gang violence, high school dropout rates, and fatherless homes?" We understand that role models are important, and Black male teachers have a strategic position to interact with Black male students 5 days a week. However, recent media coverage on the lack of Black male teachers has led to many misconceptions. Many falsely believe that Black male teachers have a primary responsibility to foster the social development of Black male students. However, increasing the presence of Black male and female teachers improves the diversity of the profession, and should be viewed as a benefit to the system, as they provide quality services to all students regardless of race or gender.

In short, the United States needs a teaching force that is drastically more diverse to represent the current demographics of the P-12 student population. However, more importantly, educational administrators should enforce the policy that every teacher, regardless of race or gender, is prepared to teach any student. White female teachers especially, as the professions' majority, should gain the tools of cultural competence to serve any student regardless of their racial background or gender. Increasing the number of Black male teachers is important, but as a minority in the teaching profession, Black male teachers should not become props for shortcoming in the educational systems. Black male teachers need to be properly trained to meet the needs of all students and all teachers need to be properly trained to teach Black students. It is prudent policy to promote diversity in the teaching force, but irresponsible practice to assign roles and responsibilities based on race.

Chance W. Lewis
Ivory A. Toldson
Volume Editors

SECTION I
INTRODUCTION

CHAPTER 1

BLACK MALE TEACHERS' PATH TO U.S. K-12 CLASSROOMS: FRAMING THE NATIONAL DISCUSSION

Chance W. Lewis

ABSTRACT

Currently, the field of education has been seeking innovative strategies to increase the representation of Black male teachers in U.S. classrooms. In this chapter, the author presents a status report of Black male teachers' path to U.S. K-12 public school classrooms at six critical stages. These stages include the following: (a) Black males with a high school diploma; (b) enrollment in educator preparation programs; (c) educator preparation program completers; (d) educator preparation programs with the highest number of Black male graduates; (e) Black male education degree holders that select teaching as a profession; and (f) the current status of Black male teachers in U.S. K-12 public schools. Based on the data presented in this chapter, recommendations are provided to the field of education to improve their representation for the benefit of all students. Additionally, the critical need for this timely book is discussed.

Black Male Teachers: Diversifying the United States' Teacher Workforce
Advances in Race and Ethnicity in Education, Volume 1, 3–14
Copyright © 2013 by Emerald Group Publishing Limited
All rights of reproduction in any form reserved
ISSN: 2051-2317/doi:10.1108/S2051-2317(2013)0000001005

Over the past 20 years, scholarly and media attention has focused on an emerging trend related to the demographic composition of the U.S. teaching force – the relatively small percentage of Black male teachers in our nation's classrooms. As an example, United States Secretary of Education Arne Duncan and Filmmaker Spike Lee, in March 2012, announced a 5-year national initiative to recruit, train, and place more than 80,000 Black male teachers into U.S. classrooms by 2015 to benefit all learners (see http://1.usa.gov/N83taH). To examine this issue, scholarly investigations over these past two decades by scholars (e.g., Dr. Marvin Lynn, Dr. H. Richard Milner, Dr. Tyrone Howard, Dr. Chance W. Lewis, Dr. Ivory A. Toldson, and countless others) have sought to understand issues related to the work lives of current Black male teachers, incentives needed to recruit this population to teaching, and how this population understands their importance as role models to all students in the field of education. However, the fundamental question for this important book is, "What does an examination of the pipeline tell us about the future representation of Black males in teaching"? To examine the future outlook of Black males in the teaching ranks, we will take a brief journey and examine the pipeline to teaching for this population.

PIPELINE STAGE 1: BLACK MALES WITH A HIGH SCHOOL DIPLOMA

As we take this brief journey, it is imperative that we know how many Black males 18 years and older in the United States currently have a high school diploma or GED. This is an important criterion in the eligibility to become a teacher – all candidates must have a high school diploma or GED and a postsecondary degree. At this stage of the pipeline, we examine the number of Black males that meet this first criterion. By having this credential, Black males are eligible to pursue postsecondary options. Considering this criterion, Fig. 1 provides us with insight on the status of Black males at this stage of the pipeline to teaching.

Table 1 highlights that 10,305,000 Black men over 18 years of age have a high school diploma or a GED. Additionally, this data illustrates that this is approximately 83% of the total Black male population. We also learn that despite misconceptions constantly portrayed by the corporate media, a large percentage of Black males have completed high school or a GED equivalent. This data allows us to understand the cohort of Black males

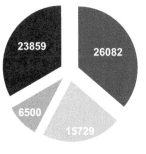

■ Black Full-Time Undergraduate
▨ Black Full-Time Graduate
▦ Black Part-Time Undergraduate
■ Black Part-Time Graduate

Fig. 1. Black Postsecondary Students in Educator Preparation Programs. *Source*: American Association of Colleges for Teacher Education (2010). Programs include all those that prepare individuals to work with P-12 schools are not exclusively preparation programs for teaching candidates.

Table 1. Black Males Educational Attainment – High School Diploma or GED Over 18 Years of Age.

No. of Black Males with a High School Diploma or GED Over 18 Years Old	Total No. of Black Males in U.S. Over 18 Years Old	Percent
10,305,000	12,351,000	83%

Source: United States Census Bureau (2010).

that pass this stage of the pipeline that meet the initial eligibility requirements to become classroom teachers in our nation's schools.

PIPELINE STAGE 2: BLACK POSTSECONDARY STUDENTS IN EDUCATOR PREPARATION PROGRAMS

The next stage of the educational pipeline highlights the number of Black postsecondary students in education programs at U.S. colleges and universities. While data is not readily available on specifically the number of Black

6

CHANCE W. LEWIS

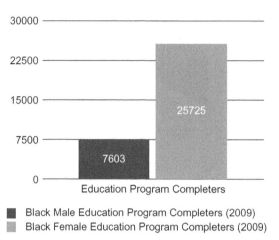

Fig. 2. Black Male Educator Program Completers (2011). *Source*: Toldson (2011a).

males in educator preparation programs, we are able to get a snapshot of Black students that are pursuing the field of education as a career option. Fig. 2 provides with a snapshot of full-time and part-time Black students by undergraduate and graduate status.

Based on current data, Fig. 1 reveals that 26,082 Black students in 2009 were enrolled as full-time undergraduate students in educator preparation programs at U.S. institutions. Additionally, another 15,729 Black students are enrolled in educator preparation programs as graduate students. When we examine part-time students that are Black, we learn that 6,500 Black students were enrolled at the undergraduate level and another 23,859 were enrolled at the graduate level in 2009. Considering the number of Black male and female students, we learn that educator preparation programs have a steady flow of Black students pursuing the field of education. It is also important to note that education is the top collegiate major choice for Black males (Toldson, 2011b). Also, it is still important to note that educator preparation programs are primarily composed of White female teachers (American Legislative Exchange Council, 2012).

PIPELINE STAGE 3: BLACK MALE EDUCATOR PROGRAM COMPLETERS

Our next stage of the pipeline provides us with data on the number of Black males that complete educator preparation programs that are now eligible to pursue teaching options after successful completion of any state testing and licensing requirements. Fig. 2 highlights that 7,603 Black males in comparison to 25,725 Black females that completed the degree requirements in 2009 to be eligible to pursue employment as classroom teachers in U.S. schools and school districts. When we focus specifically on Black teachers, we see the large disparity in the production of Black male versus Black female teachers that are completing educator preparation programs.

PIPELINE STAGE 4: UNDERGRADUATE TEACHER PREPARATION PROGRAMS WITH THE HIGHEST NUMBERS OF BLACK MALE GRADUATES (2011)

In Stage 4, data highlights the top 10 teacher preparation programs across the United States that produce the greatest number of Black male teacher graduates from educator preparation programs. Based on this data, the education community, particularly the scholarly community should investigate these educator preparation programs to understand how they are successful in recruiting, retaining, and graduating Black males and

Table 2. Undergraduate Teacher Preparation Programs with the Highest Numbers of Black Male Graduates (2011).

Rank	Institution	State	No. of Black Male Graduates
1	Southern Illinois University-Carbondale	IL	75
2	Virginia State University[a]	VA	51
3	Albany State University[a]	GA	32
4	Alabama A&M University[a]	AL	31
5	Mississippi State University	MS	30
6	Alabama State University[a]	AL	29
7	Grambling State University[a]	LA	28
8	South Carolina State University[a]	SC	26
9	Elizabeth City State University[a]	NC	25
10	Jackson State University[a]	MS	24

Source: Diverse Issues in Higher Education (2012).
[a]Indicates a historically Black college or university.

placing these students on a path to become classroom teachers in our nation's schools (Table 2) (Diverse Issues, 2012).

PIPELINE STAGE 5: BLACK MALE EDUCATOR DEGREE HOLDERS THAT SELECT TEACHING

Stage 5 is a very important stage of the pipeline given the fact that all students who complete educator preparation programs do not choose to pursue employment in the field of education. As a result, Fig. 3 provides us with the percentage of Black males who have completed postsecondary programs at U.S. colleges and universities that chose to pursue employment as teachers in public schools and school districts. According to Fig. 3, only 23% of Black males that completed educator preparation programs chose to select teaching as a career in comparison to 27% of White males, 41% of Black females, and 42% of White females. While data is not available to explain why such as small percentage chose to pursue teaching, research (Lewis, 2006) highlights many career options are now available to this population so schools and school districts must do a better job in the recruitment process for this population.

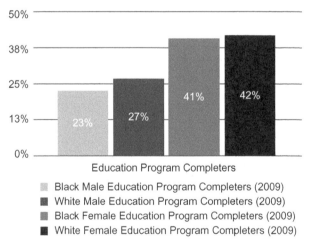

Education Program Completers

- Black Male Education Program Completers (2009)
- White Male Education Program Completers (2009)
- Black Female Education Program Completers (2009)
- White Female Education Program Completers (2009)

Fig. 3. Black Male Educator Degree Holders that Select Teaching. *Source*: Toldson (2011a).

PIPELINE STAGE 6: CURRENT STATUS OF BLACK MALES IN TEACHING IN COMPARISON TO BLACK MALE STUDENTS IN U.S. SCHOOLS

Our final stage of investigation into the pipeline to teaching for Black males allows us to examine the current status of this population in the teaching force in comparison to the number of Black male students in the U.S. public K-12 schools. This data is important for us to understand so we can examine what work needs to be done in the future. According to Fig. 4, Black male students represent 7.39% of the student population. In comparison, Black male teachers comprise 1.81% of the teaching population. This data is important to bring to our attention given that this is the largest disparity by race and gender when compared to student demographics in U.S. public schools (Toldson & Lewis, 2012).

Our final stage of investigation into the pipeline to teaching for Black males allows us to examine the current status of this population in the teaching force in comparison to the number of Black male students in the U.S. public K-12 schools. This data highlights the work that needs to be done in the future. According to Fig. 4, Black male students represent 7.39% of the student population. In comparison, Black male teachers comprise 1.81% of the teaching population.

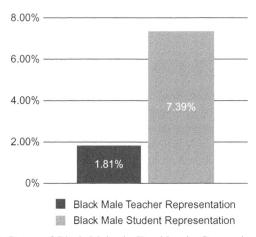

Fig. 4. Current Status of Black Males in Teaching in Comparison to Black Male Students in U.S. Schools. *Source*: Toldson (2011a).

WHAT CAN THE FIELD OF EDUCATION LEARN FROM AN EXAMINATION OF THE TEACHER PIPELINE FOR BLACK MALES?

Considering our brief examination of the pipeline to teaching for Black males, we understand from our pipeline analysis that we have to continue to encourage Black males to enter postsecondary options and pursue the field of education. As previously mentioned, the field of education is the top collegiate choice for Black males in postsecondary settings; however, we must encourage more to enter into the pipeline to teaching. To aid in this endeavor, programs such as the Call Me Mister program (see http://www.clemson.edu/hehd/departments/education/research/callmemister/) at Clemson University should be replicated nationally to encourage Black males into the field of education. Additionally, initiatives such as those started by U.S. Secretary of Education Arne Duncan are noteworthy; however, we must continue to watch closely the impact that this ambitious initiative has on the pipeline to teaching for Black males.

Finally, the research literature (Lewis, 2006) informs us that Black males are open to pursuing the field of education. So, a fundamental question that we should consider is as follows: Why do we need Black male teachers? In our opinion, we need more Black male teachers to demonstrate that this population is more than capable to educate the next generation of 21st century learners to meet their full academic potential. Additionally, since most students want to become like those they see, Black males are important role models for all students.

The Critical Need for this Edited Volume

This edited volume, *Black Male Teachers: Diversifying the United States' Teaching Force*, seeks to offer readers a comprehensive examination of the status of this population related to recruitment, retention, and the work lives of Black male teachers in U.S. classrooms. The research and ideas presented in this book expand our knowledge base to paint a clearer picture of issues surrounding this unique population in the U.S. teaching force. Across many sectors of society, different constituents, particularly school districts, have been thirsty for information and scholarly examinations as to how they can increase their recruitment and retention efforts of Black male teachers. This edited volume, hopefully, will assist readers to understand some of the complex and key issues faced by Black males who have decided to pursue a career path in the field of education. An additional hope for this publication is that it will motivate readers to make a commitment to improve education initiatives to bring more Black males into our nation's classrooms. This volume is comprised into 5 sections and 18 chapters. What follows is a brief overview of the chapters in these five sections.

SECTION I: INTRODUCTION

Section I of this edited volume comprises two chapters. It begins with this one. In Chapter 2, co-editor, Ivory A. Toldson presents snapshots of key issues as to why race matters when it comes to the race of the teacher in the K-12 classroom. The content from this chapter is timely and informative.

SECTION II: SCHOLARLY EXAMINATIONS OF BLACK MALE TEACHERS IN U.S. CLASSROOMS

Section II comprises 10 chapters. The authors are concerned with factors that impact the recruitment, retention, and work lives of Black male teachers. Each chapter makes a unique contribution to the edited volume. In Chapter 3, Ed Brockenbrough presents a chapter entitled, *Educating the Race in Postmodern Times: The Intraracial Border Crossings of Black Male Teachers*. In this chapter, he explores the intraracial divides that confounded Black male teachers with Black students and local Black communities. In Chapter 4, Erin Croke, Travis Dale, and William Ebenstein presents a chapter entitled *Recruiting Teachers from Within: Career Ladders for Paraprofessional Educators*. These authors conclude that the opportunities for Black males that are paraprofessionals are ripe opportunities for recruiting this population to become classroom teachers. Chapter 5 entitled *Teaching across Gender: The Dynamics of Black Male Teachers and Female Students* by Candice Crowell, Kamlah M. Woodson and Shafeeq Rashid provides us with important information on Black male teachers' interactions with female students. These authors highlight the dynamics of teaching across gender and present five factors for Black male teachers to consider when teaching female students. In Chapter 6 entitled, *The Case of a Black Male Mathematics Teacher Teaching in a Unique Urban Context: Implications for Recruiting Black Male Mathematics Teachers*, Julius Davis, Toya Jones, and Lawrence Clark provide a key contribution examining Black male Algebra I teachers in an urban school district. Implications from this chapter can increase the number of Black male mathematics teachers in urban schools. Chapter 7 entitled, *I Can Get at these Kids: A Narrative Study Exploring the Reasons Black Men Teach* by Dawn Nicole Hicks Tafari amplifies the voices of Black male teachers who serve as walking counter-narratives for the young males they teach. We learn from this chapter key themes that influence these Black male participants to become teachers. In Chapter 8 entitled, *No One Told Us: Recruiting and Retaining African American Males in the College of Education Program from the Urban and Rural Areas*, Camesha Hill-Carter highlights Black male perspectives as to how Predominately White Institutions (PWIs) can recruit and retain Black males in their teacher preparation programs. This chapter serves as valuable information for PWIs seeking to diversify their student populations with Black males. Chapter 9 entitled, *Double-Talking: The Complexities Surrounding Black Male Teachers as Both Problems and Solutions* by Tambra O. Jackson, Gloria S. Boutte, and Brandy S. Wilson explore the weightiness of viewing Black males as the panacea for educational and social issues in schools. This chapter provides valuable information on how Black males are seen as saviors and superheroes on issues related to Black males in urban schools. In Chapter 10, Kara Mitchell, Margarita Bianco, and Nancy Leech contribute a chapter entitled, *Pathways to Teaching: The Perspectives and Experiences of Two Black Male Teens Considering Teaching as a Career* describes a pre-collegiate course designed to explore teaching. The findings from this chapter provide substantial guidance for the improvement of educational policy and practice to increase the recruitment and retention of Black male teachers. Chapter 11 entitled, *A Call for African American Male Teachers: The Supermen Expected to Solve the Problems of Low-Performing Schools* by Vivian Gunn Morris and Curtis L. Morris explore the lives of Black teachers who serve as key mentors and balance the unfair weight of being labeled as Supermen expected to solve all problems of challenging urban schools. Based on the results of the chapter, prospective Black male teachers can be encouraged as to how to navigate the teaching profession as a Black male. In the final chapter (Chapter 12) of this section entitled, *Being Black, Being Male, and Choosing to Teach in the 21st Century: Understanding My Role, Embracing My Call*, Chezare A. Warren provides a memoir of a few significant lessons learned during his teacher preparation program and his early professional teaching practice. Based on this unique reflection, he provides recommendations to build and cultivate professional relationships with school stakeholders, capitalize on the range of professional opportunities available in the field of education, and sustain an impactful career in K-12 teaching.

SECTION III: THE VOICES OF CURRENT BLACK TEACHERS

In this section of the book, we provide valuable contributions from four current Black male teachers, in Chapters 13–16, who lend us their voices about the experiences of being a practicing teacher in K-12 classrooms. We are provided with a unique insight of the daily successes and challenges of this population. Based on the successes and challenges of our contributing Black male teachers (Justin Newell, Jamil Alhassan; Khary K. Golden, and Randy Miller), we learn that the field of education still has plenty of room for improvement for this population if we are going to dramatically increase their presence and improve their classroom experiences. Additionally, these narratives paint a picture for K-12 administrators of the realities that Black male teachers face on a daily basis. We thank these Black male teachers for lending their voices to us to shape this national discussion on issues related to Black male teachers.

SECTION IV: VOICES OF LEADING SCHOLARS

To further enhance this edited volume, we are excited to have two leading scholars to provide us with their significant contributions into framing the discourse around issues related to Black male teachers. In Chapter 17, Leslie T. Fenwick, Dean of the School of Education at Howard University and Chike Akua explore the notion as to why Black male teachers that are the best and brightest do not seek the principalship or the superintendency even though they have more preparation and experience for these posts than their white counterparts. This chapter is a must-read as it raises new questions that the field of education must consider if they are going to benefit from the skills that Black male teachers bring to the profession. Finally, in Chapter 18, Lamont A. Flowers discusses the relationship between academic self-regulation and educational gains among Black male education majors. This chapter has major significance on how we engage our Black males who have chosen to pursue the field of teaching.

SECTION V: EPILOGUE FROM SERIES EDITORS

In the final section of this book, series editors, James L. Moore, III and Chance W. Lewis provide an overview of this book and this new series with Emerald Press entitled "Advances in Race and Ethnicity in Education." These series editors lay out the contribution of this book series to the field of education and a call for future volumes in this series.

REFERENCES

American Association of Colleges for Teacher Education. (2010). *Teacher preparation: Who needs it? What do the numbers say?* Washington, DC: Author.

American Legislative Exchange Council. (2012). *Report card on American education: Ranking state K-12 performance, progress and reform.* Washington, DC: Author.

Diverse Issues in Higher Education. (2012). *Diverse issues analysis of U.S. Department of Education reports submitted by higher education institutions.* Retrieved from http://www.diverseeducation.com/top100

Lewis, C. (2006). African American male teachers in public schools: An examination of three urban school districts. *Teachers College Record, 108*(2), 224–245.

Toldson, I. A. (2011a). Diversifying the United States' teaching force: Where are we now? Where do need to go? How do we get there? *Journal of Negro Education, 80*(3), 183 186.

Toldson, I. A. (2011b). *Breaking barriers 2: Plotting the path away from Juvenile detention and toward academic success for school-age African-American males.* Washington, DC: Congressional Black Caucus Foundation, Inc.

Toldson, I. A., & Lewis, C. W. (2012). *Challenging the status quo: Academic success among school-age African American males.* Washington, DC: Congressional Black Caucus Foundation, Inc.

United States Census Bureau. (2010). *American community survey 2010.* Washington, DC: Author.

CHAPTER 2

RACE MATTERS IN THE CLASSROOM

Ivory A. Toldson

ABSTRACT

This chapter provides commentary on the causes and consequences of having a majority white and female teaching force in a diverse school system, as well as strategies to improve diversity, equity, and inclusion among P-12 teachers and students. The chapter also addresses the key reason why Black males are underrepresented in the U.S. teaching force.

DO BLACK KIDS HAVE PROBLEMS IN SCHOOLS BECAUSE SO FEW TEACHERS LOOK LIKE THEM?

After an in-service training on reducing suspensions, an assistant principal in Chicago told me that the number one reason they suspend students was for coming to school late. He said, "I just don't get it," because no matter how many times they suspend students, they keep coming to school late.

He asked me if there was anything he could do about it and I asked, "Have you ever asked them why they come to school late?"

His response was, "No, I never thought of that" – This is a typical "suspend first and ask questions *never*" approach that many educators take with black students.

Black Male Teachers: Diversifying the United States' Teacher Workforce
Advances in Race and Ethnicity in Education, Volume 1, 15–21
ISSN: 2051-2317/doi:10.1108/S2051-2317(2013)0000001006

The Chicago teachers' strike highlighted the challenges of defining teacher effectiveness in the United States. Although teaching in Chicago involves significant cross-cultural interactions between teachers and students, racial issues in the classroom was rarely discussed. In Chicago, the preschool through 12th grade student population is only 15 percent white (9 percent in public schools), yet the Chicago teaching force is 53 percent white. Blacks and Hispanics comprise more than 80 percent of Chicago schoolchildren, yet they make up only 40 percent of the teaching force (Ruggles et al., 2009).

Considering the stark contrast between the race of Chicago teachers and students, could this explain why black students in Chicago are being suspended and arrested at a rate that greatly exceeds the national average? According to the Civil Rights Data Collection Report, black students account for 76 percent of students who are suspended in Chicago public schools (Ali, 2012). Earlier this year, Voices of Youth in Chicago Education estimated that police made 2,546 school-based arrests (75 percent black) between September 2011 and February 2012 in Chicago (Harris, 2012).

In many ways, the situation in Chicago is a microcosm of the larger U.S. education landscape, whereby rapid demographic changes appear to be creating fractures in student–teacher relationships, and corrupting black students' learning experience. This chapter provides commentary on the causes and consequences of having a majority white and female teaching force in a diverse school system, as well as strategies to improve diversity, equity, and inclusion among P-12 teachers and students.

MORE THAN SIX MILLION TEACHERS IN THE UNITED STATES: WHO ARE THEY?

Today, of the more than 6 million teachers in the United States, nearly 80 percent are white, 9.3 percent are black, 7.4 percent are Hispanic, 2.3 percent are Asian, and 1.2 percent is another race. Eighty percent of all teachers are female. Relative to the composition of P-12 students in the United States, the current teaching force lacks racial and gender diversity (Ruggles et al., 2009).

Teachers comprise the largest professional occupation in the United States, accounting for the most professional employees among college-educated white women, black women, and black men. Despite the large number of teachers relative to other professions held by college-educated black men, they represent less than 2 percent of the teaching force, of a student body that is 7 percent black male. By comparison, white female teachers comprise 62 percent of the teaching force, of a student body that is 26 percent white female. Considering the entire student body, the United States has 1 white female teacher for every 15 students and 1 black male teacher for every 534 students (Ruggles et al., 2009). See Fig. 1 for a complete picture of the racial and gender diversity in the U.S. teaching force.

Males of all races are underrepresented in the U.S. teaching force. The percent of white male P-12 students is twice the percent of white male teachers; the percent of black male students is more than three times the percent of black male teachers; and the percent of Hispanic male students is almost seven times the percent of Hispanic male teachers. The over-representation of white female teachers may mitigate some issues associated with the lower number of white male teachers, because they are culturally

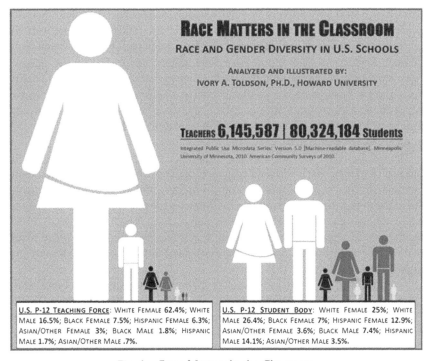

Fig. 1.   Race Matters in the Classroom.

aligned with white males. However, irrespective of gender, black and Hispanic teachers are underrepresented in the U.S. teaching force. Nationally, black and Hispanic boys will spend the majority of their school experiences under cross-gender and cross-cultural supervision.

WHY SO FEW BLACK MALE TEACHERS?

Two years ago, CNN.com proposed the question: "Is placing black men in the classroom the answer to solving some of the problems in the black community such as gang violence, high school dropout rates, and fatherless homes?"

Since then, many have speculated about why so few black males become teachers. Some assumed black males were avoiding helping professions, perhaps to pursue more lucrative opportunities. This assumption is far from the truth.

Compared to white men with college degrees, black men who are college-educated are far more likely to be a teacher, or a range of other "helping professions." Three years ago, I conducted an analysis of the top 10 occupations among black and white males who have at least a bachelor's degree. *Primary school teacher was the number 1 profession of college-educated black men* and number 3 for white men (Toldson & Snitman, 2010). Secondary school teacher was number 5 for black men and number 16 for white men. Educational administrator was number 9 for black men and number 22 for white men, and counselor was number 10 for black men and number 44 for white men.

The occupations that were in the top 10 for college-educated white men, but not in the top 10 for college-educated black men included: lawyers, chief executives, sales representatives, and physicians and surgeons. The bottom line issue is that higher paying occupations are more commonly held among white men, even when controlling for education. The nation needs more black male teachers. But given current racial income disparities, more black male teachers should not come at the expense of having more black males' in high-income positions.

Several legitimate reasons appear to account for the dearth of black male teachers. First, black males are less likely to graduate from college. In the U.S. population, 16 percent of black males and 19 percent of black females have completed college. Second, black males are less likely to major in education. In 2009, 7,603 black males and 25,725 black females graduated from college with a degree in education. Third, black males who graduate with a degree in education are less likely to become a teacher. Only 23 percent of black men with a degree in education become P-12 teachers, compared to 27 percent for white men, 41 percent for black women, and 42 percent for white women (Ruggles et al., 2009).

Interestingly, black men are more likely than any other race gender group to become educational administrators. Almost 7 percent of black males with a degree in education become educational administrators, compared to 5 percent for black females and white males, and only 2.8 percent for white females (Ruggles et al., 2009).

SO WHAT, IF MOST TEACHERS ARE WHITE?

In a perfect world, the race of a teacher would matter no more than the race of a physician. However, research evidence suggests that cultural differences between teachers and students may account for key differences between the schooling experiences of black and white students. Some school advocates suspect that teachers who lack cultural proficiency may relate to black and Hispanic students in a manner that undermines their potential.

In a recent study with my colleague, Dr. Mercedes Ebanks, we analyzed the response patterns of 8,986 students who completed the National Crime Victimization Survey: School Crime Supplement of 2009 (Toldson & Ebanks, 2012). We found that black students were less likely to perceive empathy and respect from their teachers and more likely to view the school as a punitive learning environment. White students' response patterns demonstrated a structure whereby teacher empathy and respect were central to students' academic success, school safety had no measurable influence on teachers' compassion for their students, and teacher punishment had no measurable impact on students' grades. Contrarily, black students' response patterns reflected a dynamic whereby school safety significantly diminished the overall level of empathy and respect that students perceived from teachers, and punishment from teachers significantly reduced students' grades.

These results suggest that many teachers may be operating under an implicit association bias, whereby on a subconscious level, they may view black children as security risks. Researchers at Harvard University have found that many prejudicial attitudes operate beyond our conscious awareness (Greenwald, Poehlman, Uhlmann, & Banaji, 2009). Nevertheless, they can negatively influence our judgments and behaviors. On the Implicit Association Tests, many people, both white and black, have difficulty pairing words like "delinquency" with a picture of a white person, and "wholesome" with a picture of a black person. These biases can lead teachers to have dismissive and condescending attitudes toward black culture because of negative messages they have received about black people from the media, their families, or their communities.

BEYOND BLACK AND WHITE

Importantly, any teacher regardless of race, ethnicity, or gender can teach black students. Recent media coverage on the lack of black male teachers has led to many misconceptions. The growing practice of assigning students to classes based on the race of the teacher is both unethical and misinformed. Many falsely believe that black male teachers have a primary responsibility to foster the social development of black male students. However, increasing the presence of black male teachers improves the diversity of the profession, and should be viewed as a benefit to the system, as they provide quality services to all students regardless of race or gender. In addition, black male teachers should not become a prop for failed educational and economic policies.

Another disturbing and misguided practice, recently introduced in Florida and Virginia, attempts to close the "achievement gap" by setting different performance standards for black and white students (Toppo, 2012). Interestingly, Asians outperform whites on most, if not all achievement tests, yet this well-known fact is not viewed as a deficiency among white students. But beyond race, to set fair standards based on backgrounds, we would need to separate Cambodians and Filipinos from the rest of Asians, because most indicators suggest that they underperform blacks. We would also need to separate Nigerians and Ghanaians from the rest of blacks, because most indicators suggest that they outperform whites. We should also separate poor whites from more affluent whites – or, we can simply stop betting our educational future on tests and use more legitimate measures of academic progress. Additionally, teacher performance should not be based on test scores.

Consistent with the research, teacher performance should be based on a teacher's ability to not only "teach" a student, but to "reach" a student. Effective teachers exhibit openness, unconditional positive regard, and empathy, as expressed in their ability to listen to and learn from the student. Educators' feelings toward their students and knowledge of their students' culture are important to the student's learning process. Teachers who have implicit or explicit biases toward black students, or who take a "colorblind" approach to understanding students' issues and needs, will have difficulty developing the authenticity necessary to reach black students. Students' evaluations of their teachers are the most effective method of gauging the teacher's ability to reach.

As I conclude, I reflect on Asa Fludd, a black male 11th grader, who I quoted in "Breaking Barriers: Plotting the Path to Academic Success for School-age African American Males" (Toldson, 2008). He said:

> It was at school where I met teachers who are concerned about my education. One of those teachers is my AP US History teacher, Melissa Soule. Besides making history an exciting class, Ms. Soule expressed the realities of minorities living in the United States, especially black men. She made me realize that struggle can be a luxury when you achieve, because it makes you the person who you are. Besides Ms. Soule, there are other teachers who influence me to do my best, many of them being black men.

For black male students like Asa, black male teachers who serve as models are a luxury, but committed teachers who respect and care about them as a person are a necessity.

REFERENCES

Ali, R. (2012). *Revealing new truths about our nation's schools.* Washington, DC: United States Department of Education, Office for Civil Rights.

Greenwald, A. G., Poehlman, T. A., Uhlmann, E. L., & Banaji, M. R. (2009). Understanding and using the implicit association test: III. meta-analysis of predictive validity. *Journal of Personality and Social Psychology, 97*(1), 17–41.

Harris, R. (2012). Students, CPS spar over school arrests. *Catalyst Chicago,* April 24.

Ruggles, S., Sobek, M., Alexander, T., Fitch, C. A., Goeken, R., Hall, P. K., King, M., & Ronnander, C. (2009). *Integrated public use microdata series: Version 4.0.* Minneapolis, MN: Minnesota Population Center.

Toldson, I. A. (2008). *Breaking barriers: Plotting the path to academic success for school-age African American males.* Washington, DC: Congressional Black Caucus Foundation, Inc.

Toldson, I. A., & Ebanks, M. E. (2012). Collateral damage in the classroom: How race and school environment influence teachers' attitudes and behaviors toward their students. *The National Journal of Urban Education & Practice, 6*(1), 20–40.

Toldson, I. A., & Snitman, A. (2010). Education parity and economic disparities: Correcting education-attainment discrepancies among black people in the United States. *The Journal of Negro Education, 79*(1), 1–5.

Toppo, G. (2012). Florida schools' race-based plan draws criticism, *USA TODAY,* October 11.

SECTION II
SCHOLARLY EXAMINATIONS
OF BLACK MALE TEACHERS
IN U.S. CLASSROOMS

CHAPTER 3

EDUCATING THE RACE IN POSTMODERN TIMES: THE INTRARACIAL BORDER CROSSINGS OF BLACK MALE TEACHERS

Ed Brockenbrough

ABSTRACT

Scholarly literature on Black teachers has traditionally depicted a cultural connectedness between Black teachers and Black students. Drawing upon one set of findings from a broader qualitative study on the experiences of 11 Black male teachers in a predominantly Black urban school district, this chapter explores the intraracial divides that confounded study participants' relationships with Black students and local Black communities. By charting the contested terrains of Black identity politics within urban schools and their surrounding neighborhoods, this chapter reveals the need for critical considerations of how Black male educators can respond to the heterogeneous and evolving nature of Black identities in contemporary American society. Several strategies are offered to enable Black male teachers to negotiate the intraracial differences that may emerge in their work with Black students.

Black Male Teachers: Diversifying the United States' Teacher Workforce
Advances in Race and Ethnicity in Education, Volume 1, 25–42
ISSN: 2051-2317/doi:10.1108/S2051-2317(2013)0000001007

Challenging the deficit perspectives and racist hiring practices that devalued and marginalized Black teachers in the wake of school desegregation initiatives (Foster, 1997), a rich body of scholarship has explored the culturally mediated insights that form Black teachers' unique pedagogical expertise on the education of Black children (Foster, 1994; Irvine, 2002; Ladson-Billings, 1995), providing a compelling basis for the recruitment and retention of Blacks in the teaching profession. However, as shifting socio-historical contexts transform the contours of race in twenty-first century America, much of the scholarly work on Black teachers continues to rest on an increasingly tenuous premise: namely, that Black teachers can wield a common Black cultural identity and experience to connect with and motivate Black students, despite the fissures that have disrupted and variegated constructions of culture and identity in the postmodern[1] era. Five decades since the demise of de jure Jim Crow schooling, as the cultural and political heterogeneity of Blacks in America has come increasingly to the fore, how do diverse and, at times, divergent constructions of Blackness enable and/or impede a cultural connectedness between Black teachers and Black students? This question is crucial for ongoing considerations of the cultural and pedagogical dimensions of the work of Black educators.

Drawing on a set of findings from a broader study on 11 Black male teachers in a predominantly Black urban school district, this chapter explores the intraracial divides that confounded study participants' relationships with their Black students. By exploring the contested terrains of Black identity politics, this chapter raises important questions about the pedagogical affordances and constraints of race for Black male teachers who work with Black students, and it offers several suggestions for expanding future inquiries into the lives and careers of Black men in the teaching profession.

RACIAL BONDS AND BORDER CROSSINGS: POSITIONING BLACK TEACHERS

A rich corpus of scholarly work has examined the significance of Blacks' participation in the American teaching profession. This literature has credited Black teachers for developing culturally relevant pedagogies that invoke racial bonds and emic understandings of Black culture to effectively engage Black students (Foster, 1994; Irvine, 2002; Ladson-Billings, 1994). Building upon this work, Brown (2009) and Lynn (2002, 2006a, 2006b) have explored the gendered forms of culturally relevant pedagogies enacted by Black male teachers to connect with and express care for Black youth. In addition to possessing culturally relevant pedagogical expertise, Black teachers have been credited for preparing Black youth to be critically aware of white supremacist ideologies and power structures, especially in the days of Jim Crow-era Black schools, thus operationalizing a cultural and political solidarity in their pedagogical work (Beauboeuf-Lafontant, 1999; Fairclough, 2007; Savage, 2001; Walker, 1996). By emphasizing Black educators' pedagogical insights into Black learning styles, culturally rooted modes of care for Black youth, and insider awareness of the sociopolitical contexts of Black life, this body of work has repeatedly linked Black teachers and Black students through a common Black racial identity, a shared Black cultural experience, and a collective politics of Black racial solidarity.

By contrast, an emergent set of perspectives in educational research suggests additional vantage points on the relationships between Black teachers and Black students. Fairclough's (2007) historical analysis of Blacks in teaching has unearthed cross-class tensions that complicated the rapport between middle class Black teachers and working class Black students in Jim Crow-era schools. Focusing on recent cohorts of teachers, Brockenbrough has pointed to gendered tensions, especially with Black boys (2011b), and sexual orientation (2011a) as potentially volatile divides between Black male teachers and Black students, and Achinstein and Aguirre (2008) have revealed some of the challenges experienced by novice teachers of color in their attempts to nurture a cultural match with students of color in urban schools. Casting a more expansive conceptual and thematic net, O'Connor, Lewis, and Mueller (2007) have critiqued the broader field of research on Black education for frequently ignoring historical timeframe, regional location, class status, ethnicity, and national origin as salient mediating factors in Black cultural and educational experiences. While none of these texts offers insights that would wholly discredit the claims of cultural connectedness within the larger body of scholarship on Black teachers, they do suggest that various intraracial differences, many of which have yet to be fully explored in educational research, may confound the racial solidarity traditionally imagined between Black teachers and Black students. As the sociohistorical backdrops of Black life and Black education continue to evolve, the emergent salience of intraracial differences warrants closer attention in the scholarship on Black teachers.

In order to frame encounters with intraracial differences by Black male teachers, this chapter draws upon the border crossing heuristic developed by Anzaldúa (1987). In her borderlands theory, Anzaldúa builds upon the us/them dichotomies of race and nation along the US–Mexico border to theorize the policing of numerous forms of difference across political, social, and cultural axes. Invoking the imagery of such an ominous dividing line – the heavily patrolled US–Mexico border – helps to underscore the risks entailed in certain acts of border crossing. In contrast to the discourses of racial homogeneity and solidarity that pervade much of the scholarly literature on Black teachers, this chapter relies on Anzaldúa's work to mark the multiple and consequential forms of difference, or borders, that can complicate the relationship between Black male teachers and Black students.

METHODS

In order to delve more deeply into the experiences of Black men in the teaching profession, this study employed qualitative research methods that were particularly suited for understanding how individuals make meaning of their life experiences (Maxwell, 1994). Drawing upon a regimen for in-depth interviewing developed by Seidman (1998), data collection for this study consisted of three in-depth, one-on-one interviews with each participant which focused sequentially on his Black male identity formation over his life span, his professional experiences as a Black male teacher, and his thoughts on the potential significance of emergent study findings. Additionally, two separate, one-time focus group sessions were conducted to enable study participants to collectively explore the significance of their experiences as Black male teachers. In all, data collection extended from January to October of 2007 for nine study participants, and from October of 2007 to February of 2008 for two participants who were enrolled later in the study and consequently were not included in focus group sessions. All data collection sessions were recorded with a digital audio recorder, transcribed, and coded with an eye toward two broad categories – Black male identity politics and pedagogical perspectives. Iterative phases of data analysis and triangulation across sources afforded examinations of common challenges and triumphs across participants' narratives as Black male teachers, as well as in-depth portraits of each participant's negotiations of those challenges and triumphs.

Pseudonyms for the research context and study participants are used throughout this chapter to protect participants' anonymity. All of the participants in this study were employed at the time of data collection in the

Table 1. Demographic Summary of Study Participants.

Participant	Age	Grade Level	Years of Teaching
Bill Drexler	<30	High School	<5
Damon Hubert	<30	Middle School	<5
Felix Jones	<30	High School	<5
Greg Poland	30–39	Middle School[a]	≥10
Ira Walker	30–39	High School	5–9
Karl Reardon	<30	Middle School	<5
Mitch Abrams	<30	Middle School	<5
Oliver Currington	≥40	High School	≥10
Quincy Stinson	<30	Middle School	<5
Solomon Yardley	<30	High School	<5
Victor Rollins	≥40	Middle School	5–9

[a]Grade level prior to study, comprising half of overall teaching experience.

public school system in Brewerton, a large urban center on the east coast. Black youth comprised the majority of the Brewerton School District's student body, and most Brewerton schools offered free meal programs for all of their students, indicating the impoverished socioeconomic status of the families of many Brewerton youth. Participation in this study was limited to Black male educators with middle and high school teaching experiences in order to draw upon and speak to the greater presence of male teachers at those levels. Efforts were also made to recruit teachers from schools with sizeable percentages of Black students in order to investigate claims of a special connectedness between Black male teachers and Black youth. Table 1 provides a demographic summary of the participants.

FINDINGS

In contrast to popular perceptions of Black teachers' culturally mediated rapport with Black students, some of the narratives collected through this study offered more conflictual portraits of participants' experiences as Black men in the teaching profession. In all, 9 of the 11 men in this study spoke to one or both of the following themes: (i) the identity politics across intraracial borders that placed their Black and Black male identities under scrutiny; and (ii) their disconnect with Black life in Brewerton and its influence on their teaching experiences. These themes are discussed below.[2]

Identity Politics across Intraracial Borders

Black identity politics generated challenging interactional dynamics for many of the men in this study. In fact, seven participants reported that their racial authenticity was scrutinized by Black students, and in one case by Black parents, across the intraracial borders of class, educational status, and regional background. One such participant was Solomon, a recent southern transplant to Brewerton who recalled moments when Black students would dismiss his opinions by stating "[Mr.] Yardley, you're not hood, you don't know."[3] With such remarks, Black students could question the validity of his insights into their lives because of his "non-hood" performance of Blackness. Elaborating further on this theme, Solomon stated, "I become White in [students'] minds. Like, 'He thinks he's Black, but he talks White.'" Falling beyond students' notions of normative Blackness, Solomon's seemingly inauthentic racial identity constituted an intraracial difference that distanced him at times from his students.

Like Solomon, Victor and Karl described the ways in which Black students disputed their racial authenticity. Victor noted during a focus group session that because of his demeanor and style of speech, in the eyes of his students "I act like a White dude because I'm presenting myself in a formal sense." During the same focus group session, Karl recalled similar student reactions to his speech and dress:

> [There are] perceptions of being White. Like walking in with proper English and loafers and my shirt tucked in, and like, "Who are you? Not only are you not from Brewerton but you're White. I don't care how Black your skin is, you're White," among some other things. So I feel like even though to the outside-looking-in you're viewed as a Black male – "oh, you can just come in and y'all are gonna have that connection" – in my case, I had to fight to make some of those connections because even though I was a Black male, they saw me as an outsider.

That this passage came from Karl's narrative was particularly noteworthy, as he was one of the participants who elsewhere reported having a strong rapport with Black students. Yet as Karl noted in the excerpt above, that rapport was hard-won, as his deviations from his students' particular notions of Blackness initially otherized him in their eyes. Karl thus offered a direct challenge to a central claim in popular narratives on Black men in the teaching profession.

In addition to having their racial authenticity questioned by students, some participants found themselves at odds at times with the constructs of Black masculinity that were embraced by many of their Black students. This dilemma was captured in the following comments made during a focus group session by Damon and Solomon:

D: I think there's no perception of being a worldly Black male. There's no perception of being well-spoken, articulate, well-versed in ...
S: "You haven't been to jail, Mr. [Solomon] Yardley?"
D: You know, like "you've never smoked this?" There are certain things that they don't have any perception of. And I think that there is this thing of you're supposed to be from the hood, you're supposed to dress a certain way.

After several follow-up comments from other participants, the author redirected this focus group discussion back to Solomon's interjection about having never served jail time. This led to an exchange between Solomon, Felix, and Bill that shed additional light on the possible conceptions of Black maleness among the participants' Black students:

Author: Just before I lose it, were you [*to S.*] joking when you said ...
S: No, I was being completely serious.
A: So kids have actually asked you have you been [to jail]?
S: Oh yeah, on numerous occasions.
F: I've been asked that.
S: A couple of kids were just stumped that I had never served time.
F: Yeah, I've been asked. And when they find out that I don't like or play basketball ... I could've had someone fall out the seat. They say, "What do you play, Mr. [Felix] J?" I say, "I play tennis." [*All: laughter*] One student today, he was like, "What?!"
B: Yeah, when I told them I play tennis, I got the same thing.
F: And I proved it to them. One student had a basketball. I tried to dribble, they were like "okay, we know ..." [*Others: chuckles*]

From having no previous criminal records to preferring tennis over basketball, these men deviated from the norms that their students associated with adult Black men in Brewerton. The exchange quoted above spoke to the range of experiences and issues – speech patterns, clothing, lack of jail time, athletic preferences – that could lead Black students to question participants' performances of Black masculinity.

Students were not the only potential critics of teachers' identities. One participant, Greg, pointed to intraracial borders that complicated his rapport with some Black parents. At one point in his narrative, Greg recalled a negative encounter with a Black mother at a predominantly Black middle school. When asked why this mother had behaved in an aggressive fashion toward him, Greg replied, "Well, I think it comes from, in a sense, in some way, poverty. Meaning not having a meaningful job, something that gets you up in the morning that you go to, that you enjoy." After having a little more time to warm up to the subject, Greg went on to state that "the ones [Black parents] that give me a hard time may see me as 'this uppity Negro who thinks he's better than us because he comes in with his tie, his shirt and tie on and ...' Not my problem." While not eager to dwell on the matter, Greg still pointed to class – specifically the perception of him as an uppity Negro – as a potential barrier with working class Black parents.

To be sure, the moments of dissonance catalogued thus far were not of equal severity. Students' ribbing of Felix for his interest in tennis over basketball, for instance, was a lighthearted affair; Greg's negotiation of class tensions during encounters with Black parents was not. Looking at the entire range of accounts presented above is crucial for developing a broad and nuanced understanding of how particular constructions of Blackness affected the experiences of these Black male teachers. Contrary to recurrent assumptions of the racially based connectedness between Black male teachers and Black students, the narrative passages cited above suggest that a complex amalgam of class dynamics, regional background, communicative styles, fashion sense, and masculinity politics can confound the teaching experiences of Black male educators. While participants' accounts suggested that the dissonance along intraracial divides was not necessarily insurmountable, they still attested to the need to acknowledge, explore, and contend with these divides.

"Really Kind of Foreign to Me": Disconnects with Black Life in Brewerton

The intraracial divides encountered by participants during their teaching experiences reflected the potentially conflictual nature of Black identity politics beyond school walls. While this was implicit in many of the narrative excerpts cited above, four of the men in this study spoke more directly to their sense of disconnect with the broader social context of Black life in Brewerton. One of them was Mitch. A college-educated southern transplant, Mitch characterized Brewerton as a "grimy working class city" that, unlike his prior city of residence, lacked a sizeable Black middle class presence. Mitch went on to elaborate the implications of class differences for his experience as a Black man in Brewerton:

> So here, being here now, I kind of feel a little bit socially isolated. Coming from the
> whole college bubble – where everyone is like you, everyone is in college, everyone is

about to get a degree in four years, everyone is going to be educated – into a place where most Black men definitely aren't college educated and might not even be high school educated, and possibly have spent time in a jail cell, or at least had handcuffs placed around them, is definitely a different world. Because it's definitely not one that I've lived [in]. So yeah, it creates a bit of a dissonance in being able to relate to a Black experience.

Mitch's narrative account revealed his perception of Brewerton as a working class city in which his college education and white-collar status placed him at odds with the local norms of the Black male experience. The class- and region-informed disconnects that Mitch articulated exposed intraracial dynamics in Brewerton at large that could shape one's experiences as a Black male teacher.

Also finding himself at odds with Black life in Brewerton was Bill. Like Mitch, Bill had grown up in the South and had recently relocated to Brewerton. Tracing his southern upbringing, Bill recalled the "healthy fear" of authority in the South that had ensured a certain level of respect and decorum in public. In his eyes, this healthy fear was sorely lacking amongst Black Brewertonians. Bill provided the following description of the types of behavior that illustrated the absence of a southern-bred, healthy fear of authority, and that explained his disconnect with Black life in Brewerton:

So this idea that, you know, "I'm'a do what I wanna do, and I'm not respecting anyone else, whoever it is." Just that kind of idea was something that was really kind of foreign to me. I mean obviously I had seen defiance before, but I had never really seen it as kind of just a way of life. You know, this kind of disrespect. "I'm'a throw my trash on the train, you know, just because I wanna throw my trash on the train. Well what? I don't care if there's a trash can right there, I'm'a put my trash right here because that's where I wanna put my trash." I was talking to somebody and they were saying it's kind of like how people in the North would send their kids to the South when they were having problems with their kids. "I'm'a send you to your aunt in South Carolina," right. This idea that the South equals some type of stricter code.

For Bill, the antagonistic behaviors and disregard for others that he ascribed to Black life in Brewerton made it "really kind of foreign" to him, thus challenging his sense of connectedness as a Black southern transplant to the Black Brewerton experience.

The strangeness of the antagonistic nature of Black Brewertonians affected Bill's teaching experience as well. For instance, after identifying the difference between southern and Black Brewertonian ways of living, Bill provided the following example of Black student behavior in the Brew that reflected a disregard for authority:

I was in the hall when the girl said to another girl, "Oh so-so can't go out this week, she gotta tell her mama where she wanna be, and she 15. Why she still gotta tell her mama where she going?" Like, by 15 you supposed to do whatever you want and better not nobody say nothing to you.

The mentality expressed by this girl in the hall was a source of frustration for Bill, as he went on to explain:

> I think that maybe some of my misgivings or some of my frustrations, me not understanding how can you possibly talk to [an] adult like that, comes from that idea that I'm not used to people just doing that, whereas a lot of these kids are used to it. And I talk to some of the kids, and they'll say, "My parents told me if I need to go to the bathroom and the teacher tells me I can't go to the bathroom right now, I need to get up and walk out of the class and go to the bathroom." Or, "if somebody says something to you, you better go over there and do this-that-and-the-other to them." And that was something that was really foreign to me when I came here.

Throughout his narrative, Bill repeatedly expressed his struggle to comprehend and respond to the defiant demeanors of his Black students. In the above excerpts, he framed this struggle as part of his broader attempt to grapple with a combative attitude that seemed to pervade Black life in Brewerton.

Not only did Bill report feeling at odds with certain elements of Black Brewertonian life that filtered into hallways and classrooms, but he also offered intriguing examples of how he questioned or challenged some of those elements. For instance, in the following excerpt, Bill recalled an exchange with a Black male student that brought to light conflicting notions of proper Black masculinity:

> One of my students got a tattoo over the holidays. He got a tattoo here on his neck, which just irks me so bad. And today he and I were talking about it. Because he went, "Yo, you like my tattoo?" And I was like, "I'm not big on the tattoo on the neck thing." And he was like, "Well, why?" And I was like, "Well what happens when you wanna become a doctor and you have this big tattoo on your neck? Or what happens when you wanna become a stockbroker, who's gonna want to hire you with this big tattoo on your neck?" And he went into, "Well I'll just be a drug dealer." And I was like, "Yeah because that's probably all that you'll be able to do [chuckle]."

In this passage, the student's tattoo emblemized a brand of Black masculinity that was embraced by Black youth in Brewerton. While Bill attributed his quip to the lighthearted and familiar rapport that he enjoyed with this particular student, the tattoo still was at odds with Bill's preference for the performance of a middle class Black masculinity that could enable participation in white-collar professional realms. This excerpt not only captured Bill's disaffection for the "hood" aesthetic of Black masculinity that was valorized in Black Brewerton and embraced by many of his Black students, but it also revealed his willingness to challenge that aesthetic through his position as a Black male teacher.

In a similar fashion, Damon's disaffection for Black life in Brewerton was also coupled with a willingness to challenge the worldviews of his Black students. As noted earlier, Damon felt that his students lacked a "perception of a worldly Black male." Describing the disorienting impact of his formal style of dress and professional demeanor on his students, Damon noted, "For some students, they have to now, because they've met me, question their perception of what it means to be a Black man." Raised in another city on the east coast, Damon also felt underwhelmed by what he perceived as a lack of empowerment amongst Blacks in Brewerton:

> Not to be funny but the Brew, I don't like it so I kind of close myself off from it. The Black men here, in my opinion, there are a lot of people that aren't doing ... you know. Like, there are a few that are doing something for Black people, and then there are a lot who aren't doing anything.

Damon's disenchantment with the disempowered state of Blacks in Brewerton fueled his disengagement from the local Black community. Disconnected from local community contexts, Damon was willing to model alternatives to Brewertonian constructions of Black male identity.

By contrast, Quincy, another southern transplant to Brewerton, struggled to challenge Black Brewertonian mores in the classroom. Like Bill, Quincy felt at odds with the heightened levels of hostility that he associated with Black Brewertonians, and like Damon, he reported feeling disappointed with what they perceived as Black Brewertonians' general sense of apathy. However, Quincy's dissonance with Black life in Brewerton made it difficult for him to figure out how to guide his Black students, as evident in the following passage on his frustration with what he described as an over-reliance on cursing amongst Blacks in Brewerton, including his students:

> Is it okay I try to tell you I'm real polite with y'all all the time, and that I say please, thank you, and all this? Does that make me soft or is that just me saying there's another way to do things that isn't cursing at someone all the time? Everyday I sit down, I'm like am I really doing any good by handling myself in this manner? If I just yelled all the time and cursed all the time, would that accomplish more for certain kids? Being Black in the Brew is confusing to me because I'm not a Black person from the Brew. If I had come up in it, I don't know if I'd be having these debates internally, because I may be just saying "oh well, that's what it's like here."

This passage was especially revealing, as Quincy confessed to actually questioning his effectiveness as a teacher because of his deviation from the profane and confrontational interactional style that, in his eyes, typified the

Black Brewerton experience. For Quincy, this dissonance with Black life in the Brew sometimes confounded his rapport with and insights into his Black students.

The excerpts cited above offered examples of the dissonance that several participants felt toward Black life in Brewerton. Of particular salience throughout all of these narrative accounts were the class-mediated tensions between college-educated Black male teachers and the working class Black communities they served. Like the cross-class tensions that have historically troubled Black teachers' rapport with Black students and Black communities (Fairclough, 2007), class and educational status, along with regional background, informed some study participants' disconnect with – and in some cases, disdain for – the habits and attitudes of working class Black Brewertonians. This disconnect made Black life in Brewerton "really kind of foreign" for the participants referenced above, thus further complicating their intraracial border crossings as Black male teachers working with Black students in the Brew.

DISCUSSION AND IMPLICATIONS

This chapter presented Black male teachers' accounts of their intraracial border crossings with Black students and their dissonance with the social contexts of Black Brewerton life. While these points of disconnect were provocative and important to acknowledge, it should be noted that 9 of the 11 study participants also described instances when their Blackness and Black maleness afforded culturally relevant pedagogical insights into their Black students' learning needs, and 8 participants spoke specifically to a Black cultural and political solidarity in the midst of white supremacy that informed their work with Black students.[4] This chapter's postmodern sensitivity to intraracial differences is not meant to dismiss the possibilities of Black male teachers' culturally mediated rapport with Black students. Rather, the findings presented above point to the need for more complete portraits of Black male teachers – ones that wed the affordances of cultural connectedness with the constraints of intraracial border crossings.

Throughout the presentation of findings, the scrutiny of study participants' racial authenticity emerged as a key dilemma. From being accused of "acting White" to being considered an "uppity Negro," participants sensed the boundaries that marked them as inauthentic and unrelatable in the eyes of some Black students and parents. While further exploration is needed to fully unpack the meaning of these moments across stakeholder perspectives, one cannot help but notice the class-related overtones to the tensions described by study participants. Given the potential dilemmas associated with class, it is crucial that future scholarship continue to investigate how class both enables and constrains contemporary pedagogical encounters between middle class Black male educators and working class Black students.

Class-mediated tensions that surfaced in study findings were linked to a broader sense of participant dissonance with the social contexts of Black life in Brewerton. This dissonance was expressed most explicitly by Mitch, Bill, Damon, and Quincy, all of whom were young, novice teachers and, with the exception of Damon, were recent southern transplants to the Brew. Not only did these teachers describe their sense of alienation from Black Brewerton life, but Bill, Damon, and Quincy also revealed some spill-over of this alienation into their teaching experiences. Critical scholarship on diversity in education has repeatedly asserted the dire need for urban educators to grasp the social and cultural contexts of students' out-of-school lives (Moll, Amanti, Neff, & Gonzalez, 1992; Nieto, 1999). Like Achinstein and Aguirre's (2008) work, this chapter suggests that Black male educators may not necessarily have an immediate grasp of the ways of thinking and being that characterize the Black communities served by urban schools, especially when those educators are not from the surrounding communities. Future research should not only explore this potential disconnect between Black male educators and Black urban social contexts, but it should also consider strategies for mitigating this possible divide. Doing so may be particularly beneficial for districts that rely on recruitment streams that attract Black male educators from out-of-town regions, as five study participants – Mitch, Quincy, Damon, Karl, and Solomon – were hired through alternative certification programs that place novice teachers in cities like Brewerton despite their unfamiliarity with those local contexts.

Along with familiarizing Black male teachers with local urban contexts, creating opportunities to reflect on Black identity politics may also be in order, as several narrative accounts from this study revealed participants' own determinations of acceptable and intolerable forms of Blackness and Black masculinity. As noted in the findings, Bill and Quincy expressed a palpable disdain for the poor public decorum, indifference to authority, and confrontational interactional styles that they attributed to Black youth and communities in Brewerton, and Quincy and Damon expressed a disdain for Black Brewertonian apathy. Bill and Damon also articulated a desire to model middle class forms of Black masculinity that diverged from, and in some senses corrected, the "hood" aesthetics embraced by Black male students. Through examples like these, Anzaldúa's border crossing heuristic draws attention to how Black male teachers are not only policed, but also have the potential *to police*. Just as Black male teachers' identities can be judged for their racial authenticity, the findings presented in this chapter suggest that the identities and experiences of Black students and their urban communities can fall under the moralistic scrutiny of Black male teachers. As scholars continue to explore the experiences of Black male teachers in urban contexts, a crucial task will be to further unpack how – and at what costs – Black male educators may wield their institutionally sanctioned authority within schools to validate certain forms of Blackness and Black maleness over others. It will also be imperative to explore how to create spaces where Black male educators can reflect on and revise their own potential contributions to the intraracial divides that can confound their work with Black students.

The considerations raised above collectively point to the need to reexamine the cultural connectedness traditionally ascribed to and expected of Black educators. The successes of culturally mediated pedagogies do not necessarily capture the full story of Black educators' experiences within the postmodern milieu of racial identity in today's predominantly Black urban schools. In this chapter, the scrutiny of participants' racial authenticity by Black students and parents, participants' disconnect with the social context of Black life in Brewerton, and participants' scrutiny of intolerable forms of Blackness among Black students and Brewertonians at large revealed conflictual intraracial dynamics, especially around class and regional status, that have historically complicated middle class Black educators' encounters with working class Black communities. Paying closer attention to the border crossings described in this chapter may ultimately allow educational researchers, teacher education programs, and urban school districts to help Black teachers anticipate the pitfalls of intraracial divides, consequently leaving more room to pedagogically capitalize on their potential cultural connectedness with Black students in urban schools.

FURTHER ANALYSIS

The findings presented in this chapter detailed the intraracial border crossings experienced by a set of Black male teachers in a predominantly Black urban school district. Through its spotlight on moments of intraracial disconnect, this chapter provides a framework for future research on and professional development practices with Black male teachers who must negotiate the pedagogical affordances and constraints of race in their work with Black students. The following questions may prove particularly helpful to institutions like teacher education programs and school districts, as well as to individual Black male teachers, that wish to translate this chapter's implications into practice.

(1) *What learning opportunities can teacher education programs and school districts create for Black male teachers to engage in critical analyses of (a) the shifting social constructions of Blackness in the United States and (b) the implications of those constructions for their work with Black students?* Courses provided by university teacher education departments and/or academic departments like Africana Studies, discussion-based affinity groups for Black male teachers, and Black male teacher mentors are possible strategies for creating spaces where Black male educators can examine the evolving nature of – and their own investments in – Black identity politics.

(2) *What types of connections with community stakeholders can provide Black male teachers with meaningful insights into and connections with local Black communities?* Resident-led neighborhood tours, participation in youth mentoring programs and community festivals, and attendance at key community-based institutions like churches and community centers could help to ensure that Black male teachers understand and connect with local Black community networks. Teacher education programs and school districts could coordinate such opportunities with local Black community stakeholders, and Black male teachers could seek out these opportunities on their own as well.

(3) *What strategies can Black male teachers employ within schools to negotiate intraracial differences with Black students?* Student journal-writing assignments and other instructional techniques that enable students to bring their identities and experiential narratives into the classroom could allow Black male teachers to learn about and connect with Black students across differences like class, regional background, and ethnicity. Participation as faculty advisors in extracurricular activities that invite student voice and expression also could afford Black male teachers with greater insights into the diversity of their Black students, as could strategies like school assemblies and guest speakers that are frequently engaged by schools to raise multicultural awareness.

Central to all of the questions and suggestions raised above are two premises: Black male teachers, along with the institutions that prepare and employ them, must anticipate the importance of intraracial differences in their work with Black students, and that work must be informed by intentional efforts to understand and engage local Black community contexts. Taking these two premises into account will enable Black male educators to juggle the shifting and evolving nuances of race in the classroom while still hopefully capitalizing on the pedagogical affordances of racial connectedness with Black students.

ACKNOWLEDGMENTS

The author would like to thank Dr. Logan Hazen for his feedback during the revision process. The research presented in this chapter was supported through a dissertation fellowship from the American Educational Research Association and the Institute of Educational Sciences.

NOTES

1. As an epistemological intervention, postmodernism has challenged the capacity of knowledge claims to present absolute and universalist truths, insisting instead that knowledge is always a partial, fragmented, and interested rendering produced from a particular social location (Benton & Craib, 2001; Giroux, 1988). Applied to present-day debates on identity, postmodernism has been used to critique master narratives that claim to capture the absolute truth, or the essence, of what it means to embody a particular identity and set an agenda for a particular identity group (Benton & Craib, 2001; Hall, 1996; Seidman & Alexander, 2001). In this chapter, postmodernism informs a critical attention to intraracial divides that belie conventional discourses on the racial homogeneity and solidarity mediating the relationship between Black teachers and Black students.

2. While the findings presented in this chapter identify conflictual forms of intraracial difference encountered by the men in this study, they do not always reveal how study participants actively negotiated these differences. Suggestions for how to unearth and understand those negotiations in future scholarly inquiries are offered at the end of this chapter.

3. Throughout this analysis, "hood" refers to a style or performance of Black identity that is frequently associated with Blacks in urban ghettoes, and that serves in some spaces as a mark of Black racial authenticity. See Jackson (2006) and Neal (2005) for discussions of the hood aesthetic and Black identity politics.

4. While a full discussion of these findings is beyond the scope of this chapter, it should be briefly noted that these participants described how their classroom management strategies, adaptation of curriculum, use of colloquial expressions, and mentoring of and allegiance to Black male students reflected culturally mediated moments of pedagogical and interpersonal connectedness with their Black students.

REFERENCES

Achinstein, B., & Aguirre, J. (2008). Cultural match or culturally suspect: How new teachers of color negotiate sociocultural challenges in the classroom. *Teachers College Record*, *110*(8), 1505–1540.

Anzaldúa, G. (1987). *Borderlands/La frontera: The new mestiza*. San Francisco, CA: Spinsters/ Aunt Lute.

Beauboeuf-Lafontant, T. (1999). A movement against and beyond boundaries: "Politically relevant teaching" among African American teachers. *Teachers College Record*, *100*(4), 702–723.

Benton, T., & Craib, I. (2001). *Philosophy of social science: The philosophical foundations of social thought*. New York, NY: Palgrave.

Brockenbrough, E. (2011a). Agency and abjection in the closet: The voices (and silences) of black queer male teachers. *International Journal of Qualitative Studies in Education*. doi: 10.1080/09518398.2011.590157

Brockenbrough, E. (2011b). "You ain't my daddy!": Black male teachers and the politics of surrogate fatherhood. *International Journal of Inclusive Education*. doi: 10.1080/ 13603116.2011.555091

Brown, A. L. (2009). "Brothers gonna work it out": Understanding the pedagogic performance of African American male teachers working with African American male students. *Urban Review*. Retrieved from http://www.springerlink.com/content/554g77858447r502/ fulltext.pdf

Fairclough, A. (2007). *A class of their own: Black teachers in the segregated South*. Cambridge, MA: Belknap Press of Harvard University Press.

Foster, M. (1994). Effective black teachers: A literature review. In E. Hollins, J. King & W. Hayman (Eds.), *Teaching diverse populations: Formulating a knowledge base* (pp. 225–242). Albany, NY: State University of New York Press.

Foster, M. (1997). *Black teachers on teaching*. New York, NY: The New Press.

Giroux, H. A. (1988). Border pedagogy in the age of postmodernism. *Journal of Education*, *170*(3), 162–181.

Hall, S. (1996). The question of identity. In S. Hall, D. Held, D. Hubert & K. Thompson (Eds.), *Modernity: An introduction to modern societies* (pp. 595–634). Malden, MA: Blackwell Publishers.

Irvine, J. J. (Ed.). (2002). *In search of wholeness: African American teachers and their culturally specific classroom practices*. New York, NY: Palgrave.

Jackson, R. L. (2006). *Scripting the black masculine body: Identity, discourse, and racial politics in popular media*. Albany, NY: State University of New York Press.

Ladson-Billings, G. (1994). Toward a theory of culturally relevant pedagogy. *American Educational Research Journal*, *32*(3), 465–491.

Ladson-Billings, G. (1995). But that's just good teaching!: The case for culturally relevant pedagogy. *Theory into Practice*, *34*(3), 159–165.

Lynn, M. (2002). Critical race theory and the perspectives of Black men teachers in the Los Angeles public schools. *Equity & Excellence in Education*, *35*(2), 119–130.

Lynn, M. (2006a). Dancing between two worlds: A portrait of the life of a black male teacher in South Central L.A. *International Journal of Qualitative Studies in Education*, *19*(2), 221–242.

Lynn, M. (2006b). Education for the community: Exploring the culturally relevant practices of Black male teachers. *Teachers College Record, 108*(12), 2497–2522.

Maxwell, J. A. (1994). *Qualitative research design: An interactive approach.* Thousand Oaks, CA: Sage Publications.

Moll, L. C., Amanti, C., Neff, D., & Gonzalez, N. (1992). Funds of knowledge for teaching: Using a qualitative approach to connect homes and classrooms. *Theory Into Practice, 31*(2), 132–140.

Neal, M. A. (2005). *New black man.* New York, NY: Routledge.

Nieto, S. (1999). *The light in their eyes: Creating multicultural learning communities.* New York, NY: Teachers College Press.

O'Connor, C., Lewis, A., & Mueller, J. (2007). Researching "Black" educational experiences and outcomes: Theoretical and methodological considerations. *Educational Researcher, 36*(9), 541–552.

Savage, C. (2001). "Because we did more with less": The agency of African American teachers in Franklin, Tennessee: 1860–1967. *Peabody Journal of Education, 76*(2), 170–203.

Seidman, I. (1998). *Interviewing as a qualitative research: A guide for researchers in education and the social sciences.* New York, NY: Teachers College Press.

Seidman, S., & Alexander, J. C. (Eds.). (2001). *The new social theory reader: Contemporary debates.* New York, NY: Routledge.

Walker, V. S. (1996). *Their highest potential: An African American school community in the segregated south.* Chapel Hill, NC: University of North Carolina Press.

CHAPTER 4

RECRUITING TEACHERS FROM WITHIN: CAREER LADDERS FOR PARAPROFESSIONAL EDUCATORS

Erin Croke, Travis Dale and William Ebenstein

ABSTRACT

It is vitally important that students have access to teachers who are effective and broadly representative of our society. Yet in urban areas such as New York City (NYC), many teachers lack experience or appropriate qualifications and there is a profound mismatch between the racial composition of the teacher workforce and the composition of students served. Paraprofessionals, individuals who work under the supervision of a teacher to provide instruction or other direct services to students, represent a significant pool of minority teacher candidates. In NYC, paraprofessionals employed by the Department of Education (DOE) may receive tuition support and release time as they pursue higher education. Analysis of the participation and success of NYC DOE paraprofessionals enrolled in The City University of New York (CUNY) sheds light on the potential for paraprofessionals to become teachers and diversify the teaching workforce.

Black Male Teachers: Diversifying the United States' Teacher Workforce
Advances in Race and Ethnicity in Education, Volume 1, 43–57
Copyright © 2013 by Emerald Group Publishing Limited
All rights of reproduction in any form reserved
ISSN: 2051-2317/doi:10.1108/S2051-2317(2013)0000001008

Creative teacher recruitment strategies are needed to insure an effective and diverse teacher workforce. Within the education research community there is consensus that the quality of a teacher is tied to how much students learn (Darling-Hammond, 1997; Hanushek, Kain, & Rivkin, 1998). Research suggests that it is crucially important for schools to be culturally responsive and that recruiting minority teachers may result in increased cultural sensitivity in schools (Noguera, 2008; Villegas & Lucas, 2002). Yet many schools struggle to fill teaching positions with effective teachers. And particularly in urban areas, there is a mismatch between the racial composition of the teacher workforce and the composition of students served.

In a time when it is so vital for the life chances of a child to achieve high levels of education, new mechanisms for recruiting teachers are needed. Working in NYC schools are more than 33,000 teacher assistants, and more than 1,000 of these are Black males (U.S. Census Bureau, 2000).[1] If institutions of higher education partner with schools to select, train, and support these individuals so they may become certified teachers, many will provide an outstanding service to students for years to come.

THE NEED FOR AN EFFECTIVE AND DIVERSE TEACHER WORKFORCE

The need to recruit a talented and diverse pool of teaching candidates is clear. A significant percentage of teachers are not qualified for the subjects they teach. Schools with high percentages of Black students are especially likely to employ teachers without appropriate qualifications (Aud, Fox, & KewalRamani, 2010). In 2006–2007, 11 percent of all FTE teaching assignments in New York City (NYC) were held by teachers without appropriate certification, and the percent of teachers without appropriate certification was higher in areas such as bilingual education and special education (New York State Education Department, 2008). Due to frequent teacher turnover, in any given year many classes are led by teachers without the experience needed to effect positive student outcomes. In 2006–2007 more than 8 percent of all FTE teaching assignments in NYC were held by teachers with no prior teaching experience (New York State Education Department, 2008).

High levels of teacher attrition and mobility pose significant staffing challenges for schools. Approximately 8 percent of all public school teachers in the United States left the teaching profession between 2007–2008 and 2008–2009, and an additional 8 percent of teachers moved to a different school (Aud et al., 2010). Teachers in schools serving 50 percent or more minority students were more likely to change schools compared to teachers in less diverse schools (Aud et al., 2010). Many schools have a very difficult time filling vacancies. Seventy-five percent of all schools in central cities had teaching vacancies during the 2003–2004 school year (Strizek, Pittsonberger, Riordan, Lyter, & Orlofsky, 2006). Of those schools with teaching vacancies, 19 percent hired a less than fully qualified teacher for one or more positions, 42 percent relied on long-term or short-term substitutes, 16 percent expanded class sizes, and 12 percent assigned a teacher of another subject or grade level to cover the vacancy (Strizek et al., 2006).

Changing demographics, including the aging teacher workforce and increasing percentages of minority students, pose challenges. Many teachers will be eligible to retire in the coming years: in 2006–2007 approximately 18 percent of all teachers in New York were 55 years or older (New York State Education Department, 2008). Projections indicate that by the year 2050 minority students will comprise 57 percent of the total school-age population (U.S. Department of Commerce, 1996), but the teacher work-force remains largely white. During the 2003–2004 school year, approximately 64 percent of all public school students in central cities were minority, while only 30 percent of all public school teachers in central cities were minority (Strizek et al., 2006). In New York, 40 percent of all students were Black or Hispanic while just 15 percent of all teachers were Black or Hispanic in 2006–2007, and just 6 percent of all newly issued teaching certificates went to Black or Hispanic teachers (New York State Education Department, 2008).

PARAPROFESSIONALS AS A SOURCE OF BLACK MALE TEACHER CANDIDATES

Paraprofessionals work under the supervision of a teacher to provide instruction or other direct services to students and their parents. Paraprofessionals were first introduced to help deal with teacher shortages in the 1950s. Following the Elementary and Secondary Education Act of 1965, paraprofessionals were hired for Head Start and other Title I programs to help serve economically disadvantaged students. Under the Equal Educational Opportunity Act of 1974 and the Individuals with Disabilities Education Act of 1975, it was mandated that paraprofessionals be hired to assist English language-learners and students with disabilities. As a result the number of paraprofessionals has grown exponentially.

Table 1. Teaching Assistants in the United States and New York City.

	Total	Black Males	
	#	#	%
US	915,920	14,680	1.6
NYC	33,727	1,360	4.0

Source: U.S. Census Bureau 2000, Equal Employment Opportunity Residence Data.

According to data from the U.S. Census, more than 915,000 people in the United States worked as teaching assistants in 2000, and more than 33,000 teaching assistants were employed in NYC. Approximately 2 percent of all teaching assistants nationwide were Black males, and 4 percent of all teaching assistants in NYC ($n = 1,360$) were Black males. These individuals represent a substantial pool of potential teacher candidates that could help diversify the teacher workforce (see Table 1).

EVIDENCE ABOUT THE PARAPROFESSIONAL-TO-TEACHER TRANSITION

Evidence suggests that paraprofessional-to-teacher programs may successfully increase the supply of minority teacher candidates, and that participants of such programs are likely to be retained in the teaching profession and to teach in high-need schools. In 1996, a national survey identified a total of 149 paraprofessional-to-teacher programs, and 77 percent of participating paraprofessionals were minority (Haselkorn & Fideler, 1996). Data from a national evaluation of the Pathways to Teaching Careers program conducted by Clewell and Villegas (2001) and funded by the Wallace Foundation provides further evidence. The Pathways program worked with 40 colleges and universities in 23 states to create strategies for recruiting, preparing, and certifying teachers from nontraditional backgrounds, including paraprofessionals.

After three years, 81 percent of Pathways graduates remained in the teaching field, and compared to noncertified teachers and returning Peace Corps volunteers who participated in Pathways, paraprofessionals were more likely to have remained in teaching after three years (Clewell & Villegas, 2001). Just 53 percent of those who enter teaching through a traditional four-year baccalaureate program are retained after three years

(Darling-Hammond, 2000). Pathways graduates were more likely to teach in high-need districts after receiving their certification compared to those from traditional teacher-preparation programs – 91 percent of paraprofessionals taught in high-need school districts after earning teacher certification (Clewell & Villegas, 2001).

The Pathways evaluation found that paraprofessionals who made the transition to teaching were effective in the classroom. Pathways participants were rated during student teaching by their field experience supervisors, at the end of their first year of teaching by an independent evaluator, and two years after becoming a teacher by their principals. On a five-point scale, paraprofessionals received an average rating of 3.9 for overall teacher effectiveness, compared to an average rating of 3.4 for traditionally trained novice teachers (Clewell & Villegas, 2001).

EFFORTS UNDERWAY IN NYC

NYC is an ideal location to develop a large-scale program to support paraprofessionals to become teachers. Not only is the need for qualified and diverse teachers especially salient in NYC, there are large numbers of paraprofessionals to draw upon. Tuition support has been available for paraprofessionals since 1970 through the Career Training Program (CTP), a collaborative effort between the NYC Department of Education (DOE) and the American Federation of Teachers (AFT) (Haselkorn & Fideler, 1996). CTP was created to foster opportunities within higher education for paraprofessionals and to enhance the pool of potential teachers, especially minority teachers.

Through CTP paraprofessionals may receive tuition support for up to six college credits per semester toward a bachelor's degree (New York City Department of Education, 2011). CTP will pay the initial college application fee and provide release time for participating paraprofessionals. Para-professionals who participate in the CTP are eligible for salary increases and changes in title.

The availability of tuition support for paraprofessionals employed by the NYC DOE has resulted in large numbers of paraprofessionals participating in higher education. Evidence comes from an analysis conducted by the John F. Kennedy, Jr. Institute at The City University of New York (CUNY), an organization that supports workforce development initiatives in health, education, and human services. The JFK, Jr. Institute was contracted by the NYC DOE to evaluate the participation of paraprofessionals within the CUNY system of 17 undergraduate colleges, including 6 community colleges and 11 senior colleges. As the public system of higher education in NYC serving more than 250,000 undergraduates in credited coursework each year, it can be expected that data portray overall patterns of higher education attendance and performance among paraprofessionals.

Analysis of CUNY enrollment and performance among paraprofessionals employed by the NYC DOE in 2006–2007 demonstrates a high level of involvement within the CUNY system. Of the more than 20,000 paraprofessionals employed by the NYC DOE, 67 percent of paraprofessionals attended CUNY at some point between 1990 and Fall 2010.[2] Approximately 22 percent of all paraprofessionals earned a degree from CUNY, including 573 paraprofessionals who earned a BA or higher in education (see Table 2).

Sixty-seven percent of all paraprofessionals that attended CUNY were Black or Hispanic, including 6 percent ($n = 900$) who were Black males (see Table 3). Census data show that 4 percent of all teaching assistants in NYC in 2000 were Black males (see Table 1), suggesting that CUNY participation of Black male paraprofessionals may be approximately consistent with overall representation of Black males in the workforce.

On average, data suggest Black male paraprofessionals may be especially likely to struggle within higher education. Of those with known GPA's, more than half of Black male paraprofessionals attending CUNY obtained a cumulative GPA of 2.5 or lower, compared to 35 percent of all other paraprofessionals (see Table 4). Sixty-eight percent of all paraprofessionals who attended CUNY earned some credits, but no degree. Black males were slightly less likely to have earned a degree from CUNY than other paraprofessionals. Among Black male paraprofessionals who

Table 2.   CUNY Attendance and Graduation of Paraprofessionals.

	#	%
All paras	21,523	100.0
Never attended	7,132	33.1
Some CUNY credits, no degree	9,742	45.3
Associate degree in education	674	3.1
Associate degree in other field	1,532	7.1
BA or higher in education	573	2.7
BA or higher in other field	1,871	8.7

Source: NYC DOE Career Training Program and CUNY Institutional Research Database.

attended CUNY, 162 earned a bachelor's degree, 96 earned an associate degree, and 642 did not complete a degree (see Table 5). Of those Black males who did not complete a degree, just 51 were still enrolled in Fall 2010.

Table 3. Race/Ethnicity of Paraprofessionals Attending CUNY.

	Paras Attending CUNY	
	#	%
Total[a]	14,391	100
Asian	712	4.9
Female	554	3.8
Male	158	1.1
Black	4,715	32.8
Female	3,815	26.5
Male	900	6.3
Hispanic	4,984	34.6
Female	4,268	29.7
Male	716	5.0
White	3,865	26.9
Female	3,329	23.1
Male	536	3.7

Source: NYC DOE Career Training Program and CUNY Institutional Research Database.
[a]Data for American Indian or Native Alaskan students and for those with unknown race/ethnicity are reflected in the Total only due to very small numbers.

Table 4. Average Cumulative GPA of Paraprofessionals Attending CUNY.

	Black Male Paras		All Other Paras	
	#	%	#	%
GPA				
0.0–2.0	223	31.3	1,768	16.9
2.1–2.5	169	23.7	1,863	17.8
2.6–3.0	173	24.3	2,618	25.0
3.1–3.5	102	14.3	2,295	22.0
Higher than 3.5	46	6.5	1,911	18.3

Source: NYC DOE Career Training Program and CUNY Institutional Research Database.
Note: GPA was not available for all Paras that attended CUNY.

Table 5. CUNY Attendance and Graduation of Paraprofessionals, by Race/Ethnicity and Gender.

	All	Some CUNY Credits, No Degree		Associate Degree in Education[a]		Associate Degree in Other Field[a]		BA or Higher in Education[a]		BA or Higher in Other Field[a]	
	#	#	%	#	%	#	%	#	%	#	%
Total[b]	14,391	9,741	67.7	674	4.7	1,532	10.6	573	4.0	1,871	13.0
Asian	712	491	69.0	15	2.1	69	9.7	32	4.5	105	14.7
Female	554	393	70.9	14	2.5	50	9.0	26	4.7	71	12.8
Male	158	98	62.0	1	0.6	19	12.0	6	3.8	34	21.5
Black	4,715	3,232	68.5	172	3.6	440	9.3	174	3.7	697	14.8
Female	3,815	2,590	67.9	160	4.2	356	9.3	144	3.8	565	14.8
Male	900	642	71.3	12	1.3	84	9.3	30	3.3	132	14.7
Hispanic	4,984	3,084	61.9	354	7.1	688	13.8	196	3.9	662	13.3
Female	4,268	2,604	61.0	339	7.9	613	14.4	173	4.1	539	12.6
Male	716	480	67.0	15	2.1	75	10.5	23	3.2	123	17.2
White	3,865	2,868	74.2	130	3.4	326	8.4	156	4.0	385	10.0
Female	3,329	2,497	75.0	126	3.8	272	8.2	127	3.8	307	9.2
Male	536	371	69.2	4	0.7	54	10.1	29	5.4	78	14.6

Source: NYC DOE Career Training Program and CUNY Institutional Research Database.

[a]Degree earned includes degrees from CUNY only. Paraprofessionals may hold degrees from non-CUNY institutions.

[b]Data for American Indian or Native Alaskan students and for those with unknown race/ethnicity are reflected in the Total only due to very small numbers.

Many paraprofessionals who withdrew prior to earning a degree had accumulated a substantial number of credits. On average, paraprofessionals who withdrew from a CUNY bachelor's program accumulated more than half of the credits needed to earn a bachelor's degree (see Table 6).[3] Among paraprofessionals who withdrew from a CUNY associate degree program, many had accumulated a significant number of credits. Compared to other paraprofessionals, Black males who enrolled in an associate degree program earned slightly fewer credits before withdrawing from the University (see Table 7). Outreach should be conducted and these paraprofessionals should be encouraged to reenroll and supported as they complete degree requirements.

Table 6. Average Credits Accumulated among Paraprofessionals Who Enrolled in CUNY Bachelors Programs and Withdrew Before Obtaining Degree.

	Men		Women		Total	
	#	Avg. credits	N	Avg. credits	N	Avg. credits
Asian	16	62.2	74	74.4	90	72.2
Black	119	71.2	473	72.4	592	72.2
Hispanic	115	68.6	435	71.1	550	70.6
White	65	78.6	336	70.1	401	71.5

Source: NYC DOE Career Training Program and CUNY Institutional Research Database.

Table 7. Average Credits Accumulated among Paraprofessionals Who Enrolled in CUNY Associate Programs and Withdrew Before Obtaining Degree.

	Men		Women		Total	
	#	Avg. credits	N	Avg. credits	N	Avg. credits
Asian	28	46.7	81	40.2	109	41.8
Black	274	27.5	851	36.4	1125	34.2
Hispanic	198	33.1	1135	44.1	1333	42.5
White	98	32.9	562	39.5	660	38.5

Source: NYC DOE Career Training Program and CUNY Institutional Research Database.

THE POLICY CONTEXT FOR THE PREPARATION OF PARAPROFESSIONALS AS TEACHERS

Although programs for paraprofessionals have been created in the past, and paraprofessionals have "made the list" when recruiting teachers from nontraditional sources, the trend has been to recruit college graduates without backgrounds in education for alternative route programs. In NYC, the Teaching Fellows program is an alternative route program that recruits recent college graduates and mid-career professionals. Approximately 1 in 10 teachers in NYC public schools was a Fellow during the 2006–2007 school year (NYC Teaching Fellows, 2007). Supporters of the program downplay the lack of training Fellows have when they first enter the classroom and the constant turnover the Fellows program sparks within NYC schools.

The federal No Child Left Behind law requires that all public school classes be taught by a teacher with a bachelor's degree who has met State certification requirements and has demonstrated competency in the subjects they teach. The emphasis on subject-matter competency results in alternative route programs targeting individuals that majored in a specific subject area. Additionally, the highly qualified teacher requirements set forth by the law are partially the basis of formulas that determine whether schools meet accountability standards. As a result, the long-term approach required by paraprofessional-to-teacher programs is not as attractive.

Title II of the Higher Education Act (HEA) may also influence the willingness of institutions of higher education to welcome paraprofessionals. HEA requires states to identify low-performing teacher preparation programs using pass rates on teacher licensure exams. Institutions of higher education must publicly report those pass rates. Colleges seeking accreditation of teacher preparation programs through the National Council for the Accreditation of Teacher Education (NCATE) must also prove that at least 80 percent of teacher candidates have passed subject knowledge tests required for certification. College officials may view nontraditional college students such as paraprofessionals as a group that may lower average pass rates.

In NYC, schools have faced significant budget cuts and a hiring freeze has been in effect since 2009 (Cramer, 2009; Hernandez, 2009). Vacant teaching positions, except those in high-need areas such as bilingual special education, may only be filled by those already teaching within the DOE, including teachers whose positions have been eliminated because of downsizing or school closures.

In spite of these hurdles, there is likely to continue to be strong union support for paraprofessionals to receive tuition benefits so they may climb the career ladder. According to the collective bargaining agreement between the NYC DOE and the United Federation of Teachers, entry-level paraprofessionals earned just $20,274 during the 2006–2007 school year, while paraprofessionals with experience and a bachelor's degree earned $32,250 (United Federation of Teachers, 2007). In contrast, newly hired teachers with a bachelor's degree earned $41,172 per year, and those with 8 years' experience earned $57,000 (New York City Department of Education, 2005). As they may be able to approximately double their earnings, the transition from paraprofessional to teacher represents a significant opportunity for upward mobility. School leaders should recognize that through a well-established benefit for paraprofessionals they can help foster a new cadre of effective and diverse teacher candidates.

RECOMMENDATIONS

Given the need for qualified teachers to fill vacancies in high-need districts and particular subject areas with shortages, new strategies are needed. There are significant numbers of paraprofessionals who demonstrate their passion for working with children each day. Although paraprofessional-to-teacher programs require a long-term approach because these individuals must first earn bachelor's degrees, research shows that paraprofessionals are much more likely to remain in teaching and to teach in high-need schools compared to other teacher candidates. It is recommended that additional resources be invested to support paraprofessional-to-teacher programs in NYC. Paraprofessionals have valuable experience they will bring with them after years of assisting in high-need areas such as special and bilingual education. Furthermore, paraprofessionals represent a significant pool of minority teacher candidates.

The CTP currently operating in NYC, offering tuition support and release time for paraprofessionals, provides a strong basis to support Black male paraprofessionals in pursuit of teacher certification. But much more needs to be done to create a strong and effective paraprofessional-to-teacher program. Paraprofessionals participating in teacher preparation programs should receive high-quality supports such as academic advising and tutoring. Academic counselors must especially help those paraprofessionals who begin coursework at a community college, to ensure coursework will articulate toward a bachelor's degree.

Mentors, such as paraprofessionals that have successfully made the transition to teacher, should be recruited to help guide and encourage participants. Programs must be designed so that courses are offered at convenient times and locations for working paraprofessionals. A cohort-based program may be especially effective because it creates a supportive student community for participants. Additionally, a more targeted and ambitious outreach campaign must be created to encourage paraprofessionals to work toward becoming a teacher. For example, principals could be encouraged to nominate paraprofessionals from their schools.

Creative solutions are required for the serious challenges our schools face. Opportunities should be provided for the thousands of paraprofessionals working in public schools to climb the career ladder. If such opportunities are provided, many will succeed and children attending public schools will reap the benefits.

A CASE STUDY OF THE KENNEDY FELLOWS PROGRAM

In 1989 John F. Kennedy, Jr. partnered with CUNY to create the Kennedy Fellows program for exemplary workers with little or no college experience in education, health, and human service occupations. John F. Kennedy, Jr.'s vision was to create opportunities for dedicated workers to achieve higher education and career advancement while also ensuring that students and other consumers had access to high-quality caregivers. Since the program's inception, more than 800 Fellows have received tuition support and career mentoring.

Tyrone's story demonstrates the power of the supplemental support available through the Kennedy Fellows program for paraprofessionals working toward teacher certification. Tyrone, a 35-year-old Black man had immigrated to the United States from Haiti in 2003. Eventually he secured a position as a paraprofessional educator with the NYC DOE. Tyrone found that he loved working with students with disabilities. When asked why he wanted to continue working in the field of special education Tyrone said, "You genuinely have people who are happy to see you every day. And you see the progress. It's an area or population that is underserved. It is valuable work I believe."

With tuition support from the CTP, Tyrone decided to pursue his teacher certification. He applied to three CUNY colleges and was accepted by a community college. Tyrone did well academically during his first year at CUNY, but he struggled to cover additional costs he incurred as a student, such as costs for text books and transportation. Tyrone felt lost within the large bureaucracy of the public university. He knew he would need to eventually transfer to a four-year college to earn a bachelor's degree and teacher certification, but he was uncertain of whether courses he was taking would transfer and whether he should complete his associate degree prior to transferring.

The Kennedy Fellows program provided Tyrone $1,000 for the academic year and access to a mentor. The financial support was helpful, and the mentoring was crucial. Tyrone ran into difficulty with a statistics course during his second year, and his mentor helpfully connected him to tutoring services. His mentor also helped Tyrone research the transfer process within the CUNY system. Tyrone is now close to completing his associate degree in childhood education with a high GPA and has plans to transfer to a four-year college next year.

DISCUSSION QUESTIONS

1. In what ways would it be beneficial for a school system to offer opportunities to paraprofessionals to pursue higher education? In what ways might a school system be challenged to provide such opportunities?
2. Should paraprofessionals be encouraged to become teachers?
3. How could paraprofessionals be supported during the process of deciding on a higher education program and desirable career path?
4. What supplemental supports might be needed for paraprofessionals to succeed in higher education? Are such supports available? Are paraprofessionals informed about such supports?

NOTES

1. The U.S. Census category for those employed as Teacher Assistants includes paraprofessionals and other types of school-support workers. Teacher Assistants employed in private schools are included. See: http://www.census.gov/hhes/www/ioindex/view.html.
2. At the time of the analysis, the CUNY Institutional Research Database included student enrollment records from 1990 through the Fall 2010 semester.
3. Most bachelor's degree programs require 120 credits to graduate, while most associate degree programs require 60 credits to graduate.

REFERENCES

Aud, S., Fox, M. A., & KewalRamani, A. (NCES 2010-015). *Status and trends in the education of racial and ethnic subgroups.* U.S. Department of Education. Washington, DC: U.S. Government Printing Office.

Clewell, B. C., & Villegas, A. M. (2001). *Evaluation of the DeWitt Wallace-reader's digest fund's pathways to teaching careers program.* The Urban Institute. Retrieved from http://www.urban.org/publications/410601.html

Cramer, P. (2009). No new hires, a cash-strapped DOE instructed principals today. *Gotham Schools.* Retrieved from http://gothamschools.org/2009/05/06/no-new-hires-a-cash-strapped-doe-instructed-principals-today/

Darling-Hammond, L. (1997). *Doing what matter most: Investing in teacher quality.* National Commission on Teaching and America's Future. Retrieved from http://www.eric.ed.gov/ERICWebPortal/detail?accno = ED415183

Darling-Hammond, L. (2000). *Solving the dilemmas of teacher supply, demand, and standards: How we can ensure a competent, caring, qualified teacher for ever child.* National Commission on Teacher and America's Future. Retrieved from http://eric.ed.gov/ERICWebPortal/custom/portlets/recordDetails/detailmini.jsp?_nfpb = true&_&ERICExt Search_SearchValue_0=ED463337&ERICExtSearch_SearchType_0=eric_accno&accno= ED463337

Hanushek, E. A., Kain, J. F., & Rivkin, S. G. (1998). *Teachers, schools, and academic achievement.* NBER Working Paper No. W6691. Retrieved from http://ssrn.com/abstract=122569

Haselkorn, D., & Fideler, E. (1996). *Breaking the class ceiling: Paraeducator pathways to teaching.* Belmont, MA: Recruiting New Teachers, Inc.

Hernandez, J. C. (2009). Schools chief bans hiring of teachers from outside. *The New York Times,* May 6. Retrieved from http://www.nytimes.com/2009/05/07/nyregion/07hiring.html?adxnnl=1&ref=joeliklein&adxnnlx=1313461477-g2jSy0rhmEmT1JZJ3YaYfw

New York City Department of Education. (2005). *Salary schedules effective November 1, 2005. Certified teachers schedule.* Office of Salary Status. Retrieved from http://schools.nyc.gov/NR/rdonlyres/4C4CE78C-CC16-43C2-BB1C-66BA7FD74BE4/0/SalarySchedule teacher1105increase.pdf

New York City Department of Education. (2011). *Career training program.* Retrieved from http://www.teachnycprograms.net/getpage.php?page_id = 84

New York City Teaching Fellows. (2007). *Program history and statistics.* Retrieved from http://www.nycteachingfellows.org

New York State Education Department. (2008). *Teacher supply and demand in New York State.* Albany, NY: Office of Higher Education. Retrieved from http://www.highered.nysed.gov/oris/stats/documents/tsd2008finalreport508.pdf

Noguera, P. (2008). *The trouble with black boys: ...And other reflections on race, equity, and the future of public education.* San Francisco, CA: Jossey-Bass.

Strizek, G. A., Pittsonberger, J. L., Riordan, K. E., Lyter, D. M., & Orlofsky, G. F. (NCES 2006-313). *Characteristics of schools, districts, teachers, principals, and school libraries in the United States: 2003–04 Schools and Staffing Survey.* U.S. Department of Education. Washington, DC: U.S. Government Printing Office.

United Federation of Teachers. (2007). *Agreement between the Board of Education of the City School District of the City of New York and United Federation of Teachers Local 2,*

American Federation of Teachers, AFL-CIO, covering Teacher Aide, Educational Assistant, Educational Associate, Auxiliary Trainer, Bilingual Professional Assistant, June 1, 2003–October 12, 2007. Retrieved from http://www.uft.org/member/contracts/paraprofessional/para_contract_07.pdf

U.S. Census Bureau. (2000). *Equal employment opportunity residence data.* Retrieved from http://www.census.gov/eeo2000/index.html

U.S. Department of Commerce. (1996). *Current population reports: Population projections of the United States by age, sex, race, and Hispanic origin: 1995 to 2050.* Washington, DC: U.S. Depaetment of Commerce.

Villegas, A. M., & Lucas, T. (2002). *Educating culturally responsive teachers.* Albany, NY: State University of New York Press.

CHAPTER 5

TEACHING ACROSS GENDER: THE DYNAMICS OF BLACK MALE TEACHERS AND FEMALE STUDENTS

Candice Crowell, Kamilah M. Woodson and Shafeeq Rashid

ABSTRACT

Black male teachers represent between two and five percent of the teaching force, yet many research studies have suggested the importance of their presence in the classroom. While most research focuses on the necessity of a larger force of Black male teachers to serve as role models for Black male students, minimal research examines their importance in teaching Black female students. In addition to this lack of research, teacher-training programs, even those that tailor their programming toward Black men, do little to address issues of teaching across gender. This phenomenon has implications for Black male teacher retention, Black female student success, and improved gender dynamics in the Black community. This chapter highlights the dynamics of teaching across gender through review of the literature and a case study. It presents

Black Male Teachers: Diversifying the United States' Teacher Workforce
Advances in Race and Ethnicity in Education, Volume 1, 59–75
Copyright © 2013 by Emerald Group Publishing Limited
All rights of reproduction in any form reserved
ISSN: 2051-2317/doi:10.1108/S2051-2317(2013)0000001009

the Gender Dynamic Awareness Model, a conceptual framework for use in teacher training that addresses five factors for Black men to consider when teaching Black female students.

Estimates of Black male teachers in elementary and secondary schools range from two to seven percent (National Center for Education Statistics, 2010; US Bureau of Labor Statistics). The lack of Black male teachers has had implications for a variety of issues in primary and secondary schools. Few accessible role models for Black male students, overrepresentation of Black students in special education, disproportionate dropout rates for students of color, and underrepresentation of culturally relevant material in the curriculum exemplify just some of the issues related to the lack of Black male presence as teachers (Brown, 2009a, 2009b). Additionally, gender dynamics between male teachers and female students, as well as male teachers and female staff, play a significant role in the effectiveness of retention efforts for male teachers. For the few Black male teachers that remain committed to the field, there are several difficulties requiring attention in teacher-training programs, such as the perception of Black male teachers as dangerous, especially when teaching across gender (Lynn, 2006).

Teaching across gender refers to the process of being educationally responsive to students of the opposite sex, while maintaining appropriate boundaries to facilitate optimum success in learning. Teaching across gender stands as an issue that remains minimally addressed in both teacher-training programs and the literature. Sinclair (2004) discusses the "extrapsychodynamics" of teaching across gender and suggest that educators often avoid acknowledgment of the sexual dynamics involved in teaching. This is a great need in considering how to retain male teachers. She states, "Mostly we have been reluctant, perhaps with good reason, to look at the dynamics of attraction, gender and sexuality in the teaching context" (p. 227). This reluctance leaves a gap in the literature and the development of pedagogy that fully supports male teachers. Compound that with the developmental milestones, as it relates to the aforementioned dynamics, that female students undergo while under the instruction of their male teachers, such as puberty, increased interest in the opposite sex, and sexual curiosity, and researchers have a glaring responsibility to articulate how this phenomena plays out at each level of education.

This chapter will explore a specific Black male teacher's experience with teaching across gender. It considers how issues of attraction and gender manifest in the classroom between female students and male teachers across the K-12 educational experience, but specifically in high school. This chapter also explores variables such as performance and masculinity among Black male teachers, and it seeks to improve their skill sets in negotiating gender related dynamics, student needs, and academic success. Finally, it introduces the Gender Dynamic Awareness Model (GDAM), a framework developed to assist Black male teachers in managing the above dynamics involved in teaching across gender.

ATTRACTION IN TEACHING

The examination of attraction in the teacher–student relationship is lacking due to the stigma associated with sexual relationships between adults and minors. Johnson (2004) refers to attraction between students and teachers as the "elephant in education's closet that has been assiduously ignored in educational research" (p. 84). Studies that explore this dynamic often use case studies or journaling (Sikes, 2006), as finding large numbers of people who will admit to experiencing attraction to their students is difficult. Johnson's (2004) study reflects on the experience of a female teacher attracted to a male student, a phenomenon less stigmatized than the dynamics of which this chapter speaks. Still, she articulates the need to give voice to this dynamic in teacher training, so as to avoid the mistake of not addressing it. She suggests that the power differential can become attractive to both teachers and students, and that while discussion or consultation about it may further foster the attraction, it is also likely to normalize, removing some of the "forbidden fruit" appeal associated with doing something dangerous. She quotes Hooks (1995), who suggests that denying feelings of attraction to a student allow for irresponsibility and a lack of accountability, because the desire is not disclosed to anyone.

The literature in psychology is slightly more open to investigating attachment to clients, as most clients are also adults. Given the power differential and ethics around relating to clients in a sexual manner, there are similarities useful for comparison in attraction between teachers and students. Bridges (1994) states, "Unrecognized, misunderstood, or inappropriately handled, sexual feelings in psychotherapy may lead to a variety of unintended and untherapeutic outcomes" (p. 424). The same can be said for teaching, where if a male teacher is unaware of or reluctant to process his attraction to a student with a trusted colleague, the strain can be taxing and eventually problematic.

BLACK GENDER DYNAMICS AND PERFORMANCE IN SCHOOLS

Lynn and Jennings (2009) suggest that public schools are "hostile territory" for some Black men. Given the highly publicized challenges, real or media-marketed, between Black women and men, there is reason to believe that these challenges express themselves in the classroom as well. As mentioned above, Black male teachers account for a small percentage of the teaching population. This ratio mimics the widely held perception that there is an absence of Black men, which has implications for how female students and teachers approach and respond to them. Another gender dynamic that has been popularly discussed in the Black community is that Black women have taken on more masculine roles, having had to learn independence earlier than their other female counterparts. This phenomenon has been said to emasculate Black men, and so hostility may arise in environments where the Black males and females buy into these stereotypes. Whether the school is predominantly White, culturally diverse, or predominantly Black, Black male teachers find themselves having to create performances to manage the hostility they experience from their colleagues, administrators, and students. Maylor (2009) brings up another relevant issue for Black male teachers, as they negotiate gender. Gender dynamics differ across class, and the class differences between students and their teachers, particularly in high poverty schools, may add an additional complication to teaching across gender. Martino (2008) underscores the significance of masculinity as a classed phenomenon. The subject of Martino's case study, Steve, suggests that the working class or working poor class of students are used to a misogynistic, sexist, aggressive masculinity. Thus, a part of the performance is presenting a masculinity that is different from that to which the students are more consistently exposed.

Brown (2009a) notes how a part of Black pedagogical performance includes using personal power to garner respect with Black students. Although Brown (2009a) focuses on the relationship between Black male teachers and Black male students, it is especially important to recognize how Black male teacher's experience of gender dynamics with Black women in their personal lives influences their performance with Black female students.

Their assumptions about the emotional and social needs of their female students determine what performances are possible and appropriate. Also, given those same dynamics, the female students' expectations of Black men and their projections of their experiences all set the stage for performance. Brown (2009a) found three performance styles that Black male teachers use with Black male students: the enforcer, the negotiator, and the playful. One could argue that for interactions with female students, additional performance styles may be necessary and useful. There is no panacea when it comes to teaching Black children, so the use of a variety of styles and pedagogical performances is meaningful for Black male teachers.

DEVELOPMENT OF BLACK TEENAGE GIRLS

While the focus of this chapter is teaching across gender, it is important to briefly consider the population they are most likely to serve: Black girls. Although this section predominantly considers the experiences of high school girls, which is where the majority of teaching across gender issues occur, we recognize that there are issues across the spectrum of K-12 education. For men who teach in elementary schools, administrators and colleagues may question their sexuality and professional motives. Martino (2008) notes that male teachers, especially in elementary settings, are often viewed suspiciously for their commitment to teaching. There may be assumptions that male teachers of young girls are going to prey upon them sexually. However, from another perspective, little girls who may lack father figures, or who have complicated relationships with the men in their lives, may present challenging situations for male teachers to navigate, including precocious sexual advances or projecting negative emotions on to the teacher. Teacher training should address these situations openly and prepare male teachers to confidently, armed with information, deal with them in developmentally appropriate ways relative to the age of their students.

For Black male teachers of high school girls, more complex challenges arise, some of which stem from the teacher's relationships with women and some from the students' relationships with men. Muhammad and Dixson (2008) profile the lives of Black girls in high school. They argue that there is more literature available on teaching Black boys than Black girls. Based on this argument, and the paucity of research on Black male teachers, what we offer in this chapter is the exploration of the interaction between two of the least studied groups in educational research: Black male teachers and Black female students. We are investigating the nature of this research through a heterosexual lens, but future research should consider how homosexuality (teacher or student) influences the dynamics of teaching across gender in the Black community.

Despite media representations of Black females, Muhammad and Dixson (2008) find that Black girls in high school are resilient, self-reliant, and able to navigate peer pressure better than their counter parts. Maylor (2009) asserts that Black girls tend to outperform Black boys in the classroom. Muhammad and Dixson (2008) also articulate how teachers often depict Black female students as loud and "ghetto," without a critical consideration of how their assertive behavior contributes to their academic success. Black male teachers must negotiate a delicate balance in encouraging their Black female students without "adultifying" them, where they "oversubscribe and interpret these students' confidence, assertiveness, and academic eagerness as inappropriate or 'overly mature' behaviors that 'normal' children should and do not display" (p. 166). It may be easier to misinterpret the behaviors, attitudes, and intentions of Black female students without proper training in teaching across gender. The GDAM provides a framework for how to interact with and understand the dynamics of teaching across gender.

GENDER DYNAMIC AWARENESS MODEL

There are three main ways that Black males have traditionally interacted with Black females: mate, matron, and child. We propose that for the teacher–student relationship, another way of relating be considered: mentee. Gormley (2008) defines the mentee–mentor relationship as one in which the "mentors are both friends and teachers to their mentees and are expected to somehow manage highly intimate, mutual relationships without compromising their objective evaluation of mentee performance" (p. 45). The GDAM of relating to female students recommends that Black male teachers see their female students as mentees in this light. It requires that they endorse a progressive awareness of gender dynamics in the Black community and how they relate to women in their personal lives, a concerted effort to understand the female student's relationship with her father or other male figures, an internal acknowledgment of any attraction that may be present between the teacher and student, and a commitment to navigate the above variables, consulting with trusted colleagues as needed, with the intention to assist the student in reaching academic and social success in school and life (Fig. 1).

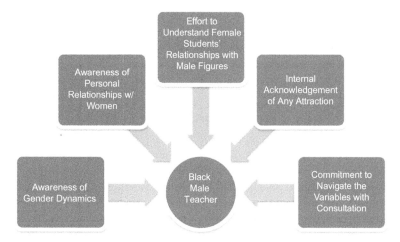

Fig. 1. Gender Dynamic Awareness Model.

AWARENESS OF GENDER DYNAMICS

This model centers the Black male teacher's understanding of female students in a conscientious and committed manner. With awareness of gender dynamics, he can thoughtfully perform the teaching role because he knows what the underlying societal messages are about men and women, and how those have played out in his life. Whether he endorses a belief in the popular stereotypes about Black men and women impacts his perception of what students might expect of him. For example, if he recognizes that a popular misconception about gender relations is that Black women do not need Black men, he is better prepared to carefully confront the manifestation of that in a female student who has internalized it.

AWARENESS OF PERSONAL RELATIONSHIPS WITH WOMEN

Gormley (2008) suggests that elements of attachment influence the relationship between mentees and mentors. Thus, an awareness of one's personal relationships with women provides insight into what attitudes may transfer in interaction with female students. If the male teacher has consistently struggled in his interactions with Black women in the past, this may be an area of exploration for him to investigate the nature of these soured relationships. His improved insight will reflect in his ability to respond to his female students as individuals, rather than as members of a group with whom he struggles.

EFFORT TO UNDERSTAND FEMALE STUDENTS' RELATIONSHIPS WITH MALES

Along the same vein, making the effort to understand his female student's relationships with her male figures allows him to establish rapport by demonstrating interest in her life. This interest becomes useful in how he responds to her academic and behavioral needs. He is also privy to how her negative or positive relationships may affect her communication style with him, as well as her classroom behavior. If she has had difficult relationships with the men in her life, then he may have to persistently work through her resistance to his attempts to connect.

INTERNAL ACKNOWLEDGMENT OF ATTRACTION

Acknowledgment of attraction, in either direction, should not be shared with the student. If he recognizes his attraction, then he must process that with a trusted colleague and determine whether he can maintain professional boundaries. If not, he may ask that the student be transferred. Although this may compromise the relationship, it is a protective measure. He may also need to seek professional counseling to address the dynamics behind the attraction to prevent it from becoming unmanageable with other students in the future. If the attraction is from student to teacher, he may need to consult with a trusted colleague or supervisor to determine the extent of the student's expression of the attraction. On the milder end, he may be able to manage it by clearly stating his romantic unavailability, but highlighting his commitment to her academic success. On the more pronounced end, he may need to ask that the student be referred for counseling to address her difficulties with boundaries. She may also need to be transferred.

COMMITMENT TO NAVIGATE THE VARIABLES WITH CONSULTATION

A commitment to navigate these complex factors must be engendered and maintained throughout his tenure as a teacher. This should occur through professional development and consultation with colleagues. While the authors recognize that many schools avoid this topic in their teacher in-services, finding a trusted colleague with whom to converse or seeking therapy around these issues may prove invaluable in developing one's ability to respond to any issues that arise in a way that promotes the student's growth and teacher professionalism. An example of how these variables present in the classroom is evident in the following case study.

CASE STUDY

The goal of this case study is to provide a baseline experience with a female student who exhibited several behaviors that Black male teachers encounter. Although not all aspects of the GDAM were employed, through analysis of the case study the model was developed.

VIGNETTE

Shanda was a 14-year-old freshmen girl with origins in rural Georgia, by way of several lower income housing projects. She initially entered Temper, a low performing urban high school with Black students representing 95 percent of the student body, with less than half of the semester left in the school year. Although quiet, she displayed the negative traits of many girls her age with her background, such as combative body language in the face of redirection, low tolerance for completing difficult tasks, and a short and easily provoked temper. It also became clear that Shanda's reading and writing skills were not up to 9th grade standards. She often struggled with critical thinking concepts and analysis in literature. She was a very slow starter when it came to independent writing, and when she was finally able to write, she did not venture beyond simple sentences and low-level vocabulary. However these issues put her on the same level as the majority of her classmates at Temper.

Shanda came from a nonnuclear and troubled family background. Shanda's mother has been incarcerated several times since she was in grade school. Her father has been the main caretaker, along with his longtime girlfriend. The resulting issues of her mother's absence, combined with the typical angst of teenage girls, made her difficult to handle. Because she was coming from a lower income family, she did not have nicer clothes or maintain her hair or nails. Unfortunately, Shanda's appearance was generally dowdy, and her buckteeth exposed her to ridicule by classmates.

Most preeminently, however, was the fact that she had physically matured early and possessed a curvaceous and voluptuous figure that garnered her nonhostile attention, so like many teenage girls she flaunted it when she could.

Shanda often erupted violently into outbursts whenever she felt challenged or disrespected by another student. As with many teenagers, especially those with troubled backgrounds hailing from urban environments, a sense of bravado and a feared reputation were of high importance, and she placed the preservation of that reputation above all things. She also had trouble asking for help, or would often get frustrated at difficult work and act out in order to have a reason to not do her assignments. Thus, it was not odd to have to reprimand Shanda for an outburst or separate her from another student before a situation escalated. Shanda's main positive attribute was that she was generally quiet and did not go out of her way to bother others or reciprocate negative behavior.

CASE ANALYSIS – TEACHER PERSPECTIVE

Strategies Attempted with Shanda

I made a conscious decision to soften my demeanor in an effort to create a more nurturing learning environment. I observed that some female students constantly acted out to receive reprimands for negative behavior, but what they wanted more than anything was attention, whether positive or negative. A simple strategy to use was to give positive attention before negative behaviors started.

Eventually through this approach, I developed what almost became a character to use with my female students. Many of the students that required this character had the same problems of poor parental oversight on their appearance, absent or problematic male figures, and low self-esteem. To combat this I actively turned up the charisma and became a more supportive and solid male figure. I complimented them without flattering. I always smiled and spoke to them with a distinctly even and "smooth" tone of voice. This made it much easier to correct their behaviors and work without evoking their wrath or fudging a line. In special cases, such as Shanda's, it became necessary to provide one on one attention in order for this "character" to yield the best results. I decided that I would begin pulling Shanda aside whenever possible for a few pep talks. Conversations ranged from the silly, to the work at hand, to the deeply philosophical and personal.

This helped build trust and a connection that would be needed to begin altering and correcting her behavior in my class.

Once trust was established, I would often set goals for her as she came in. Some goals were work-based, but most were behavioral. It was important to present the idea to her as an option as opposed to a command. Like many people, it became clear that Shanda appreciated the feeling of autonomy. Over the semester, outbursts greatly diminished and she began to display elements of self-efficacy in my class. She became a motivated self-starter and had little problem staying on task. Shanda finished the class with a well-earned B and a refreshing attitude. She left me with an intense, yet short-lived, spirit of confidence and accomplishment.

Upon returning to school the following year as a sophomore, Shanda was several months pregnant. Initially, she still displayed traces of the positive attitude she had during my time with her. However, by the time she reentered my class the second semester of her sophomore year, now a mother, she had severely regressed back to her previous combative and angry state. None of the characteristics that I had displayed the previous year seemed to have a lasting effect on her behavior or her work ethic. It is hard to say if it was the burden of parenting or home conflict that forced her to regress so drastically, as both seemed to be preeminent fixtures for her, evidenced through our conversations and her work. She had become even more combative, less effectual in her work, and more inappropriate in her dress and appearance. By the latter half of the semester, I was forced to resort to typical disciplinary action with her, which often resulted in her being removed from class.

Reflections from a Black Male Teacher

This case is highly indicative of the many delicate and unique challenges that male teachers encounter when working with young female students. Aside from the obvious issues related to social standards and norms, such as the perception of teaching being a feminine profession, or the likelihood of being in a small minority of male teachers in a given school, there is also an unfamiliarity with young women as a whole. There are few resources or systems, whether professional or social, for male teachers to hone their abilities to learn from or relate to young women. General male culture and social norms do little to prepare men for this foreign realm. Many men will claim to struggle to relate to their wives, daughters, and girlfriends, so relating to young ladies where there is no other bond is doubly difficult.

Furthermore, one might consider the large percentage of male teachers who are also coaches and come into teaching for the specific purpose of being a coach. The world of athletics is not known for progressive understandings of gender dynamics. Simply put, there is the potential for large schisms between male familiarity and expectations when it comes to female students.

Another significant issue is the constant threat and danger of crossing boundaries of appropriateness with female students. Many male teachers spoke to me in my first days of teaching about how it only takes an accusation of inappropriate behavior from a student to end your career. The case study spoke on Shanda's proclivity for wearing clothing that accentuated her figure. At age 14, it is unlikely that Shanda understood exactly why she was doing this except for the fact that it garnered her attention. This puts a male teacher in an uncomfortable position. It is unrealistic for most male teachers not to notice when a female is trying to dress provocatively. On the other hand, it is completely reasonable and expected that a male teacher will not act in a way to promote such behavior or cross the line for what's appropriate. Still this conflict creates tension.

To address this tension, some male teachers purposely avoid dealing with attractive female students. Many teachers will be lackadaisical with dress code reinforcement, for fear of drawing attention to the student's appearance. The truth is that many males typically know how to relate to women through three lenses: matron, mate, or my child. Clearly, none of these roles fits in the context of the classroom. It begs the question of how a teacher builds a productive teaching relationship with a student without opening himself up to problems. The uncontrollable and unpredictable behavior of a typical teenage girl creates a veritable minefield of possible career threatening dangers that many men avoid by simply being cold and limiting the emotional connections that are often needed to teach at a high level. Thus, teaching across gender proves to be not just an issue of professional development, but of common social structure.

Gender dynamics become even more significant when dealing with female students who lack positive or constructive men in their personal lives. One often deals with misplaced anger, confusion, fear, inappropriate attention seeking, and other barriers to doing the job effectively. This case is not at all unique in its challenges, however said challenges are still difficult to address, and there is a severe dearth of support and help for those faced with similar situations. Aside from gender gaps and misunderstandings, one of the biggest challenges in this situation was the overall ineffectual nature of Temper high school and its lack of resources and support for Black male teachers dealing with issues of teaching across gender. The culture of the school expects the teacher to handle everything on his own. With that unspoken understanding in mind, the "character" creation strategy, or performance, was more a desperate act of self-preservation than a calculated strategy for addressing the issue.

The traits and characteristics displayed in the "character" are not natural to me. In general, I am not what one would consider "smooth" or "cool." My early students often described me as dry and stoic, and normally I would adopt a hard-line stance toward students who consistently broke rules. Fortunately, I quickly recognized that this was highly ineffective in a setting where authority and self-efficacy are not functioning properly. Furthermore, young ladies who have not had any male authority figures in their lives often react aggressively and negatively when faced with rigid discipline. I understood that girls at this age throughout generations have always idealized that image of men being cool, witty, charming, and independent, so in addition to Brown's (2009a) three pedagogical performance types, I might add the "nonchalant/cool" character. In a way it created a dynamic where female students often went out of their way to please me. This is an important dynamic in the student–teacher relationship, as it promotes compliance in students, but it may backfire when their self-efficacy is not intrinsic and based exclusively on a desire to please born out of insecure attachment.

As stated earlier, many males' baseline experiences with women are born out of courting and flirtation. The basic principles of those behaviors were still very much at work, but without the ulterior intentions in mind. I did my best to make her feel special, and conversely she acted in a way that reinforced the behaviors I desired. When dealing with members of the opposite sex, it can often be beneficial to find out what they appreciate about men and display that behavior in order to make them devoted allies. It is actually a very similar representation in regards to the common goals that are inherent in work relationships, as well the delicate line of appropriateness in male/female dynamics in the work place. With students it is no different; it is only made more difficult by the fact that with up to 20 different girls in a classroom, you cannot always display every characteristic that appeals to every student.

The biggest question I still hold is why there was such a sharp regression by Shanda after she had her child. A possible conclusion came to me when I asked her about the baby's father, to which she often responded with expletives. The same oddity that had made Shanda unique amongst her peers, the presence of her father, had possibly created a situation where her attitude toward men could be potentially worse than other students. Because

Shanda's father was around, she naturally may have expected that her child's father would have done the same. It is clear, however, that the father of Shanda's child had not been around at all. This greatly intensified the sense of anger and resentment that was present in her the previous year. It was also during this semester that I first heard her begin to denigrate her own father. With the relationships she had with the two most significant men in her life broken, it seemed impossible for me to play the role of positive character "part time" and expect to see results. To truly remedy the issues of Shanda, a comprehensive approach involving counseling, social services, and additional assistance may have been needed.

CASE ANALYSIS – ADDITIONAL PERSPECTIVES

The teacher and Shanda were met with some challenges that were largely based in teaching across gender. Shanda came from a socioeconomic background different than the teacher, and they seemingly held different views about masculinity, as the teacher felt he must perform to be an effective teacher. Also, Shanda engaged in some attention-seeking behaviors, such as dressing provocatively and outbursting to cover up some issues with self-esteem and self-efficacy. Although the teacher recognized them as attention-seeking behaviors, he felt helpless and unsupported in dealing with them. Unequipped with appropriate training around teaching across gender, he was left to try skills that were not always grounded in best practices. Kenny (2002) examines this question in his exploration of teaching across gender with female nursing students. He argues that the employing institution must provide the support necessary for a male teacher to be effective with his female students. This resulted in hit or miss successes, and then an overall decline in Shanda's behavior and academic performance. The teacher used Brown's (2009a) idea of pedagogical performance, but admittedly felt uncomfortable and inauthentic in its execution. He possessed a certain level of cultural awareness, but perhaps socioeconomic status differences between him and Shanda created a block in his perception of her culture and her perception of his. Finally, he took the time to provide individual attention and worked to build rapport with Shanda. The extraneous situation of her relationships with men, however, may have put a block up on how she perceived his earnest efforts to help her succeed.

From the GDAM, the teacher engaged the student in an effort to understand her relationships with other males and possessed an awareness of gender dynamics in the Black community. He also demonstrated a commitment to navigate the variables involved in teaching across gender, but reported an unsupportive environment, not conducive to consultation, which may have proved helpful. The teacher provided some awareness of his personal relationships with women, but that may have been further considered and explored through consultation or counseling to determine how those difficulties manifested from his end. Also, there was acknowledgment that the student dressed provocatively, but limited insight into whether there was attraction based on a fear instilled by other male teachers early in his career. Discussion questions that lend themselves to deeper exploration of this case using the GDAM and the dynamics of teaching across gender follow.

DISCUSSION QUESTIONS

- What can be done to deal with the misconceptions that both teachers and students may have about each other, based on personal relationships with members of the opposite sex and gender dynamics in the Black community?
- As a teacher, how do I assert boundaries, especially if attraction exists, yet still remain open to developing a teaching relationship?
- How do Black male teachers identify trusted colleagues and supervisors with whom to discuss issues around teaching across gender?
- How do my relationships with women influence the way I perceive and interact with my female students?
- What resources are available to support Black male teachers in navigating cross gender dynamics?

IMPLICATIONS FOR TEACHER-TRAINING AND FUTURE RESEARCH

Developing teacher-training curriculum for Black men that enhances their skills in these areas has the potential to reduce the complications that arise when teaching across gender. Many Black male teachers get into the profession because they are looking to be a role model for the Black male students. Although Black men may feel competent in their abilities to relate to young Black men, their ambivalence about relating to young Black women has implications for the teacher's retention, as well as the student's academic advancement. When Black male teachers are trained well in all areas, they are more likely to perform well in the classroom and continue in their positions. When teachers interact well with students and are attuned to their life experiences, they can step back and depersonalize the seemingly intentional aggressive or seductive acts. It allows them a healthy objectivity, from which they can connect to the student and not the situation.

The teacher in the case study endorsed an understanding of what the GDAM promotes, but he acknowledges that support and training around teaching across gender would have further developed his ability to work with Shanda. We suggest that this model be tested in training programs that specifically target Black male teachers, and that research around its effectiveness be conducted and promoted to move teachers toward a stronger understanding of teaching across gender dynamics. Additionally, it seems that the bulk of research has been put in place to address giving women better tools to teach males. More work investigating the reverse is needed. Finally, this chapter attends to the relationship between Black male teachers and Black female students. Research should pursue how the phenomenon of teaching across gender manifests between Black male teachers and non-Black female students, as well as how homosexuality of the teacher, student, or both interacts with this experience.

Policy around teaching and teacher training might begin to consider implications of cross gender experiences and how they impact the learning environment. With alternative teaching certifications becoming more popular, these organizations may enhance their curriculum around this issue, which may fit well in coursework on multicultural education. Further, schools may incorporate professional development specific to teaching across gender for novice and veteran teachers alike, as veterans may have been educated in a time that did not promote respectful male/female interactions at any level.

CONCLUSION

In some situations students will struggle to maintain positive behavior no matter what one does. The "character," or performance, strategy is not one that can or should be replicated for every male teacher; however, its basic premise, along with the GDAM, lies in building relationships and learning one's self and one's students. It reinforces the fact that in order to be effective as a male teacher of female students, a teacher has to evaluate his experiences and values, as well as his students', in relation to gender. There is little room for rigidity in education, thus different aspects of the model may be more germane depending on the situation. Different pedagogical performances may be required depending on the student, but it is important to negotiate the performance in relation to maintaining a comfortable level of authenticity. The GDAM promotes the balance and flexibility required of all teachers, but as the need for Black male teachers is especially pressing, the implementation of the model is suggested for programs that train high numbers of Black male teachers.

REFERENCES

Bridges, N. A. (1994). Meaning and management of attraction: Neglected areas of psychotherapy training and practice. *Psychotherapy, 31*(3), 424–433.

Brown, A. L. (2009a). "Brothers gonna work it out": Understanding the pedagogic performance of African American male teachers working with African American male students. *Urban Review, 41*, 416–435.

Brown, A. L. (2009b). "O brother where art thou?" Examining the ideological discourses of African American male teachers working with African American male students. *Race, Ethnicity, and Education, 12*(4), 473–493.

Gormley, B. (2008). An application of attachment theory: Mentoring relationship dynamics and ethical concerns. *Mentoring & Tutoring: Partnership in Learning, 16*(1), 45–62.

Hooks, B. (1995). In praise of student/teacher romances. *Utne Reader, 68*, 37–38.

Johnson, T. S. (2004). "I secretly relished that delicious feeling of excitement": A rhizoanalysis of teacher-student attraction. *Taboo, 8*, 84–95.

Kenny, G. (2002). Male teacher female students: A novice teacher reflects. *Nurse Education Today, 22*, 571–577.

Lynn, M. (2006). Education for the community: Exploring the culturally relevant practices of Black male teachers. *Teachers College Record, 108*(12), 2497–2522.

Lynn, M., & Jennings, M. E. (2009). Power, politics, and critical race pedagogy: A critical race analysis of Black male teachers' pedagogy. *Race, Ethnicity, and Education, 12*(2), 173–196.

Martino, W. (2008). The lure of hegemonic masculinity: Investigating the dynamics of gender relations in two male elementary school teachers' lives. *International Journal of Qualitative Studies in Education, 21*(6), 575–603.

Maylor, U. (2009). "They do not relate to Black people like us": Black teachers as role models for Black pupils. *Journal of Education Policy, 24*(1), 1–21.

Muhammad, C. G., & Dixson, A. D. (2008). Black females in high school: A statistical educational profile. *The Negro Educational Review, 59*(3–4), 163–180.

Sikes, P. (2006). Scandalous stories and dangerous liaisons: When female pupils and male teachers fall in love. *Sex Education, 6*(3), 265–280.

Sinclair, A. (2004). Teaching managers about masculinities: Are you kidding? In C. Grey & E. Antonacopoulou (Eds.), *Essential readings in management learning* (pp. 217–236). London: Sage.

U.S. Department of Education, National Center for Education Statistics. (2010). *Teacher attrition and mobility: Results from the 2008–09 teacher follow-up survey.* NCES.

CHAPTER 6

THE CASE OF A BLACK MALE MATHEMATICS TEACHER TEACHING IN A UNIQUE URBAN CONTEXT: IMPLICATIONS FOR RECRUITING BLACK MALE MATHEMATICS TEACHERS

Julius Davis, Toya Jones Frank and Lawrence M. Clark

ABSTRACT

In an effort to diversify the nation's teaching force, the U.S. Department of Education has initiated programs to increase teachers of color in U.S. schools, particularly Black male teachers in subject areas like mathematics. In that Black male mathematics teachers continue to be under researched, particularly in urban school contexts, it was critical that their cases were (1) documented and analyzed in an effort to better understand their experiences and practices, and (2) utilized to inform teacher recruitment efforts. In this chapter, we present the case of Floyd Lee, a Black male mathematics teacher who participated in an NSF-funded research study of Black Algebra 1 teachers teaching in an urban school district. We present experiences that appear to influence his practice

Black Male Teachers: Diversifying the United States' Teacher Workforce
Advances in Race and Ethnicity in Education, Volume 1, 77–92
Copyright © 2013 by Emerald Group Publishing Limited
All rights of reproduction in any form reserved
ISSN: 2051-2317/doi:10.1108/S2051-2317(2013)0000001010

and consider how his case, and other cases like Floyd's, might inform
efforts to increase the number of Black male mathematics teachers in
U.S. schools.

The U.S. Department of Education has been advancing a new policy
initiative called the Teach Campaign to recruit more Black teachers,
particularly Black male teachers in critical subject areas like mathematics
(Duncan, 2011). This policy initiative has targeted Historically Black
Colleges and Universities (HBCUs) and urban high schools as places to
recruit more Black teachers. The campaign has sought to increase the
number of Black teachers and has placed emphasis on recruiting more Black
male teachers nationally to 5% of the teaching force by 2015, which
amounts to 80,000 Black male teachers who will be recent college graduates
and career changers over the next four years (Gordy, 2011). Although the
campaign has sought to recruit Black male teachers and teachers of
mathematics, it has been unclear how many Black male mathematics
teachers were expected to be among the 80,000. Overall, the Teach
Campaign has been heralded as an important program, and both opponents
and supporters of President Barack Obama have congratulated him for
advancing such an innovative policy (Cottman, 2011).
   As graduates of HBCUs and former middle and high school mathematics
teachers, we applaud the President's efforts. However, as mathematics
educational researchers interested in issues of equity, race, and teacher
identity, several questions and cautions came to mind in light of the
campaign. An important question that emerged for us was "To what extent
was the research base on the experiences and practices of Black male
teachers consulted to structure the goals of the campaign?" In that Black
male mathematics teachers continue to be an under-researched population
in mathematics education (Brown, 2000; Leavitt, 2010; Peterek, 2010;
Weaver, 2001), it was important to have some sense of how the goals of the
campaign were framed against the limited research literature available.
Furthermore, this was an important question to consider given that research
has moved beyond characterizing Black teachers as simply "role models"
and has shifted to exploring the varied culturally specific practices teachers
of color brought to their classrooms (Irvine, 1989). A related caution that
emerged for us was to consider how the Teach Campaign might promote the
message that increasing the number of Black male teachers may be perceived
as the most effective solution to a complicated problem – the problem of
Black student underachievement. We believe that we must be careful to

manage the expectations placed upon Black mathematics teachers and their benefit to Black students as well as their role in promoting Black student achievement. Issues that plague Black student achievement were influenced by a multitude of factors (Jencks & Phillips, 1998; Martin, 2009) at multiple levels, thus the quest for a solution should be a shared enterprise through initiatives at the social, legislative, community, and individual levels. Lastly, despite a shared history, it was important to recognize that Black teachers, including Black male teachers, were a highly varied group that may not all possess characteristics that will be effective with all Black students, especially Black male students (Rezai-Rashti & Martino, 2009).

In this chapter, we first briefly examine the Teach Campaign initiative and explore the research literature on experiences and practices of Black teachers and Black male teachers. We follow this discussion with the presentation of a case of a Black male mathematics teacher, Floyd Lee, and discuss how our understanding of his influences to teach, personal perspectives and experiences, and classroom practices may inform the Teach Campaign and similar efforts.

THE TEACH CAMPAIGN

In early 2011, Arne Duncan, Secretary of the U.S. Department of Education, held town hall meetings at Morehouse College in Atlanta, GA and Howard University in Washington, DC to announce and discuss a federally funded teacher recruiting initiative titled The Teach Campaign. The sites of the meetings were purposefully scheduled at the two HBCUs due to the Teach Campaign's explicit focus on recruiting Black males into teaching. According to *The Root's* Cynthia Gordy (2011):

> A big piece of the TEACH campaign pitch is that, for talented, dedicated black college students, teaching is a moral imperative. With nearly 50 percent of African-Americans dropping out of high school, Duncan contends, teaching is a way to be part of the solution. It's an opportunity to give back to your community. It's a way to make a difference for young boys who desperately need positive role models in their lives. (Para. 5)

The Teach Campaign was casting "the moral imperative" and "the need for positive role models" as central rationales for Blacks to begin a teaching career, yet there was some empirical evidence to support the need for more Black teachers, and particularly Black male teachers. Klopfenstein (2005) found that Black female teachers positively affected Black male students' advancement to rigorous mathematics courses beyond Geometry and likewise for Black male teachers teaching Black female students. She also found that as the percentage of Black mathematics teachers increased so did the number of Black students enrolled in Algebra II after completing Geometry. Dee's (2004) research indicated that Black students' academic performance increased when taught by Black teachers for at least a year. Other researchers have found that Black teachers who teach Black students increased their academic performance, minimized behavior problems, and prepared them for life (Foster, 1994a, 1994b; Walker, 1996).

Yet a review of other research studies of Black teachers revealed a complicated picture. Howse (2006), for example, found that not all Black mathematics teachers possessed positive beliefs about Black students' ability to do mathematics. Others have cautioned that there was a tendency in the research literature to essentialize Black teachers' experiences and practices and that the heterogeneity of their experiences was often ignored (Clark, Johnson, & Chazan, 2009). Furthermore, Lynn (2001) cautioned against developing strict formulas that outline the elements of Black teachers' practices because doing so would suggest that Black teachers' practice was monolithic. In short, as suggested by Villegas and Irvine (2010), a comprehensive research base was needed to support efforts to increase the number of Black teachers.

EXPLORING THE LITERATURE TO PROVIDE INSIGHT INTO BLACK MALE MATHEMATICS TEACHERS

Our examination of the literature provided further insight into the experiences and practices that Black teachers brought to the profession. The practices that Black teachers brought to the profession were multi-dimensional, multifaceted, and heavily influenced by their life and educational experiences (Mitchell, 1998; Patterson, Mickelson, Hester, & Wyrick, 2011; Ramsey, 2008). These experiences included growing up in diverse family structures, coming from differing socioeconomic back-grounds, and living in communities of varying urbanicity and demo-graphics. Black teachers' academic experiences also played a major role in shaping their practice, including their attitudes toward school, academic performance, and relationships with their teachers and peers. The types of colleges and universities that Black teachers attended also shaped their identity and practice. Most Black teachers, including Black mathematics teachers, attended HBCUs (Foster, 1994a; Lewis, 2006). Teachers who attend HBCUs may have different racialized experiences than those attending predominately White institutions. Thus, teachers' racialized experiences, both in and out of school, may influence their identity and practice (Martin, 2009). Further, teachers' professional experiences (e.g., teaching in diverse school contexts and working with students from particular demographics) may also shape their practice.

The unique experiences of being a Black person may provide Black teachers with qualitatively different life experiences than their counterparts of other races. Some argue that these experiences may help Black teachers connect and build relationships with their students (Davis, 2010; Moody, 2003); however, there was danger in generalizing this assertion to all Black teachers. The literature points to the value of having Black teachers in classrooms that serve Black children (Irvine, 1989), especially Black boys (Foster & Peele, 1999). We caution that this does not mean that Black teachers were a panacea that will eliminate all of the challenges facing Black students' educational attainment and performance (Toldson, 2008, 2011). Lynn (2001) noted that, "Studies of Black teachers become inconsequential if [researchers] cannot provide some evidence that what these teachers do in classrooms actually make a difference in the lives of Black students" (p. 43). Black teachers' practices were not monolithic. In fact, their practices were just as varied and diverse as the teachers themselves.

While there has been a growing body of literature about Black teachers in general, there continues to be very little research about the experiences and practices of Black mathematics teachers (Clark, Jones, & Davis, 2011). Most of what has been gathered about Black mathematics teachers, has come primarily from four lines of research including: (1) studies focusing solely on Black mathematics teachers (Brown, 2000; Leavitt, 2010; Peterek, 2010; Weaver, 2001); (2) studies of Black students who described their Black mathematics teachers (Davis, 2010; Ellington, 2006; Moody, 2003); (3) research and reports of teachers taken as a whole that provide partial insight into Black mathematics teachers' practice and experiences (Haberman, 2004); and (4) broader studies of Black teachers that include Black mathematics teachers (Foster, 1997; Lynn, 2001; Walker, 1996). Although these studies have provided some insight about Black mathematics teachers, little has been gathered that specifically address Black male mathematics teachers. This may be attributed to their small number in the teaching force. Most studies have examined the experiences and practices of Black female teachers (Lynn, 2001).

Dwyer (2011) estimated that only 1.7% of today's K-12 teachers were Black men, which suggests that Black male mathematics teachers comprise less than 1% of all U.S. teachers. Black male teachers have been sought after for numerous reasons including: (1) their ability to develop meaningful relationships with their students; (2) their ability to serve as role models and shatter stereotypes for all youth, especially Black male youth; (3) their ability to be strict, yet caring, classroom managers and disciplinarians; (4) their ability to improve the academic performance of their students while preparing them for life; (5) their ability use cultural references to teach and reach their students; and (6) their ability to be advocates for Black students, especially Black male students (Foster, 1995; James, 2002; Lewis, 2006; Lynn, 2006; Martino & Rezai-Rashti, 2010). Lewis (2006) contended that Black male teachers were needed to expand conceptualizations of Black males beyond athletes, entertainers, and criminals for all students.

Foster (1997) and Lynn (2001) captured the experiences and practices of two Black male mathematics teachers who taught in different time periods and community contexts. Their stories were illustrative of the findings in the literature about Black teachers, both in general and in mathematics education. Foster captured the experiences and practices of Everett Dawson, a Black male mathematics teacher and 41-year teaching veteran who taught in segregated and integrated schools in rural North Carolina. Lynn provided a contemporary portrait of the experiences and practices of Leon, a Black male mathematics teacher and former gang member of mixed heritage who taught in an urban school in Los Angeles. The time periods in which Everett and Leon taught were also salient to their experiences.

Everett and Leon had distinct pathways to becoming certified mathematics teachers. Because he loved math, Everett decided to major in mathematics at North Carolina A&T, an HBCU. Despite a lucrative offer to work with computers for the War Department, he decided to become a teacher at the request of his foster mother. Boswell (2010) and Lewis (2006) indicated that Black male teachers' family members and former teachers were important allies in persuading them to go into teaching. Everett was initially resistant, but grew to enjoy the profession. After graduating from a small religious college, working in business and as a substitute teacher, Leon changed careers to become a mathematics teacher. Leon and Everett's stories highlight the diversity of pathways to teaching mathematics for Black men.

Everett and Leon's racialized experiences illustrated how Black teachers' race and context influence their decisions to teach, as well as their identity and practice (Martin, 2009). Everett, who spent the majority of his teaching career in all-Black, rural segregated schools, believed that his colleagues did a remarkable job with the resources they had available. As he reflected on his experiences teaching in segregated and desegregated schools, Everett believed that Black teachers were able to support Black students better in all-Black schools. He also believed that Black students in desegregated schools were not being prepared for the challenges of being in a racist society. When assigned to teach a course for Black students characterized as difficult and academically incapable, Everett developed an applied mathematics course that connected mathematical concepts to these students' lives to help them succeed.

Leon's story presented a totally different perspective of Blackness and racialized experiences based on his upbringing and family structure. Leon's father was African American and his mother was Japanese. He was comfortable with both his African American and Japanese heritage. Lynn (2001) admitted to almost overlooking Leon as a research participant because he did not look Black to him. This experience reminded Lynn to expand his conceptualization of what it means to be Black and to acknowledge the heterogeneity and variation of Black people. Leon's portrait forces us to recognize African American as an ethnicity or cultural identity and not a race (Lynn, 2001). Leon's sociopolitical consciousness, ethnic pride, and sense of community development as a Black person emerged as he left the gang and engaged with Black educators who were active in the civil rights movement. These racialized experiences became salient in his teaching practice. He integrated mathematics and social justice topics in his teaching. He connected history, racism, and mathematics to teach his students that Black people had to prove that injustices actually occurred to them by supporting their claims with facts.

The differing experiences across racial, community, academic, and familial experiences of Leon and Everett point to the heterogeneity and variation of Black male mathematics teachers. Further, this literature suggests implications to consider when recruiting Black men into the teaching force. Drawing upon this literature, we present the case of Floyd, a Black male teacher and participant in a larger study of well-respected Black mathematics teachers who participated in an NSF-funded research project of urban Algebra I teachers. When we examine his case in light of the literature reviewed, we suggest issues to consider in the recruitment of Black male mathematics teachers that may inform the Teach Campaign's efforts.

METHODOLOGY: THE CASE STUDY OF FLOYD LEE

We utilized a descriptive case study to understand the experiences of Floyd Lee, a young Black male mathematics teacher who was in the first two years of his teaching career at the time of this study. The guiding research question was: How does a Black male mathematics teacher draw on his experiences and worldview to develop practices to teach Black students in an urban school? We employed case study research methodologies to intensely study Floyd and the complex phenomena of the shortage of Black male mathematics teachers. We collected data as interviews, observations, videos, field notes, memos, and documents. The data corpus consisted of approximately 9 interviews and 25 classroom observations. Using the data sources, we focused on details that provided a rich description of Floyd and his practice. Our analysis of the data focused on the development of an in-depth case description of Floyd's experiences and practices (Creswell, 1998; Yin, 2009). Additionally, we used the data sources from this study to triangulate findings to increase construct validity (Yin, 1994). The findings from this study were limited due to our focus on a single case that presented a challenge for generalizing the findings to Black male mathematics teachers in other settings.

FINDINGS

Floyd Lee was a 24-year-old Black male who was heavily influenced by his parents. He described his childhood community as all Black, middle class, and blue collar. He was raised as an only child in a two-parent household with parents that guided him through life, instilled discipline, and helped him make important life decisions that included becoming a mathematics teacher. Floyd noted that his father was very stern and that his parents insisted that he do the things that they asked of him, such as dressing neatly, even if he thought they were senseless requests. He believed his childhood experiences taught him life lessons that carried over into his adult life and teaching.

Floyd's family structure and upbringing played a major role in his decision to teach. After graduating from high school, he attended a local HBCU. While he was in college, his mother suggested that he pursue a career in teaching. Floyd followed his mother's suggestion, but was torn about whether to teach high school English or mathematics. He chose to teach mathematics because he thought his skills were stronger in mathematics than in English. He also decided to teach in the district where he grew up. He did this out of his concern that the district and the students were underserved and in need. He believed teaching was a means to give back to his community. Floyd taught in a very unique urban school district.

Urban, in this context, refers to the district's geographical proximity to a large, metropolitan city that enrolls predominantly Black and/or Latino students and also enrolls a high percentage of students participating in a free and reduced lunch program. The district Floyd taught in was unique given its location to three other urban school districts, the relative wealth in this school district was higher than most urban school districts in the area and nation and the racial composition of the area. The urban school districts were fairly large in comparison to school districts in the state and nation.

Floyd attributed his success in mathematics primarily to high expectations placed on him by others. "When you are successful in mathematics," Floyd stated, "I think people see you as like this really super smart person. I never really thought I was, like, super smart. I thought I was, like, an average guy." He graduated from college having earned a 3.6 GPA, a bachelor's degree in mathematics, and teaching certification in secondary mathematics through a traditional teacher education program.

During his academic career, Floyd succeeded in mathematics but struggled to come to terms with courses that emphasized proof and conceptual understanding. He acknowledged: "The proof classes were the ones I probably had the most difficulty with." Floyd was more interested in getting mathematical tasks done for the purposes of fulfilling the requirements to earn his bachelor's degree, rather than for the admiration of the discipline. Floyd sent a similar message about learning mathematics to his students. Floyd felt that his students should learn mathematics to accomplish long- and short-term goals, specifically to graduate from high school. He did not feel that teaching mathematics was the most important aspect of his job. He stated, "People might ask, 'Well, so why does he teach math?' But for real, and I don't know if you notice this in my teaching ... the math is so insignificant." He felt that it was more important to influence his students' life and educational choices, much like his parents did for him. Floyd wanted his students to earn grades that would help them get to the next step in life, whether it was college, a trade school, or a job.

Floyd acknowledged his contextual and experiential limitations and considered them in guiding his students. First, Floyd and his colleagues felt tremendous pressure to have students pass the statewide high school mathematics exit exam. Second, Floyd felt like he had to combat the broader societal messages being communicated to students about their ability to do mathematics. Third, he viewed the images of Black people portrayed in the media as a challenge to his efforts to positively influence his students. To combat these messages of limited ability and negative stereotypes, Floyd used speeches to deliberately address issues about the social, academic, and mathematical behaviors that could potentially interfere with his students' futures. Floyd was concerned that his students were choosing to represent themselves in ways that closely identified with hip-hop culture and this association would ultimately deny them social and professional opportunities later in life.

While he felt it was important to counter the negative images students faced, he did not see his role as being a surrogate father. He acknowledged his youth and inability to talk to students about issues beyond his own life experience. Floyd stated, "I do try to model ... if nothing else that, you can get through this high school thing ... and ... start to develop your life. Cause that's really about as far as I could tell you ... I've gotten through high school; I've gotten through college. And I'm working on establishing my career ... I can't tell you about starting a family ... I don't know nothing about that – haven't started that." Floyd openly admits that he cannot tell his students about starting a family because he has not gotten to that point in his life.

Floyd shared the collective racial/ethnic identity and cultural heritage of his Black students. Floyd's classes were 77% Black, 18% Latino, and 5% White. Floyd's familiarity with the community and school and his closeness in age to his students provided Floyd with an emic perspective of his students' personal and academic life. Floyd took pride in having insight into his students' personal and academic lives. In summary, Floyd's case illuminated practices from the literature of Black teachers. His case illustrated that his upbringing, views about mathematics, views about his students' life, academic and mathematical choices, and views about the influences of broader society's messages on his students heavily influenced his practice as a mathematics teacher. While many of his experiences and practices aligned with the literature, we raise several issues that were not prevalent in the existing literature base.

CASE ANALYSIS: DISCUSSION, IMPLICATIONS, AND CONCLUSION

We present three points for consideration that arise from the examination of Floyd Lee's case that may inform the Teach Campaign's efforts to recruit and retain Black male mathematics teachers. First, we suggest that the Teach Campaign reexamine the expectations placed upon young Black male teachers. Black male teachers are often recruited to serve as teachers so that they may benefit underserved communities and be role models for Black boys. Young Black male teachers should not be expected to be "other fathers" (Lynn, 2002) or be burdened with the responsibility of saving young Black boys or the Black community. Consideration needs to be given to the fact that many of these young men are recent college graduates and career starters who may not have children or families. Many of them are also getting acclimated to the idea of being on their own, building their careers, and managing their finances and household responsibilities. Young Black male teachers have experiential limitations that need to be considered and respected. The campaign should think of ways to help young Black men manage the expectations and pressure being put on them. Young Black male teachers should able to decide what expectations and responsibilities they can realistically take on in their career without the external pressure. Floyd's case supports our recommendation. He recognized his limitations in teaching life lessons to his students beyond where he was in his own life and openly discussed this in his interviews.

Second, the Teach Campaign should consider multiple pathways to teaching that could encourage more Black men to become mathematics teachers. Floyd's case helps us to think about ways to get more Black male teachers into the profession by rethinking certification routes and the supports put in place to help prospective Black male mathematics teachers matriculate through higher-level mathematics courses. Floyd did not necessarily see himself as being a "math person" or good at mathematics. He noted his struggles in higher-level mathematics courses in college. Further, he did not think that teaching mathematics was the most important part of his job. We surmise that there are probably a number of young Black men who do not see themselves as stereotypical "math persons" or exceptionally good in mathematics (Thompson, 2010). However, if given the proper supports, they could be promising additions to the teaching profession.

Moreover, we have to provide Black males who do not see themselves as "math persons" or who are uncomfortable with higher level mathematics courses with options and support structures to get them certified to become mathematics teachers. Thus, we propose that the Teach Campaign encourage these Black males to purse alternative certification routes for middle school to enter the profession. These programs do not require prospective teachers to major in mathematics or take the same number of mathematics courses as traditional mathematics majors seeking secondary certification. This area of certification will also allow interested Black men to assume responsibility for making a difference in the mathematical experiences of

Black boys at the middle school level. Middle school mathematics is an important juncture for boys, especially Black boys (Berry, 2008; Davis, 2010; Thompson, 2010) because it provides a needed foundation for them to be able to purse higher-level mathematics in high school and college.

We also recommend that the Teach Campaign examine the support structures provided to Black males majoring in mathematics to become teachers in traditional secondary teacher education programs. Floyd's case illustrates that he experienced problems with higher-level mathematics in his teacher education program that may have shaped his perspective about the nature of mathematics and teaching mathematics. Floyd's case suggests that he may have benefited from a cohort structure in his higher-level mathematics courses similar to the model advanced by Fullilove and Tresiman (1990). The Teach Campaign should consider investing in developing a cohort model to support young Black men in successfully completing higher-level mathematics courses and to increase their confidence and self-efficacy in higher-level mathematics. This model should be examined to figure out how to create a learning community that Black men find useful to support their learning of mathematics and enhance their peer interactions in the cohort.

Finally, we suggest that the Teach Campaign think of ways to leverage the support of families to encourage more young Black men to become mathematics teachers. As previously mentioned, researchers have found that family members of Black men were important allies in increasing the number of Black male teachers (Boswell, 2010; Lewis, 2006). Floyd's case supports these research findings. Similar to Everett's case in the literature review, his mother encouraged him to pursue a career in teaching. One challenge for programs like the Teach Campaign in leveraging family support is figuring out how to build meaningful relationships with them. Another challenge for these programs may be the difficulty in dealing with family members' past negative experiences as students and as mathematics learners and how these experiences may have shaped their views of mathematics (Martin, 2006). Nevertheless, the Teach Campaign should figure out how to encourage family members to support this effort and to encourage young men to pursue a career in teaching mathematics.

Floyd's case provides a window into issues that need to be further discussed about recruiting, supporting, and retaining Black male mathematics teachers. The following discussion questions come to mind: (1) How do programs such as the Teach Campaign build and leverage relationships with the families of Black men in the teacher recruitment process? (2) How do university programs designed to develop Black mathematics teachers build and manage cohort-based experiences for them? (3) What types of professional development experiences should teacher recruitment programs offer young Black male teachers to prepare them for the complexities of teaching in underserved school and community settings? (4) How should university-based teacher education programs acculturate Black male mathematics teachers into the experience of teaching young, Black male students? (5) How should programs like the Teach Campaign as well as university-based teacher education programs help young Black male teachers manage the negative stereotypical messages about Black students in the media with their responsibilities as teachers? By reflecting on the literature presented, Floyd's case, and the issues raised in these questions, programs such as the Teach Campaign and teacher education programs may potentially recruit Black men who have not considered teaching mathematics as a viable career option. Furthermore, attending to the cultural nuances inherit in the experiences of Black male mathematics teachers, these programs may have more success in recruiting, retaining, and supporting them in the profession.

ACKNOWLEDGMENT

The Case Studies of Urban Algebra I Teachers Project is funded by the National Science Foundation (NSF) Centers for Learning and Teaching program grant awarded to The Mid-Atlantic Center for Mathematics Teaching and Learning (MACMTL). The views expressed here are those of the authors and do not reflect those of NSF or MACMTL.

REFERENCES

Berry, R. (2008). Access to upper-level mathematics: The stories of African American middle school boys who are successful with school mathematics. *Journal for Research in Mathematics Education, 39*(5), 464–488.

Boswell, D. S. (2010). *"Missing in action": A study of the underrepresentation of African American male kindergarten through grade 12 educators in public school systems.* Minneapolis, MN: Capella University.

Brown, A. H. (2000). Creative pedagogy to enhance the academic achievement of minority students in mathematics: Lessons from African American mathematics teachers. In S. T. Gregory (Ed.), *The academic achievement of minority students: Perspectives, practices, and prescriptions.* Lanham, MD: University Press of America.

Clark, L. M., Johnson, W., & Chazan, D. (2009). Researching African American mathematics teachers of African American students: Conceptual and methodological considerations.

In D. B. Martin (Ed.), *Mathematics teaching, learning and liberation in the lives of Black children* (pp. 39–62). New York, NY: Routledge.

Clark, L. M., Jones, T. & Davis, J. (2011). *Conceptualizing the African American mathematics teacher: Utilizing historical context.* Manuscript submitted for publication.

Cottman, M. H. (2011, February 1). *Analysis: Black men, our classrooms need you.* Retrieved from http://www.blackamericaweb.com/?q=articles/news/baw_commentary_news/25556

Creswell, J. W. (1998). *Qualitative inquiry and research design: Choosing among five traditions.* Thousand Oaks, CA: Sage.

Davis, J. (2010). *A critical ethnography of Black middle school students' mathematics education and lived realities.* Unpublished dissertation, Morgan State University, Baltimore, MD.

Dee, T. S. (2004). Teachers, race, and student achievement in a randomized experiment. *The Review of Economics and Statistics, 86*(1), 195–210.

Duncan, A. (2011, February 1). *The next generation of teachers.* Retrieved from http://www.whitehouse.gov/blog/2011/02/01/next-generation-teachers

Dwyer, L. (2011, March 9). *Spike Lee wants more Black male teachers.* Retrieved from http://2025bmb.org/connect-read.php?id=14798

Ellington, R. (2006). *Having their say: Eight high achieving African-American undergraduate mathematics majors discuss their success and persistence in mathematics.* Unpublished dissertation, University of Maryland, College Park, MD.

Foster, M. (1994a). Chapter 12: Effective black teachers: A literature review. In E. R. Hollins, J. E. King & W. C. Hayman (Eds.), *Teaching diverse populations: Formulating a knowledge base.* Albany, NY: State of New York Press.

Foster, M. (1994b). Educating for competence in community and culture: Exploring the views of exemplary African American teachers. In M. J. Shujaa (Ed.), *Too much schooling, too little education: A paradox of black life in white societies* (pp. 221–244). Trenton, NJ: Africa World Press.

Foster, M. (1995). African American teachers and culturally relevant pedagogy. In J. A. Banks & C. A. M. Banks (Eds.), *Handbook of research on multicultural education* (pp. 570–581). New York, NY: Macmillan.

Foster, M. (1997). *Black teachers on teaching.* New York, NY: Carroll & Graf Publishers.

Foster, M., & Peele, T. P. (1999). Teaching Black males: Lessons from the experts. In V. Polite & J. Davis (Eds.), *African American males in school and society: Practices and policies.* New York, NY: Teachers College Press.

Fullilove, R. E., & Tresiman, P. U. (1990). Mathematics achievement among African American undergraduates at the University of California, Berkeley: An evaluation of the mathematics workshop program. *Journal of Negro Education, 59*, 463–478.

Gordy, C. (2011). Arne Duncan wants you as a new recruit. *The Root*, January 31. Retrieved from http://www.theroot.com/blogs/black-college-students/arne-duncan-wants-you-new-recruit

Haberman, M. (2004). *Teacher burnout in black and white.* Milwaukee, WI: The Haberman Foundation.

Howse, M. (2006). *What is the nature of African American teachers' beliefs about mathematics and how do these beliefs relate to their beliefs about the performance of African American students?* Unpublished dissertation, Florida State University, Tallahassee, FL.

Irvine, J. (1989). Beyond role models: An examination of cultural influences on the pedagogical perspectives of black teachers. *Peabody Journal of Education, 66*(4), 51–63.

James, C. (2002). Achieving desire: Narrative of a black male teacher. *International Journal of Qualitative Studies in Education, 15*(2), 171–186.

Jencks, C., & Philips, M. (1998). *The black-white test score gap.* Washington, DC: Brookings Institution Press.

Klopfenstein, K. (2005). Beyond test scores: The impact of black teacher role models on rigorous math-taking. *Contemporary Economic Policy, 23*(3), 416–428.

Leavitt, D. R. (2010). *"Meek, but not weak!" A resilient Black female mathematics teacher composes a purposeful life.* Unpublished dissertation, University of Illinois at Chicago, IL.

Lewis, C. (2006). African American male teachers in public schools: An examination of three urban school districts. *Teachers College Record, 108*(2), 224–245.

Lynn, M. (2001). *Portraits in black.* Unpublished dissertation, University of California, Los Angeles, CA.

Lynn, M. (2002). Critical race theory and the perspectives of Black men teachers in the Los Angeles public schools. *Equity and Excellence in Education, 35*(2), 87–92.

Lynn, M. (2006). Education in the community: Exploring the culturally relevant practices of Black male teachers. *The Teachers College of Record, 108*(12), 2497–2522.

Martin, D. (2006). Mathematics learning and participations as racialized forms of experience: African American parents speak on the struggle for mathematics literacy. *Mathematical Thinking and Learning, 8*(3), 197–229.

Martin, D. (2009). Researching race in mathematics education. *Teachers College Record, 111*(2), 295–338.

Martino, W., & Rezai-Rashti, G. M. (2010). Male teacher shortage: Black teachers' perspectives. *Gender and Education, 22*(3), 247–262.

Mitchell, A. (1998). African American teachers: Unique roles and universal lessons. *Education and Urban Society, 31*(1), 104–122.

Moody, V. R. (2003). The ins and outs of succeeding in mathematics: African American students' notions and perceptions. *Multicultural Perspectives, 5*(1), 33–37.

Patterson, J., Mickelson, K., Hester, M., & Wyrick, J. (2011). Remembering teachers in a segregated south: Narratives of womanist pedagogy. *Urban Education, 46*(3), 267–291.

Peterek, E. (2010). *Culturally responsive teaching in the context of mathematics: A grounded theory approach.* Unpublished dissertation, University of Florida, Gainesville, FL.

Ramsey, S. (2008). *Reading, writing and segregation: A century of Black women teachers in Nashville.* Urbana, IL: University of Illinois Press.

Rezai-Rashti, G. M., & Martino, W. J. (2009). Black male teachers as role models: Resisting the homogenizing impulse of gender and racial affiliation. *American Educational Research Journal, 47*, 37–64.

Thompson, L. R. (2010). *A phenomenological study of mathematics meaning: A possible factor affecting the mathematics achievement of African American male high school students.* Unpublished dissertation, Morgan State University, Baltimore, MD.

Toldson, I. A. (2008). *Breaking barriers: Plotting the path to academic success for school-age African American males.* Washington, DC: Congressional Black Caucus Foundation, Inc.

Toldson, I. A. (2011). *Breaking barriers 2: Plotting the path away from juvenile detention and toward academic success for school-age African American males.* Washington, DC: Congressional Black Caucus Foundation, Inc.

Villegas, A., & Irvine, J. (2010). Diversifying the teaching force: An examination of major arguments. *Urban Review, 42*, 175–192.

Walker, V. S. (1996). *Their highest potential: An African American school community in the segregated south.* Chapel Hill, NC: The University of North Carolina Press.

Weaver, T. B. (2001). *Case studies of two African American middle grades mathematics teachers who taught African American students.* Unpublished dissertation, Georgia State University, Atlanta, GA.

Yin, R. K. (1994). *Case study research: Design and methods* (2nd edn.). Thousand Oaks, CA: Sage.

Yin, R. K. (2009). *Case study research: Design and methods* (4th edn.). Thousand Oaks, CA: Sage.

CHAPTER 7

"I CAN GET AT THESE KIDS": A NARRATIVE STUDY EXPLORING THE REASONS BLACK MEN TEACH

Dawn Nicole Hicks Tafari

ABSTRACT

In response to the crisis affecting black boys in public schools (skewed numbers of black boys out of school on suspension and referred for special education services, as well as low high school graduation rates), the researcher sought to amplify the voices of black male teachers who serve as walking counter-narratives for the boys they teach and with whom they interact on a daily basis (Lynn, 2006). This narrative study focuses on the interviews of four black male K-12 teachers, born between 1972 and 1987. The researcher listened to these teachers' stories, observed selectivities, and silences (Casey, 1993), and looked for the patterns that arose among the educational, experiential, and cultural experiences that these teachers have had. Four themes emerged that addressed the influences on these men's decisions to become K-12 teachers: the separate becomes connected, and the self is transformed; Black woman as inspiration; it takes a village; and transforming society by fighting students.

Black Male Teachers: Diversifying the United States' Teacher Workforce
Advances in Race and Ethnicity in Education, Volume 1, 93–106
Copyright © 2013 by Emerald Group Publishing Limited
All rights of reproduction in any form reserved
ISSN: 2051-2317/doi:10.1108/S2051-2317(2013)0000001011

I walk into the facility, and there was a little kid. He walks up to me and he, like he hits me on my arm, and he said, you know, uh, "Come and help me with my homework." The kid doesn't know me; I don't know who this kid is and uh ... I walk over, and I begin to help the kid with his homework, and when I started doing that, it was like, almost like immediately I knew for the first time this was the thing, this was the area I really wanted to be a part of ... uhm ... words can't really explain it, but it was like something within myself I really knew this was the thing I've been missing. You know, this was the part that's been missing for a while. This was the avenue that I been searching for.
                                                                    —Mr. Matthew Jamison

INTRODUCTION

As a young woman, I watched my little brother struggle in school as he tried to navigate the educational system's frequent suspensions and special education referrals. When I became an elementary school teacher in Brooklyn, New York, I witnessed firsthand how black boys were over-represented in the dean's office. Most teachers struggled with them; I struggled with them. Simultaneously, I was intrigued. I was first turned on to teaching when I joined Walton High School's Pre-Teaching Academy as a junior. I remember working with this one black male student in particular (while a pre-teacher); I remember feeling good about helping him learn science. You see, I have always had an intense love and concern for black men; I see a light inside of them that often goes unnoticed by most others.

Throughout my 13 years of experience as a public school teacher and as a teacher trainer, I have known two black male elementary school (classroom) teachers, and I can't help but wonder if there is a connection between the skewed numbers of black boys in special education and out-of-school suspension (Haggerty, 2009), the high number of black males who drop out of high school (Schott, 2011), and the low number of black male teachers. This wondering compelled me to talk to those men who succeeded despite the odds and became teachers. I want to know why they decided to work with children. What happened in their lives to make them choose education? Does it happen in an instant like for Mr. Jamison? This is important to me because I believe that black male teachers can serve as walking counter-narratives for the boys and girls they teach and for the adults with whom they interact on a daily basis. Furthermore, their positive presence in the classroom can add diversity to a teaching force that is quite homogeneous as it is predominantly white and female (Kunjufu, 2011).

METHOD

I utilized a narrative methodology to listen to the stories of black male teachers. I conducted a narrative study in order "to capture storied knowledge" (Hatch, 2002, p. 28) and gather a fuller understanding of my participants' experiences. Collins' Afrocentric Feminist Epistemology (2003) explores the idea that the "narrative method requires that the story be told, not torn apart in analysis, and trusted as core belief" (p. 56). I do not strive to "give voice" to black male teachers; they already have voices. What I do hope to do, however, is to broadcast their voices loudly and clearly and, hopefully, shed some light on "the words of [these] ordinary teachers" (Casey, 1993, p. 28). According to Riessman (1993), narrative research is a valuable "addition to the stock pot of social science methods, bringing critical flavors to the forefront that otherwise get lost. Narrative analysis allows for systematic study of personal experience and meaning: how events have been constructed by active subjects" (p. 70). My four storytellers have used language to make sense of their lives, constructing stories as a way of sharing their personal experiences with me. In order to learn of these personal experiences, I asked the "grand tour question" (Quantz, 1992, p. 189 as cited in Casey, 1995, p. 233): "Tell me the story of your life." This question is "designed to be directive enough to require concrete and precise responses, yet open enough to allow the interviewee to go in any direction ... Such questions allow the interviewees to recall anything they think might be important or amusing" (p. 233). When asked this "grand tour question," these storytellers took their interviews in various directions – approaching their stories from unique angles and perspectives. Because of this, the stories were not easily "knitted together" as in "traditional qualitative methods" (Riessman, 1993, p. vi). Instead, I looked for connections among the stories and identified unifying themes.

To acquire my pool of participants, I utilized a snowball approach. I talked to black male teachers I knew; e-mailed my invitation to participate to friends and colleagues, asking them to spread the word; and posted invitations to participate on my FaceBook page and on a website dedicated to "actively promoting a black male image." The participants whose stories I will share follow in Table 1.

The variety in teaching assignments and location added an intriguing element of diversity to this study. However, because of their various geographic locations, I conducted all interviews over the telephone and recorded them with participant permission. I transcribed each interview after listening to the tape recording two to three times. True to the narrative

Table 1.   Participant Profiles.

Teacher Name (Pseudonym)	Year Born	Grade Taught	Subject	Type of School	Geographic Area (U.S.)
Matthew Jamison	1976	5	All	Public elementary school	South
Benjamin First	1987	7	English	All-boys private school	Northeast
Craig Michaels	1972	10	Math	Alternative high school	Northeast
Donovan Easely	1984	11	English	Public high school	Southeast

tradition (Casey, 1993, 1995; Collins, 2003; Hatch, 2002; Riessman, 1993), I did not seek to "validate" or "[tear] apart" my participants' stories. Instead, I reviewed the transcripts several times, uncovering the themes that were present amongst the participants and then supported their ideas with current literature on the topic. My findings and my interpretations of those findings follow.

FINDINGS AND INTERPRETATION

The four gentlemen who talked with me all shared very interesting and lively stories that highlight a myriad of life experiences. However, four themes emerged as I reviewed my participants' stories. These themes represent the patterns most prevalent within the stories and the intertextuality visible when I compare my storytellers with other narrative studies on black male teachers. The four themes are as follows:

- The separate becomes connected, and the self is transformed,
- Black woman as inspiration,
- It takes a village ..., and
- Transforming society by fighting *for* students.

The Separate Becomes Connected, and the Self is Transformed

This first theme comes out of all four interviews. All four storytellers tell of how the separate became connected and how they were personally transformed as a result. Matthew Jamison explained his transformation process:

> I'm going through a transformation in my life when I had time to really understand that life wasn't just about me; it wasn't just about what I wanted to do. It wasn't just about everyone catering to me. And I began to learn some of these principles and life lessons through washing cars and driving the limousine service. The more I began to do it, I really wanted to provide a good service for the customers, and the more I began to develop, I guess this particular mindset, my life really began to change. It was like a shift, you know, coming from a standpoint of thinking everything was about me, going to the point …; how can I make life better for someone else?

For Matthew, transformation of the self meant an evolving mindset – going from being concerned only about himself to being concerned for others. He learned the importance of "service" and making life better for others by washing cars and driving limousines. Other studies on black male teachers also show this desire to "be of service." For example, Bridges (2009) asserts that "African American males possess a commitment to teaching African American children, particularly males who live in difficult circumstances, because in many ways they see themselves in the students" (p. 22). For Benjamin First, transformation of the self came through a different kind of service – his experience mentoring a younger black male. He shared,

> through me mentoring a young boy, meeting his family, helping him out, I was able to reconnect with my father. It all came through me mentoring a young boy, and now I look at myself. I'm a black male teacher, and I'm working with young boys, and trying to kind of rectify or re-imagine the image of the black man in people's minds.

Benjamin's transformation also resulted from how he saw what appeared to be two entirely separate entities impacting each other – mentoring and meeting his father. This connection made it clear to him that he needed to teach. And like Mr. Jackson in Milner's (2008) study, Benjamin sees the concept of "image" at the forefront of his responsibilities within the classroom.

Craig Michaels' transformation of self was constructed from several stimuli. He underwent this transformation because of how he interpreted the various messages that he was receiving.

> While I was in the car business, I was a sales manager, and I often found myself teaching my sales people over and over and over again. They would have to chase me out of the sales office. And the Lord, he just was directing – he just was saying, "Go into teaching, go into teaching, go into teaching." Plus, my wife is an educator. She's an elementary schoolteacher. So between that, pulling on my spirit by the Lord, and reading my wife's articles, reading her papers, I became interested in education.

For Craig, these exchanges were meaningful and served as the impetus for his becoming "interested in education." Craig was the only teacher in this group to specifically speak of a spiritual calling to teach. However, this "pulling on [the] spirit" is not uncommon among black male teachers. Bridges affirms that "many teachers of color draw from a rich spiritual tradition, which, they assert, played a significant role in their decision to become educators" (Bridges, 2009, p. 19). Hence, Craig, at the age of 30, deciding to no longer deny the compulsion, allowed the transformation to take place.

Unlike the other black male teachers in this study, Donovan Easely did not speak of any preservice transformation. Instead, his transformation came after he became a teacher. He expresses, "teaching English at a predominantly African-American school ... has been life-learning, and it's been a challenge." He goes on to explain that "what makes teaching rewarding for me is that I think you, through relationships and commitment, can get a chance to grow." Donovan's experiences as a new teacher in an urban setting have challenged him. However, he embraced the opportunity to grow and change as a result of his interactions with his students. Each of these men recognized a transformation happening within and not only acknowledged it, but they also welcomed it.

Black Woman as Inspiration

The second theme to emerge was that of black women as a source of inspiration. Each of the storytellers was impacted by a black woman in one way or another. During his interview, Matthew talked a lot about his mother. She was the first to ask him about becoming a school teacher when he was about eight or nine years old, but she didn't stop there. Jamison explains, "and she would ... every once in a while, make mention of me becoming a school teacher, and I would always make faces, and refer to her, like that's the craziest idea I've ever heard in my life." Most importantly, when Matthew did decide to become a teacher, his mother supported him wholeheartedly:

> I told my mother, I said, "Well, you know what?" I said, "You know all those times when you told me about becoming an elementary school teacher? I think it's time." And she and I, we joked about it ..., and I told her that I'm gonna enroll in the local college and become an elementary school teacher. That's the progress I wanted to make. And she was so excited, and I think it was about a week later, she gives me a call, and she tells me, "Well, there's a program out of Clemson that's called Call Me Mister, and it's a program designed to place more African-American males in the classroom."

Matthew's mother saw something in him early in his life that he denied and circumvented until he was a young adult. I can't help but think that her foresight was always in the back of his mind and had something to do with his eventual transformation.

Benjamin also talks about his mother in his story. However, her role was very different; she served more as a connector than as a predictor. Benjamin was with his mom when the separate began to become connected. He explained,

> one day, I was walking with my mom through the gym and [the] young boy [I was mentoring and his father were] in the gym as well, and my mom sees him, and he sees my mom, and ... I was like, "Okay, so they know each other." ... Within two to five minutes of them meeting, I basically put together that they went to school together. My mom had me while she was in college. So that being said, this guy knows my dad. But I don't know my dad ... but through me, potentially me mentoring a young boy, meeting his family helping him out, I was able to reconnect with my father.

Though this is the most that Benjamin talked about his mother during his entire story, I feel his vivid recall of this scene is important. The fact that he began painting the picture of *how* the connection between his mentee and his father was made with "I was walking with my mom" demonstrates her centrality in his life.

There is also a sense of centrality regarding the lady in Craig's life. However, she serves more as a respected source of information. As previously mentioned, his "reading my wife's articles, reading her papers," was a part of what incited him to pursue a career in education. Craig also begins his story by making direct mention of his mother and the many black female teachers and black female principals with which he came in contact as boy. He also talks briefly about how his mother takes in her two siblings when her mother dies. Then, he moves quickly along in his story to when he met his wife. He explained,

> at an early age, my mother lost her both of her parents, and her brother and sister came to live with us, so I've always had people around me – community-focused. I came to Springfield, Massachusetts on a football scholarship, and I played football for 4 years. And I met my wife at American International College my senior year.

I find it interesting how Craig associated his being "community-focused" with his large family. Furthermore, he seemed to imply that he learned to be "community-focused" from his mom in addition to being around so many influential black men and women in his community.

Like Craig, but unlike Matthew and Benjamin, the lady in Donovan's life is his wife. Newly married, Donovan speaks highly and positively of his wife. Like Craig's wife, Donovan's wife is a teacher as well. However, Donovan's wife became a teacher one year after he did.

> I'm married also. My wife is an English teacher at Stephens High School. We've been married for going on a year now ... And she's been enjoying teaching as well. She inspires me through what she does each and every day.

I find it particularly interesting that even though Donovan has two years more experience as a teacher than his wife does, it is she who "inspires" him. Additionally, I noticed that though he does make mention of his family early in his narrative, he never directly mentions his mother as the other teachers in this study do.

It Takes a Village ...

The third theme to emerge among these stories was the African proverb, "It takes a village to raise a child." In other words, each of the black male teachers received some sort of support from people other than members of their immediate families. As previously mentioned, Matthew Jamison's mother was a huge supporter of his decision to become a teacher. However, she was not alone. He explained that in the Call Me Mister program, he was

> a part of a program where, you know, you're also developing – you're partnering with other African-American males who, they're after the same goals. They're trying to achieve those same things that you're trying to achieve, and not only wanting to make a better life for yourself, but wanting to, you know, provide a better community from, you know what we came from, a better situation for other kids.

Being surrounded with like-minded individuals, other black men who were "after the same goals," provided Matthew with the much needed "village" that contributed to his success.

Benjamin did not have a "village" where he lived; however, his support system presented itself in the form of his basketball coach. It was his basketball coach who created the opportunity for Benjamin to support another boy.

> But my senior year I was working. I was playing basketball, and my coach told me, "You should work with this freshman. You know, I think you'd be a good fit for him." So I was already kind of tapped. You know as a senior in high school to like mentor this young boy, and I didn't even really understand that concept at the time.

It is through this support system that Benjamin eventually finds his path. He even recognizes, in retrospect, that by setting him up to mentor a younger student, Benjamin was being "tapped" by his coach to go into teaching.

Craig also talked much about his "village." Early in his narrative, he talked about having a "very strong ... big family," about his neighborhood being a "tight-knit community," and about having "many black role models" in his neighborhood and, later on, in his fraternity. Furthermore, he discussed how he "bumped into" a friend of a principal, and ... asked, "Do you know anybody in the school system I can talk to and can point me in the right direction to get into teaching?" It is through this friend that Craig is connected with a principal who offers him a teaching position.

Donovan did not talk openly about having any kind of strong support system at home. Though he came from a big family, he explained that his independence set him apart from his siblings:

> life for me was, in some ways, difficult being one of the few to graduate college out of my family, and being the baby out of all of my brothers and sisters. I was definitely the youngest one that graduated. And one of the first to venture out and to do some things that – to be a trendsetter – to do things that my family never did. And so, for me, it was in some ways very, very rewarding, but in some ways the road was difficult, but I'm definitely proud to say that I made it.

Donovan's silence about any direct form of familial support here is very interesting. However, like Craig, Donovan also "had a good friend" who referred him to a principal who promptly offered him a teaching position. Moreover, Donovan asserts that his "village" has manifested since he has been teaching:

> I'm so glad that I'm able to work with some of the colleagues that I'm able to work with. I can say, honestly, that I know that I wouldn't be in this place right now if it weren't for people that encouraged me and kept me on the right path when I wanted to quit.

Like his transformation of self, Donovan's support system developed after he began teaching.

Transforming Society by Fighting for *Students*

The final theme, and perhaps the most profound, to emerge was that of transforming society by fighting *for* students. Each of the black male teachers in this study sought to fight for students in some way. Matthew Jamison's first experience in the elementary school was working as a teacher's assistant in a special education classroom. He was assigned to work one-on-one with a male fifth grade student who had "some serious

emotional issues," who "everyone in the building was afraid of," and who
had "threatened to do [him] bodily harm." Ironically, when reflecting on
this experience, Matthew explains

> I loved every minute of it, and the thing that really stood out to me was that the kids in
> that class, no one was, I found out that no one was an advocate for them. You know, no
> one was really fighting for them. You know, it was always seen that they were the
> troublemakers. They were the ones who were always in trouble. You know, but there
> was no one trying to, you know, fight for them and fight for their rights. And I think
> with that in mind, that really propelled me to really make the decision to you know want
> to become an elementary school teacher ... uhm ... because I was really concerned about
> the students in that class.

Matthew was seriously compelled to teach because he wanted to help these
children. Matthew's authentic knowledge and experience about the
communities from which many of these students came fueled his desire to
want to transform society by fighting "*for* them." Lynn (2006) sustains this
concept. He asserts that "black male teachers, many of whom possess an
intimate knowledge of their students' living conditions, must be partners in
our struggle to transform our world, one classroom at a time" (p. 12). This
intimate connection was a major impetus for Jamison from the onset.

Benjamin also wanted to transform society in some way. Early in his
narrative, he talks about his experience living in the "second poorest city in
the country" but going to a private school in "one of the top five towns in
the country":

> So at school I was a little bit kind of one person. I could still be myself, but when I came
> home, you know, I came home in a uniform every day so I was kind of teased and
> ostracized for, you know, going to a private school. And, you know, kids used to tease
> me and [say] "why do you talk like that?" and "you talk white" and etcetera. And
> I didn't feel like that. I was like, "I just learned this in English class."

Benjamin's desire to fight for students comes more in the form of changing
the image of black men. The teasing he underwent as a young man
compelled him to want to work hard to "rectify or reimagine the image of
the black man in people's minds." I find this desire to change people's minds
was quite common among the literature on black male teachers. In Milner's
(2008) narrative study exploring the counter-narratives of teachers in urban
school settings, he shares the story of one black male teacher: Mr. Jackson.
Mr. Jackson was committed to social change, and his desire to teach was
shaped by "the idea that he needed to help his students find value and
relevance of school for their lives" (p. 1580). Mr. Jackson wanted his
students to be successful in life, beyond the school building's walls. In this

study, "Mr. Jackson was consistently pointing to issues of image and perceptions between and among students as well as between the teacher and the students ... [and he] worked to make sure that his students had a positive image of him ... " (p. 1581). He hoped to demonstrate to his students that they had control over how people perceived them.

Craig also desires to transform society by helping students. He talks in depth about one specific situation that happened when he was 30 years old:

> a couple of things were going on in our community. Bill Cosby had just come to Springfield, and he, basically, adopted 4 boys and sent them down to Georgia for school, paid for their education. Uhm ... 2 boys in our city, who were twins, had just gotten killed – Black young men – and the crime rate was crazy. It was just, it was just wild. And I said, "Well, I can get at these kids."

On the surface, it seems that these situations have nothing to do with Craig. He was from New York, and he did not know any of these young men personally. However, he felt compelled to "get at these kids." His concern for the community and young black men, in particular, was selfless. He wants to make a difference; he wants to transform society. Likewise, a study completed with participants in the African American Males Into Teaching (Brown & Butty, 1999) – exposed that one of "the reasons Black men enter[ed] the field of teaching [was because] they sought to make a difference in their communities and felt that teaching was a key way in which to do this" (Lynn, 2006, p. 3). Other studies on black male teachers (James, 2002; Lynn, 2002) also support this finding. In addition, the studies identify this "underlying commitment to social change" (Lynn, 2006, p. 3) as another reason why black men become teachers.

Donovan also talked of wanting to change the world by fighting for students. He talked, however, about very specific experiences that he had with his students over the last three years.

> If you only got maybe one or two children ... to see them and take them up under your wing, and for them to kind of reproduce yourself into them. Then, I would say that has been the most rewarding piece for me. And I can honestly say that I've done that. I've grabbed about 3 males that I know that comes to mind right now that I know that they have a very bright future, and I mentor them outside of teaching. We've done community service together. We've done church, and we've done dinners, and we've done a lot of things together. And I've poured into their lives throughout my life and allowed them to see the mistakes and things that I've made and, you know, to try to redirect them down a different path. So to see them doing that, and to go forward and press forward is very, very rewarding for me.

Donovan's commitment to truly changing his students' lives was apparent in his actions. Like the black male teachers in Bridges' study, Easely was "motivated to impart knowledge and prepare students to survive in a racialized society" (Bridges, 2009, p. 22). Donovan mentors his black male students and shares his life with them by being transparent and by inviting them into his world. He tries to help them transform their lives by being an example – by showing them how he has transformed his own life.

CONCLUSION

This collection of the stories of four black male teachers led to the emergence of four themes addressing the factors that influence these men's decisions to become K-12 teachers Their narratives are powerful testimonies that clearly expressed why they have decided to follow their chosen paths. These men were driven by their desires to transform themselves and society impacted by the positive influence of black women and support systems that include their families, friends, colleagues, and an athletic coach. Three of the four men pursued teaching as an alternative career after being transformed, or "called," in one way or another. The remaining teacher, though he became a teacher right after graduating from college, continues to allow himself to be transformed through his experiences with his students and colleagues.

As this is a qualitative study in the narrative tradition, my results are not generalizable. Therefore, more studies like this one need to be done because the voices of more black male teachers need to be amplified. My goal was to highlight these four black male teachers and to share their stories. Each of these stories is unique and passionate, and I hope that more black men will be "called" to take this important path. It is also my hope that black women will continue to support and inspire the black men with whom they come in contact because this is a powerful connection that should not be ignored. In addition, I hope that school districts and teacher education programs will pay attention to the reasons why these black men teach and put the support systems in place to help more black boys become successful students and more black men become successful teachers. Why? Well, I believe Matthew Jamison said it best:

> I knew how a lot of students they quickly related to the athlete, and I really wanted to do something different for not just for black students, but for all students. I really wanted to make a difference, and I wanted to give them a different picture of, you know, what a male educator looks like, you know, especially a male educator who is really concerned, *who's really concerned about them* – someone who really wants them to be successful.

CASE ANALYSIS

In the Greenson City School District (GCSD) black male students have higher suspension rates, higher percentage of referrals to special education, and lower high school graduation rates than any other racial or gender group in the district. Concerned with the underachievement of its black male students, the GCSD Board of Education held a public meeting to ascertain ideas on the steps it should take to bridge the achievement gap between its black male students and their white counterparts. As a result of the meeting and much deliberation, GCSD decided to focus much of its forthcoming recruitment efforts on hiring and retaining black male teachers in order to diversify the teaching population so that it mirrors the student body. The GCSD Board of Education has determined that the following recruitment strategies will be put in place:

- recruit black males from local universities within teacher education programs;
- offer cash incentives to black males who contractually agree to teach in GCSD for at least three years after they graduate from college;
- offer tuition reimbursement for black male teachers who pursue graduate degrees in education while teaching in the GCSD; and
- add a $2,500 increase to the GCSD salary schedule in an effort to attract more black male teachers to Greenson City.

The recruitment plan is to begin effective the next academic year. Its effectiveness will be evaluated after five years.

DISCUSSION QUESTIONS

1. What are the policy implications for GCSD's new recruitment strategy? Explain.
2. Targeting universities with teacher education programs and offering a cash incentive, or signing bonus, are GCSD's first two plans of attack. Many districts do this, especially in times of severe teacher shortage. Discuss the possible outcomes of putting strategies such as these in place.
3. The GCSD Board of Education believes that tuition reimbursement for black male teachers can help increase retention. Do you agree? Why or why not?
4. Which strategy on GCSD's recruitment plan would be the most effective? Explain.

5. Is GCSD in line with the motivations of black men who teach? If yes, how so? If no, devise a recruitment plan that you believe would be more effective. Justify your response.

REFERENCES

Bridges, T. L. (2009). *Peace, love, unity and having fun: Storying the life histories and pedagogical beliefs of African American male teachers form the hip hop generation.* Unpublished dissertation, University of Maryland, College Park, MD.

Brown, J. W., & Butty, J.-A. M. (1999). Education factors that influence African American male teachers' educational and career aspirations: Implications for school district recruitment and retention efforts. *The Journal of Negro Education, 68*(3), 280–292.

Casey, K. (1993). *I answer with my life: Life histories of women teachers working for social change.* New York, NY: Routledge.

Casey, K. (1995). The new narrative research in education. *Review of Research in Education, 21*, 211–253.

Collins, P. H. (2003). Toward an Afrocentric feminist epistemology. In Y. Lincoln & N. Denzin (Eds.), *Turning points in qualitative research* (pp. 47–72). Walnut Creek, CA: Altamira Press.

Haggerty, J. (2009, October). *From the selected works of Jennifer J.* Retrieved from http://works.bepress.com/jennifer_haggerty/1. Accessed on April 21, 2011.

Hatch, J. (2002). *Doing qualitative research in education settings.* New York, NY: New York Press.

James, C. (2002). Achieving desire: A narrative of a black male teacher. *International Journal of Qualitative Studies in Education, 15*, 171–186.

Kunjufu, D. J. (2011). *Understanding black male learning styles.* Chicago, IL: African American Images.

Lynn, M. (2002). Critical race theory and the perspectives of black male teachers in the Los Angeles public schools. *Equity & Excellence in Education, 35*(2), 87–92.

Lynn, M. (2006). Education for the community: Exploring the culturally relevant practices of black male teachers. *Teachers College Record, 108*(12), 2497–2522.

Milner, H. R., IV. (2008). Disrupting deficit notions of difference: Counter-narratives of teachers and community in Urban education. *Teaching and Teacher Education, 24*(6), 1573–1598.

Riessman, C. K. (1993). *Narrative analysis.* Newbury Park, CA: Sage.

The Schott Foundation for Public Education. (2011). *Yes we can: The 2010 Schott 50 State Report on black males in public education.* Retrieved from http://blackboysreport.org/?page_id = 14. Accessed on August 21, 2011.

CHAPTER 8

NO ONE TOLD US: RECRUITING AND RETAINING AFRICAN AMERICAN MALES IN THE COLLEGE OF EDUCATION PROGRAM FROM THE URBAN AND RURAL AREAS

Camesha Hill-Carter

ABSTRACT

African American male teachers are increasingly becoming an endangered species among the profession of education in the public, private, and higher sectors. Working with African American males at a predominately white institution (PWI), these students are often overlooked and overburdened with outliving stereotypes that are expected of them via the media montage that has been presented by mainstream America. Fortunately, these men often arise and surpass the status quo and become what W.E.B. DuBois surmises as the talented tenth. In a candid interview with the two African American males, out of the 1,200 students who are in the teacher education program at this PWI, the students talk explicitly

Black Male Teachers: Diversifying the United States' Teacher Workforce
Advances in Race and Ethnicity in Education, Volume 1, 107–116
Copyright © 2013 by Emerald Group Publishing Limited
All rights of reproduction in any form reserved
ISSN: 2051-2317/doi:10.1108/S2051-2317(2013)0000001012

on how to recruit and retain African American males, like themselves, through examples, mentors, and role models that will affect the decision of future male teachers and cultivate the African American male teachers who are currently in the program. Using a qualitative research design, the students will answer several hypotheses that will allow one a closer look into the world of young African American male teacher perspectives in the PWI.

According to Powell, 94% of all teachers in the United States are white female (2009). Minorities and white males take up the other 6%. Of that 6%, African American males are represented by a resounding 1.98% (U.S. Department of Education, 2010). One can surmise that African American male teachers are becoming rare as well as extinct. With the number of African American males dwindling to less than 40% of the graduation rate (Alexander, 2004), more of these students are choosing fields outside of education (Hill-Carter, 2010). Colleges and universities are requesting ways and information on how to recruit and retain African American males to become a part of a field that shapes and molds the future of the free world (Acthstien, Ogwa, Sexton, & Freitas, 2010). Being a teacher is not as glamorous as other professions that seem attainable by African American males. Media saturation of other occupations (e.g. recording artist or athlete) makes recruiting African American males a very daunting task (Gause, 2005).

At the predominately white institution (PWI) of this study, the current teacher education program views this dilemma as an acute problem and is looking at ways on how to rectify this issue. The census of the program lists three African American males in the entire teacher education program of 1,200 students. Only two of the three students were able to be interviewed due to full acceptance in the teacher education program (NCATE Standard 6 Institutional Report [NCATE], 2010).

The two students are from very different areas of the state. One of the students (Student 1) comes to the education program to help students like him. He was raised in one of the roughest areas in his city, where his parent put him in the bussing program for better educational opportunities. The other student (Student 2) comes from a very rural area where the lines of race still divide the city. This student stated that his educational system did not have any African American teachers or African American administrators. In a candid interview, with these students, they discuss how the university can recruit African American males to the teacher education program and retain these same students through graduation into the field of education.

NO ONE TOLD US: RECRUITING

While recruiting is the responsibility of the admissions department, many students come to a university or college because of a parent being an alumnus or the student's particular field brings him or her to a school (Behnke, Piercy, & Diversi, 2004; Rowan-Keyon, Perna, & Swan, 2011). Many students have full scale counselor offices, with colleges coming into the school for recruitment, in their high schools that help students get to the institution of higher learning that best facilitate their needs (Curry & Lamble, 2007). Other students try to figure out and find their way to a particular educational setting and/or field by sheer miracle (Curry & Lamble, 2007). This is the case for the two young men who have entered the field of education at the predominantly white institution of this study.

Their entrance into the educational field is purely purposed to affect a change in the community to which they serve. This part of the interview introduces the ideas of these students who often feel alone, until this interview, did not know that the other student existed.

Interviewer: Why did you choose education?

Student 1: I had no clue as to what I wanted to be. When I really searched myself, I did not want other students to go through what I went through as a student. I loved school but I didn't like my experiences at school. I really want to inspire students who look like me. That's why I want to become a teacher.

Student 2: Where I come from, there are not many positive role models. I have never had a male teacher. I feel that this is my calling.

Interviewer: So, you feel a sense of urgency to give back to your community?

Student 1 and 2: Yes!

Interviewer: Answer this, as an African American male in a predominately white institution (PWI) program, what can professors do to help you or facilitate a need to make our program more attractive to African American males?

Student 1: I have arrived at becoming a teacher on my own. No one really told me that I could be a teacher.

Student 2: Me either.

Student 1 con'td: You guys need to make the program more positive. We never see anyone like us. So, show us (African American Males) that you really want us here. Instead of trying to make us down play the stereotypes of being a star or an athlete, embrace us as the intellectuals that we are.

Student 2: I liked what he said, but also have a club for African American male teachers, so that we know that we are not the only males out there and the only African Americans. I really would like someone that I can relate too and they relate to me as being a man. Not trying to say Interviewer, that as a woman you couldn't help me but as a black man there is only so much you can give me. I need another black man.

Student 1: No offense, we need a man.

Interviewer: I am fine with that. You know I would hook you guys up with a program and everything but the leadership of someone that looks like you and understands your trial has a far more greater impact on your life than any woman of any race could possibly do once you have made the interaction with her. On another note, how can we recruit more African American males into this program?

Student 2: Start early and do it often.

Interviewer: Do what often?

Student 2: Getting into the schools especially rural schools as earlier as possible. The more we see, men like us, doing and saying teaching is one of the best fields to go into and you can be a teacher too. You can spotlight the benefits – show the perks. As a teacher you can, (1) affect a change, (2) have a Monday – Friday work schedule, (3) have your weekends off, (4) have holidays off and things like that.

Student 1: Yeah, like go into the high school and recruit students not only for the university but for the education program. You got to get the word out. A lot my friends now want to be teachers. They say that if [Student 1] is doing it then, I can do it too. Another thought, like pitching education as a realistic job for African-Americans. Most people don't think about education as a good living. They want to be NFL stars or make quick money. But being a teacher will not have you always watching your back or being worried about what to do if you have break someone off because they are messing around on your spot. You have to make people aware of the good living teaching provides. The media is saying there is no positive role models. By becoming a teacher, you become a role model. I can be a difference maker.

Interviewer: Yes, you can be and are a difference maker.

Student 2: Yeah, people are asking me have you made it yet! Keep working to your goal! Its like when I become a teacher then the whole community will be a teacher. That is wild.

Interviewer: No, you are the community's hope.

The underlying theme is that these students were not exposed to teaching in a very positive light. Each student felt that if they would have had a conversation about being a teacher from someone who looks like them in the position, negative forces such as not wanting other students to go through what they have gone through, would not have been the deciding factor for them to enter into education Each student had his reasoning as to why he became a teacher. One student did not think that one could make a "good living" as a teacher. The other wants to become a teacher so that other students in his old school district can see that they too can become a teacher and work in a predominately white environment. These young men were full of ideas as to how to recruit more African American males to the educational program. African American men , who are in education program, should go out into the schools, very early and very often, to advertise being a teacher (Dee, 2004). Targeting urban and rural schools, those men will begin to plant seeds into other males to become teachers as an alternative to what their environment dictates them to become. It is crucial to have organizations that meet the needs of the African American males led by African American males. This builds unity and allows students to have identity with a person by gender and race (Tatum, 2003). These students forged their way despite the obstacles they had to cross to get to this teacher preparation program. Each agreed that if someone had told them early that they could become teachers, they would have made the choice earlier and would have brought others with them.

HOW TO KEEP US: RETENTION

At this particular PWI, students take exploratory classes to explore the field to which he or she may want to enter. Through these classes, our two

African American students found themselves in a field experience class for education, which gave them positive results. In this part of the interview, the students talk about their experiences and how African American males could be retained in college and in the teacher education program.

Interviewer: Ok, let's talk about your experience in the educational system especially the teacher education program. How can we matriculate you through this program?

Student 1: I haven't had any problem with any of the instructors but I have found that instructors expect less of me or my work. I see that often when I raise my hand, the professor will look my way and call on someone else; even when my hand is the only one up.

Student 2: You too

Student 1 cont'd: I think the best thing about this training is that we are able to go into the field early on to experience teaching, too. It lets us know if teaching is really for us or not. This is what it [teaching] is going to be like whether you like it or not. I went to one school, and they were asking when was I coming back because the children just adored me.

Student 2: Yeah me too. Here is the first part of the question first. Some teachers will embrace you while others expect less from you. Those are the instructors that make me drive to prove them wrong. I am not the stereotype that they see on the television or hear on the news. Part two of your question is that I was raised in a rural community. I returned to that community to do my field experience. The students were so excited to see me especially the boys white or black. I became a part of the school in that I was the lunch and recess monitor even after my field experience. If I missed a class or something like that, then when I came the next week, the students will say things like where have you been; we've missed you.

Interviewer: So what I hear you saying is that the teacher program should not teach you as a stereotype but as a human being as well as allow others to get to know you in the communities through field experiences. How does that retain you in education?

Student 1: There is no better feeling than to know you have and will make a difference in someone's life regardless of skin color. I did my field experience in an all-white school. The only minorities were me and an Asian girl. The children wanted to learn and were excited about me. I would like to go to more urban settings to have the same effect.

Student 2: Yeah me too. We all need to be exposed to different types of environments. So, that we can have a worldwide view of how that environment looks and this environment and so on. This why we need an organization for African American males teachers period; where they can share these experiences.

From the commentary of these two men, once accepted in the program and the student's individual experiences made a difference in someone's life as well as their lives, they were hooked into becoming a teacher. They have both experienced the reverence that some of society still gives educators. Their matriculation through their individual K-12 schools has prepared them to think in a particular way about school and its people. Through experiencing different environments, communities, and schools, these students learned that people are people and they make a difference because of who they are not by their outer covering. So, retention is easy in the program once the student saw that they were needed (Dee, 2004).

CONCLUSION

There were several trends that emerged from this conversation with these two very bright African American men. One trend is identity. African American men need other positive African American men to help guide them. The students were very poignant and précised that they needed a positive African American man to lead them. Cultural identity is one of the ways student of color can identify and acculturate in difficult education arenas (Dee, 2004).

Second, the trend of solidarity became an emerging theme. The two students wanted an organization specifically for them and their field. The purpose of this organization is to galvanize strength by knowing that there are others out there like them. Organizing a professional organization that will allow them to learn their craft, without stigmatization, would be a plus for these students (Anhorn, 2008; Hill-Carter, 2010). Another trend that emerged is students are not being told that they can become a teacher. "A teacher makes a good living" as stated by one of the students. African American students are often bombarded with images from the media that deem NFL stars and/or rappers as role models (Gause, 2005). Colleges and universities must go into schools and talk to kids as early as possible and as often as possible to tell them about being an educator (Loza, 2003). The last trend of this study is when African American males arrive on the college or university campus. There must be some type of program, that is all inclusive, that will provide the students a methodology to follow when encountering instructors and/or professors who engage in unethical practices to discourage the students from achieving their total potential (Tatum, 2003).

In closing, Brown stated, "African American teachers possess specific beliefs, attitudes and dispositions needed to reach the African American learner" (2009, p. 418). To delve further in the premise, African American male teachers emanate specific beliefs, skills, attitudes, dispositions, and identity that are crucial for all learners, especially the African American male (Dee, 2004). Socialization is one of the major trends in this study. Students would prefer an organization that caters to them individually as well as ethnically and educationally. Unique to their situation, many African American males are not privy to knowing other African American males that are in the same college or even the same department. An organization mentored by an African American male will bring African American males together to form a cohesive bond as they matriculate through the teacher education program (Brown, 2009). However, there is a need of taking the information back to the community to which these students come from. As one of the students suggested, "Colleges and Universities must recruit often and early" and encourage other students from elementary through high school that they too can become teachers (Loza, 2003). Students should be exposed to different environments as well as role models who do not portray a fast lifestyle (Gause, 2005). Surprisingly enough, these students stated that once they encountered the field program and how students were drawn to them, they each began to find their true purpose of education and that is to inspire the next generation.

CASE STUDY

Raymond is a student from an urban area in one of the toughest cities in the United States. By description, Raymond has the mannerisms as well as the look of a typical media street hustler. Graduating 5th in his class, Raymond was offered a full tuition scholarship to TZTU, a PWI. Raymond knows that he wants to become a teacher to help his community but feels awkward because he is always the only male and often times the only African American in his classes.

At an all-student meeting, in the college of education, Raymond finds out that there are five other African American men that are also in the college. Raymond rushes over to meet the others students to talk with them. As soon as Raymond began to talk to the other African American males that are in the meeting, the meeting begins. Raymond pulls out his cell phone to turn the volume down, while other students are coming in and others who are talking. The professor, who is leading the meeting, yells at the African American men, "We will not have that chaos you people bring in from the streets in here." Feeling frustrated and ashamed, Raymond and the other African American males melted into their chairs and did not make a sound because this meeting was about their placement in the field, which puts them one step closer to becoming a teacher. Raymond wanted to retaliate, but he knew he would have only caused more trouble for himself. He really doesn't know if these other students will support him. After the meeting, Tyrone stated to all of the men, "I am sick of being treated like this!" "You too!" said Raymond.

DISCUSSION QUESTIONS

1. How can these students rectify the above situation?
2. Would an African American male professor make a difference? Why or why not?
3. If you were a professor listening to this meeting, what would you say to your colleague? To the students? To the chair? To the Dean?
4. What would these students need now, after being unethically accosted?
5. What would you have done if you were Raymond? Why?

REFERENCES

Acthstien, B., Ogwa, R. T., Sexton, D., & Freitas, C. (2010). Retaining teachers of color: A pressing problem and a potential strategy for "hard-to-staff" schools. *Review of Educational Research, 80*(71), 72–104.

Alexander, B. (2004, January 14). *Race and ethnicity: Number of black men dwindle in college.* Retrieved from http://www.msnbc.msn.com/id/3919177/ns/us_news-life/t/number-black-men-college-dwindle/from/toolbar. Accessed on August 28, 2011.

Anhorn, R. (2008). The professions that eats its young. *The Delta Kappa Gamma Bulletin, 74*(3), 15–26.

Behnke, A., Piercy, K. W., & Diversi, M. (2004). Educational and occupational aspirations of Latino youth and their parents. *Hispanic Journal of Behavioral Sciences, 26*, 16–35.

Brown, A. L. (2009). Brothers gonna work it out: Understanding the pedagogic performance of African American male teachers working with African American male students. *Urban Review: Issues and Ideas in Public Education, 41*(5), 416–435.

Curry, J., & Lamble, G. W. (2007). Enhancing school counselor accountability: The large group guidance portfolio. *Professional School Counselor, 11*(2), 145–148.

Dee, T. S. (2004). Teacher, race, and student achievement in a randomized experiment. *The Review of Economics and Statistics, 86*(1), 195–210.

Gause, C. P. (2005). The Ghetto sophisticates: Performing black masculinity, saving lost souls, and serving as leaders of the new school. *Taboo, 9*(1), 17–31.

Hill-Carter, C. (2010). *The effects of teacher mentoring on teacher retention.* Ann Arbor, MI: ProQuest.

Loza, P. (2003, Mar). A system at risk: College outreach programs and the educational neglect of underachieving Latino high school students. *Urban Review, 35*(1), 43–57.

NCATE Standard 6 Institutional Report [NCATE]. (2010). Retrieved from http://www.semo.edu/search.asp?q=teacher+education+program+disaggregated+information&x=7&y=12. Accessed December 2011.

Powell, S. D. (2009). *Introduction to education: Choosing your teaching path.* Upper Saddle River, NJ: Pearson Education.

Rowan-Keyon, H. T., Perna, L. W., & Swan, A. K. (2011). Structuring opportunity: The role of school context in shaping high school students' occupational aspirations. *Career Development, 59*(4), 330–344.

Tatum, B. D. (2003). *Why are all the black kids sitting together in the cafeteria.* New York, NY: Basic Books.

U.S. Department of Education. (2010). Retrieved from http://nces.ed.gov/fastfacts/display.asp?id=28. Accessed December 2011.

CHAPTER 9

DOUBLE-TALKING: THE COMPLEXITIES SURROUNDING BLACK MALE TEACHERS AS BOTH PROBLEMS AND SOLUTIONS

Tambra O. Jackson, Gloria S. Boutte and Brandy S. Wilson

ABSTRACT

Simultaneously drawing from DuBois' timeless question, "How does it feel to be a problem?" (DuBois, 1990[1903], p. 7) and contemporary notions that Black males are the solution to solving social and educational troubles in the Black community such as gang violence, high school dropout rates, and fatherless homes (Duncan, 2011), we focus on the positioning of Black males in the discourse on teacher recruitment and retention. While acknowledging the need to recruit and retain Black male teachers, we explore the weightiness of viewing Black males as the panacea for educational and social issues in schools such as disproportionate dropout and expulsion rates for students of color and youth involvement in gangs. We identify both challenges and opportunities faced by Black males and capture the complex and sometimes contradictory discourses. Particular attention is given to deconstructing the "double-talk" (Black males as

Black Male Teachers: Diversifying the United States' Teacher Workforce
Advances in Race and Ethnicity in Education, Volume 1, 117–131
ISSN: 2051-2317/doi:10.1108/S2051-2317(2013)0000001013

both a problem and a solution) which positions Black male teachers as both the crisis and the savior/superhero.

INTRODUCTION

(T)he people with the problem are the people with the solution.
                              –Myles Horton (as cited in Nordin, 2011)

Over a century ago, DuBois (1990[1903]) noted that issues pertaining to Black folks do not receive a critical eye of analysis and suggested that is the least that is owed. He wrote, "We must not forget that most Americans answer all queries regarding the Negro *a priori*, and that the least that human courtesy can do is to listen to evidence" (p. 75). Honoring DuBois' call, we turn a critical eye of analysis to the Black male crisis narrative in regard to the ways in which Black males are positioned in teaching, particularly with regard to recruitment and retention. Since Black male teachers are rarely illuminated in the research, leaving the impression that they are virtually nonexistent, this chapter examines what it means for Black males to be considered both a problem and a solution. Simultaneously drawing from DuBois' timeless question, "How does it feel to be a problem?" (DuBois, 1990[1903], p. 7) and contemporary notions that Black males are the solution to solving social and educational troubles in the Black community such as gang violence, high school dropout rates, and fatherless homes (Duncan, 2011), we focus on the positioning of Black males in the discourse of teacher recruitment and retention. We identify the challenges and opportunities that Black male teachers face. Our intent is to capture complex and sometimes contradictory discourses surrounding recruitment and retention of Black males in teaching. Particular attention is given to deconstructing the "double-talk" (Black males as both a problem and a solution). That is, Black male teachers are positioned as both the villains and the saviors/superheroes. While acknowledging the need to recruit and retain Black male teachers, we explore the weightiness of viewing Black males as the panacea for educational issues as well as how this effort may inadvertently give the impression of assuaging White teachers from their responsibilities of effectively educating all students.
   There is ample rhetoric in mass media about Black men and *their* issues. Black men are positioned as having all sorts of problems – unemployment, lack of education, imprisonment, drug abuse, domestic abuse, father-absent homes, and so forth. These issues are often presented as being innately synonymous with Black maleness and do not acknowledge institutional forces or influences (Brown & Donnor, 2011). For example, one dominant

storyline is that Black men are absent fathers because that is just how they are. The fact that the Black family has been under assault since slavery, and Black men in particular have been systematically denied opportunities to provide for their families, is rarely considered. Examining the Black male crisis narrative, Brown and Donnor (2011) argued that this narrative has not resulted in systematic improvement for the group.

> The young Black male crisis narrative overlooks the significance of the historical and structural interrelationship between race and social inequity. Thus, programs, policies, forums, and trade publications asserting to address the young Black male crisis are unlikely to produce meaningful outcomes because they lack a structural critique of racial inequity. As a result of this omission, targeted responses to the young Black male crisis narrative inadvertently recapitulate a larger societal discourse of African American males as a population needing to be saved from themselves. (p. 18)

The Black male crisis narrative has been especially prevalent in education. While Black children, especially males, lead the statistics for all things negative when it comes to schooling experiences, few colleges and schools of education explicitly explore these phenomena in their preparation programs which inadvertently leads new teachers to remain uninformed or to believe there is little they can do. For instance, when one of the authors recently shared statistics about the schooling experiences of Black children, that 85 percent of Black children are reading below grade level and not performing on grade level in math; 46 percent of Black high school students attend the 2,000 "dropout factories" (schools) in this country where approximately 60 percent or fewer of the freshmen class will graduate with a regular diploma (Children's Defense Fund, 2010) with her class of preservice teachers, many said that they did not know it was "*that* bad." The rhetoric of an achievement gap was so familiar to them that they simply assumed that Black children were just behind, not failing. Ironically, against the dismal backdrop of this pervasive Black male crises narrative, Black males' influence on youth culture and social mores is powerful. While people hold multiple and sometimes contradictory identities, this paradox regarding Black males as both thugs who are dangerous *and* superheroes who lead fashion and entertainment trends and who have the potential to powerfully impact schools is worth probing.

THUGS AND SUPERHEROES: BLACK MALES AS PROBLEMS AND SOLUTIONS

Ladson-Billings (2011) suggests that America and the world have a love–hate relationship with Black males. She notes how Black male youth culture is marketed around the world. Youth of various ethnicities in American suburbs and around the world consume and co-opt styles, clothes, and language used by Black male youth. On the other hand, Black males are often negatively stereotyped and those very same things about Black male youth are often hated and criticized by the general public. Indeed, the image and perception of Black males as criminals is pervasive and widespread in contemporary society. The terms "Black males" and "thugs" are erroneously perceived as being synonymous. For instance, a Google image search of the word "thug" yields results depicting mostly Black males. Several rap artists such as Tupac, Slim Thug, Bone Thugs-n-Harmony, and 50 Cent are among the most notable images. However, there are many young Black male faces not on any record label that are defined by mass media as being representative of a thug.

Barrett (2006) explains that contemporary media imagery produces and reproduces stereotypes. In particular, Barrett argues, video games – common spaces where Black youth are often (mis)represented – are "formative in terms of individual and social understandings of race, youth, and citizenship in the modern, neoliberal, globalized world" (p. 96). In his analysis of the popular video game, *Grand Theft Auto: San Andreas*, Barrett found that youth's social understandings of race – particularly Blackness – are shaped by the Black main character's missions in the game which usually involve beating, shooting, killing, and robbing other gang members, who are typically Black or Latino. These violent acts in the video game represent Black neighborhoods in South Central Los Angeles as "sites of fear and terror" (p. 102) produced by Black male youth on their own accord without requiring video game players to contemplate inequitable social arrangements. Preparing for their violent missions, players (typically White and middle-class), choose from an array of "Black styles" of clothing and accessories with a few clicks of their game controller paired with the beats and rhymes of rap music. Barrett argues that the implication here is that "Black culture" can be taken on and off. Importantly, one-dimensional, reductionist portrayals reify pervasive and persistent stereotypes of Black males.

Exploring the prevalence and consequences of racial stereotyping in video games, Burgess, Dill, Stermer, Burgess, and Brown (2011) conducted a content analysis of video game magazines and 149 video game covers. They found that "minority males" were more likely to be portrayed as athletes or as aggressive and found evidence of the "dangerous minority male stereotype" in video game covers. Moreover, males of color were overrepresented as thugs. Simultaneously, the authors conducted an experimental study exposing video game players to violent and nonviolent games with both White and Black characters. Participants were faster at classifying violent stimuli following games with Black characters and at classifying nonviolent stimuli following games with White characters, indicating that images of popular video game characters evoke racial stereotypes of the Black male as criminal and "thug."

In contrast, Black males who are married, college educated, gainfully employed, and own their homes are lauded as superheroes. They are viewed as being *different* than other Black males, and there is curiosity around how they "made it," intimating that being a law abiding, educated citizen is not a normative characteristic associated with Black maleness. A constant subtext is that these "upstanding" men are considered to be anomalies. Paradoxically, these "superheroes" can be readily profiled when they are at a convenience store in their sweats at night or if people do not know that they are married, educated, and gainfully employed. In these cases, they are more likely to be perceived as "just another thug" than as educated Black men. Likewise, Black male teachers are also often placed in this superhero category while at the same time unfairly treated and scrutinized.

CHALLENGES FOR BLACK MALES IN SCHOOLS AND SOCIETY

As a group, Black males make for a provocative and interesting case study with a storyline that is frequently full of contradictions about their roles in schools and society. For instance, they spend most of their schooling year being on the long end of disproportional suspensions, expulsions, disciplinary actions, and special education placements (Monroe, 2005; Morris, 2005; Noguera, 2008; Planty et al., 2009; Skiba, 2006). Indeed, Noguera (2008) suggests that for many Black males, schools increasingly resemble prisons. Given the picture that these inequitable school arrangements paints, it is no wonder that Black males are consistently framed as a problem. Contrastingly (and recently), Black males in high school and college are being told that they are a central part of the solution faced by young Black males (and others) in schools. The incomprehensibleness and incongruity of this dilemma is enough to make anyone want to holler (McCall, 1995). And yet, as we shall discuss later, many Black males have responded to the call for teachers.

Pervasive negative representations of Black males in society exist in the media and extend into schools. It should not be surprising that many educators internalize these messages of Black male criminality and intellectual inferiority and contribute to the reproduction of societal notions of "the Black male problem" through schooling policies and practices (Ladson-Billings, 2011). Under the prevailing influence of deficit perceptions of Black male culture and appearances, educators often place Black youth into lower ability groups or tracks in schools (Kao & Thompson, 2003; Oakes, 2005[1985]; Watanbe, 2008). Black males also experience under-representation in gifted education programs as a result of educators' deficit thinking about their (males) intelligence (Ford & Grantham, 2003; Tyson, 2008). Unfortunately, it is not only members of society and educators who buy into deficit thinking about Black men. Black males, themselves, may also internalize negative images and perceive themselves as a problem (Kirkland, 2011).

The ways that Black males respond to the endemic low expectations of them has been explained in a variety of ways. For example, Fordham and Ogbu (1986) and Ogbu and Simons (1998) explained that Black males devalue or disown education in order to preserve Black male pride and to avoid "acting White." Others agree with the idea that Black males may assume oppositional identities and disidentify with schooling, but also acknowledge that negative stereotypes can contribute to lower levels of motivation and performance in school (Noguera, 2003; Steele, 2003). Still others examine the role of families and social environments of Black youth as the impetus for disconnections between school and Black youth. All too often, however, these are conceived from a deficit and deprivational framework (e.g., Rothstein, 2004) which fail to take structural inequities into account.

THE COMPLEX ROLES OF BLACK MALES TEACHERS

Commenting on the shortage of Black male teachers in a June 2010 interview with CNN, U.S. Department of Education Secretary Arne Duncan advocated for more African American men to enter the teaching profession in order to decrease gaps in achievement and increase graduation rates for young Black men (Cable News Network, 2010). Duncan attributed the lack of Black male teachers to a shortage of Black males graduating from high school, completing college, and entering the teaching profession. He challenged Black men to "step-up" and "be part of the solution."

Indicative of the "double-talk" surrounding this topic, CNN asked, "Is placing black men in the classroom the answer to solving some of the problems in the black community such as gang violence, high school dropout rates, and fatherless homes? Secretary Duncan thinks so" (Cable News Network, 2010). Framing and positioning Black males as both the problem and the solution fails to address the true roots of the issue (i.e., the persistent and pervasive structural barriers that Black males face in educational institutions and society that confound the current state of affairs). In fact, Duncan was challenged three months later by a Black male high school student who was interviewed by CNN's Carl Azuz, "I've seen in most schools where they have a separation system where 20% of the class is given the most opportunity and everyone else is left out. So schools aren't doing their best in pushing everyone to their fullest potential." This student's reflection, and the experiences that give rise to it, demonstrate the complex relationship between schooling and Black males.

So what do Black male teachers have to say about all of this? The next section shares work by scholars who used critical race theory to illuminate the voices of Black male teachers. Marvin Lynn (2006a) employed Critical Race Methodology (CRM) to explore the lived experiences and meaning-making of young Black male teachers in South Central Los Angeles. Acknowledging the centrality of race and relying on the experience and knowledge of people of Color, Lynn captured the educational stories of one Black male teacher through ongoing in-depth interviews. Providing an account of the teacher's academic success despite his experiences of societal and educational marginalization, Lynn reveals the complexities involved in teaching for Black males. Indeed, the title of Lynn's article, *Dancing Between Two Worlds*, signifies Black male teachers' complex arrangements in a society where to teach is to create an opportunity to overcome racial inequality for African Americans while the process involved in becoming teachers "devalues their ways of knowing, being, thinking, feeling, and acting" (p. 238). But despite the dehumanizing process of teacher education that many Black male teachers face, Lynn found that the decision to pursue a career in teaching was grounded in the persistent influence of African American male teachers.

In another scholarly piece pointing to the complexities of Black male teachers' roles, Lynn (2006b) argued that Black men remain excluded from the classroom because of the socio-historical arrangement of schools and societal expectations for Black men. Pointing to the work of Mabokela and Madsen (2003) who found that Black male teachers experienced a double burden of being both Black and male in a profession comprised mostly by

White women, Lynn explained that Black male teachers "operate on a continuum between resistance and accommodation to White patriarchal norms and practices as a way in which to survive the profession" (p. 2500). Indeed, Lynn found, that a major contribution to the success of the three Black male teachers in his study was their cultural knowledge produced from their communities — knowledge that was generally not valued nor taught in their teacher education programs. One specific example of cultural knowledge that made the Black male teachers in Lynn's study successful was their knowledge of "street culture" — a term that Lynn borrows from Dance (2002). In other words, these teachers used students' street knowledge as a rich and relevant resource from which they connected students' existing knowledge to school curriculum. This particular finding from Lynn's study, then, begs the question whether African American male teachers without this "street knowledge" would prove as successful as the teachers in his study. Posed differently, are Black male teachers framed as solutions to the Black-male problem because it is assumed in dominant discourse that they share a personal history of lived experience and cultural knowledge?

The plot becomes even more complex when the employability of Black male teachers is examined vis-à-vis the rhetoric that Black males are the solution. While Lewis (2006) contends that school districts need more Black male teachers and outlined recruitment and retention strategies, Bell (2011) captured the essence of the double messages that are sent to Black male teachers in a narrative study about a Black male sixth-grade English/Language Arts teacher in eastern North Carolina, who tries to obtain a teaching position after graduation from college. Bell shares that as a Black male, with a Master's degree in education, the participant in his study learned that being prepared to teach did not mean that getting a teaching position would be easy. Bell captured the subtle role that racism and/or cultural hiring practices play with new Black male teachers seeking employment. The hype about the need for Black male teachers was confirmed as Bell's participant narrated that he was readily invited for interviews. However, out of eight interviews, he was offered only one job — and very late into the interview process. Most interviewers conveyed that the Black male sixth-grade teacher was well qualified and would patronizingly encourage him by saying that he would get a job quickly as a Black male teacher in high demand. It is noteworthy that most of the schools that he interviewed had no Black male teachers (or maybe only one in some cases). As expected, the interviewing process was disheartening and he often felt that he was not being seriously considered. The experience of Bell's participant not only illuminates the complexities of his lived experiences but can be extrapolated to other Black male teachers by providing a contextual perspective in understanding the multifaceted issues surrounding Black male teachers (Bell, 2011). At the same time, we recognize that his experience may or may not be typical. This is an area where additional research would be beneficial.

The research on the lives of Black male teachers indicates that they have stepped up to be part of the solution well before the Secretary of Education's call. While we do not yet have sufficient information as to how many Black male teachers encounter experiences like those described by Bell (2011), there is documentation of the kinds of programs that funnel candidates into the teacher education pipeline. We question the "double-talk" of such programs and give attention to our state as a case in point.

OPPORTUNITIES: BLACK MALE TEACHER RECRUITMENT IN SOUTH CAROLINA

Two popular recruitment programs in South Carolina – *Call Me MISTER* and *Teaching Fellows* – have the potential to address the dilemmas faced by Black males interested in teaching or entering teacher preparation programs. Given their ability to financially support preservice teachers' education and their partnerships with colleges and universities across the state, both of these programs are positioned as key gatekeepers of the teaching profession for the state.

The "Call Me MISTER" program began at Clemson University and is funded by federal, private grants, and donations. Thirteen colleges and universities within the state participate inclusive of 4 historically Black colleges and universities (HBCUs) and 4 technical colleges. The program has an expanded consortium of national partners that extend beyond South Carolina to states such as Pennsylvania, Florida, Kentucky, Missouri, and Virginia. In essence, the program specifically targets the recruitment of Black males from "underserved, socio-economically disadvantaged, and educationally at-risk communities" (Call Me MISTER, 2011, Welcome section, para. 1) into the profession at the elementary school level. The project provides tuition assistance through loan forgiveness programs, academic support, and a cohort system for social and cultural support. Over the past decade the program had over 150 participants in the teacher preparation pipeline. A 2007 report cited that 20 Black male teachers who completed the program were currently teaching in South Carolina schools (Holsendolph, 2007). Congruent with the "Black males as saviors" mantra, principals of the Black male teachers from the "Call Me MISTER" program express high praise for the impact that the "Misters" have had on the social development of their students. Once long-term impact data from this program is available, it can provide data regarding whether or not the prophecy of Black male teachers as "superheroes" can be fulfilled. Importantly, these new Black male teachers will need to receive support and mentoring necessary to succeed and should not be expected to perform miraculous changes without support from administrators and other teachers as well as changes in school policies which currently privilege certain groups of students and teachers.

Teaching Fellows is a state funded recruitment program involving 11 colleges and universities (one HBCU). The program was created in response to the state's teacher shortage. Their mission is "to recruit talented high school seniors into the teaching profession and help them develop leadership qualities" (Center for Educator Recruitment, Retention and Advancement [CERRA], 2011a). Each year scholarships of upto $6,000 per year over four years are awarded to high school seniors who demonstrate high academic achievement, service to their school and community, and a desire to teach. Recipients owe one year of teaching in South Carolina public school for every year they receive funding, and they must complete this obligation within five years of graduation. The program boasts of its track record to recruit and retain teachers for the state's public schools. Seventy-one percent of Teaching Fellow graduates are employed in South Carolina public schools.

Ten-year demographic data (2000–2010) from the South Carolina Teaching Fellows programs indicated that only 9 percent of the fellows were African American (Center for Educator Recruitment, Retention and Advancement [CERRA], 2011b). While the report did not disaggregate the demographics to show the number of Black males, it is evident that the percentage is likely low since only 1 percent of the 1,781 fellows were males. There is an opportunity for the Fellows program to aggressively recruit and graduate more African American male teachers since they are disproportionately underrepresented among the fellows. Blatant disparities such as this one make the sincerity of efforts to recruit Black males into teaching questionable. Whether because of cumulative effects of unequal schooling, policies which are not flexible and Black-male teacher friendly, pervasive stereotypes, lack of interest among Black males, or other factors, there is evidence that vigilant efforts to recruit Black males into teaching are needed if the profession seriously sees Black males as promising teachers who can make a difference in the lives of all students.

Though both programs are aimed at recruitment, the rationales stated in their mission statements position Black males differently. The "Call Me MISTER" program positions Black males as a solution to their mission to "increase the pool of available teachers from a broader more diverse background particularly among the State's lowest performing elementary schools" (Clemson University website). Contrastingly, the Teaching Fellows program positions Black males as needing to prove themselves "talented" as their mission is "to recruit talented high school seniors into the teaching profession and help them develop leadership qualities" (CERRA website). Considering that over the past 11 years, less than 10 percent of the fellows have been Black, one can surmise that either there is not a pool of talented Black male high school students or there is a lack of commitment to invest the resources in Black males.

RECOMMENDATIONS AND CONCLUSION

The positioning of Black men in the discourse of teacher recruitment and retention is consistent with macro perceptions of Black masculinity. Accounting for these broader societal notions of Black maleness, Lynn (2006a) explains that, "Black men represent irrationality, disorder, hyper-sexuality, and economic depravity" in a society where manhood is conceptualized through a "Eurocentric conception of gender, [one that] represents, order, rationality, and economic, social and political dominance" (p. 238). Like the broader societal discourse, Black males are positioned as deficient (both in their presence and in their capabilities) in teacher recruitment and retention discourse. This pervasive negative stereotype must be interrupted and deconstructed.

Future research necessitates extensive and long-term efforts to examine teacher recruitment and retention programs' mission statements, goals, and actions to determine the extent to which Black males are specifically included in program initiatives. Further, scholarship that deepens our understanding of teacher recruitment programs and colleges of education which have demonstrated success in recruiting and retaining Black males in teacher education may offer models for programs and colleges dedicated to increasing the number of Black males in the teaching profession. Additional extensive and recent statistical analysis of program and college of education demographics and recruitment efforts are necessary to gain a more complete picture of recruitment and retention. Further qualitative research efforts aimed at understanding the experiences of Black male teachers, teacher candidates, and Black males who have left teacher education programs and the teaching field could offer insights into Black males' perceptions of their positioning as problem and solution, their motivations to enter the teaching profession, and insights to improve Black male teacher recruitment and retention efforts.

From the countless task forces, reports, books, articles, and efforts such as single gender classes/academies to educate Black males at all levels (pre-k–higher education), rhetoric abounds. Therefore, a subtextual question of this chapter has been, "How can we get past the recurrent and pervasive pontification and speechifying to devise viable, sustainable, systemic, and funded solutions which can reverse and eradicate negative performance trends for pre-K-12 students?" In seeking solutions, we suggest going to the source – Black males, since they are the experts of their own lives. This suggestion is not intended to add yet another burden to Black males, but to solicit their voices instead of having others to speak for them. At the same time, we hasten to note that no one group can solve this mammoth problem; however, Black males may just lead the way – as they have done in other arenas (e.g., music, athletics, science).

> Herein the longing of black men must have respect: the rich and bitter depth of their experience, the unknown treasures of their inner life, the strange rendings of nature they have seen, may give the world new points of view and make their loving, living, and doing precious to all human hearts. (DuBois, 1990, p. 82)

DISCUSSION QUESTIONS

1. How does the positioning of Black males as saviors in education connect to broader societal gender stereotypes?
2. What are some of the social, cultural, historical, and economic issues that teacher recruitment and retention programs should pay attention to if they are serious about increasing the number of Black males in the teaching profession?
3. What are possible explanations for differences in perceptions of the need for more Black males versus White males into the teaching profession?

4. In what ways do Black males perceive and understand their positioning in society and schooling as both a problem and a solution? How do these understandings influence motivations to enter the teaching profession?
5. How might a deeper understanding of the dilemmas that Black males face in society and education inform educational policy to increase recruitment, retention, and successful teaching for Black males?
6. How might schools and teacher education programs counter the prevailing negative narratives about Black males?
7. Discuss the complexities involved in enlisting the support of the majority White and female teaching profession to recruit and retain Black male teachers?

REFERENCES

Barrett, P. (2006). White thumbs, black bodies: Race, violence, and neoliberal fantasies in Grand Theft auto: San Andreas. *The Review of Education, Pedagogy, and Cultural Studies, 28*, 95–119.

Bell, E. E. (2011). *A qualitative study/A narrative analysis of a Black male looking to teach.* Retrieved from http://www.eric.ed.gov/contentdelivery/servlet/ERICServlet?accno=ED 520106

Brown, A. L., & Donnor, J. K. (2011). Toward a new narrative on Black males, education, and public policy. *Race Ethnicity and Education, 14*(1), 17–32.

Burgess, M. R., Dill, K. E., Stermer, S., Burgess, S. R., & Brown, B. P. (2011). Playing with prejudice: The prevalence and consequences of racial stereotypes in video games. *Media Psychology, 14*(3), 289–311.

Cable News Network. (2010). Retrieved from http://newsroom.blogs.cnn.com/2010/06/21/ duncan-black-male-teachers-needed-2/

Call Me MISTER. (2011). Retrieved from http://www.clemson.edu/hehd/departments/education/ research-service/callmemister/

Center for Educator Recruitment, Retention and Advancement. (2011a). Retrieved from http:// www.cerra.org/teachingFellows

Center for Educator Recruitment, Retention and Advancement. (2011b). *Teaching fellows data.* Retrieved from http://www.cerra.org/teachingfellows/data.aspx. Accessed on August 30, 2011.

Children's Defense Fund. (2010). *The state of America's children 2010.* Washington, DC: Author.

Dance, L. J. (2002). *Tough fronts: The impact of street culture on schooling.* New York, NY: Routledge.

DuBois, W. E. B. (1990[1903]). *The souls of Black folk.* New York, NY: First Vintage Books/ The Library of America Edition.

Duncan, A. (2011). *Arne Duncan, Spike Lee urge Black men to become teachers.* Retrieved from http://www.huffingtonpost.com/2011/01/31/arne-duncan-spike-lee-black-male-teachers_ n_816597.html. Accessed on April 16, 2011.

Ford, D., & Grantham, T. (2003). Providing access for culturally diverse gifted students: From deficit to dynamic thinking. *Theory into Practice, 42*(3), 217–225.

Fordham, S., & Ogbu, J. U. (1986). Black students' school success: Coping with the "Burden of 'Acting White'". *Urban Review, 18*(3), 176–206.

Holsendolph, E. (2007, June 14). Each one, teach one. *Diverse Issues in Higher Education.* Retrieved from www.diverseeducation.com. Accessed on September 6, 2011.

Kao, G., & Thompson, J. (2003). Racial and ethnic stratification in educational achievement and attainment. *Annual Review of Sociology, 29*, 417–442.

Kirkland, D. (2011). "Something to brag about": Black males, literacy, and diversity in teacher education. In A. F. Ball & C. A. Tyson (Eds.), *Studying diversity in teacher education* (pp. 183–199). Lanham, MD: Rowman & Littlefield.

Ladson-Billings, G. (2011). Boyz to men? Teaching to restore Black boys' childhood. *Race Ethnicity and Education, 14*(1), 7–15.

Lewis, C. W. (2006). African American male teachers in public schools: An examination of three urban school districts. *Teachers College Record, 108*(2), 224–245.

Lynn, M. (2006a). Dancing between two worlds: A portrait of the life of a Black male in South Central LA. *International Journal of Qualitative Studies in Education, 19*(2), 221–242.

Lynn, M. (2006b). Education for the community: Exploring the culturally relevant practices of Black male teachers. *Teachers College Record, 108*(12), 2497–2522.

Mabokela, R. O., & Madsen, J. A. (2003). Crossing boundaries: African American teachers in suburban schools. *Comparative Education Review, 47*, 90–111.

McCall, N. (1995). *Makes me wanna holler: A young Black man in America.* New York, NY: Vintage Books.

Monroe, C. (2005). Why are "bad boys" always Black? Causes of disproportionality in school discipline and recommendations for change. *The Clearing House, 79*(1), 45–50.

Morris, E. (2005). "Tuck in That Shirt!" Race, class, gender and discipline in an urban school. *Sociological Perspectives, 48*(1), 25–48.

Noguera, P. A. (2003). The trouble with Black boys: The role and influence of environmental and cultural factors on the academic performance of African American males. *Urban Education, 38*(4), 431–459.

Noguera, P. (2008). What discipline is for: Connecting students to the benefits of learning. In M. Pollock (Ed.), *Everyday antiracism: Getting real about race in school* (pp. 132–137). New York, NY: The New Press.

Nordin, K. (2011). The politics of stigma: Starving in a land of poverty. *Human Rights Magazine Home, 37*(1). Retrieved from http://www.americanbar.org/publications/ human_rights_magazine_home/human_rights_vol37_2010/winter2010/the_politics_of_ stigma_starving_in_a_land_of_plenty.html. Accessed on September 1, 2011.

Oakes, J. (2005[1985]). *Keeping track: How schools structure inequality.* New York, NY: Yale University Press.

Ogbu, J. U., & Simons, H. D. (1998). Voluntary and involuntary minorities: A cultural-ecological theory of school performance with some implications for education. *Anthropology and Education Quarterly, 29*(2), 155–188.

Planty, M., Hussar, W., Snyder, T., Kena, G., KewalRamani, A., Kemp, J., ... Bianco, K. (2009). *The condition of education 2009* (NCES 2009-081). National Center for Education Statistics, Institute of Education Sciences, U.S. Department of Education, Washington, DC.

Rothstein, R. (2004). *Class and schools: Using social, economic, and educational reform to close the Black-White achievement gap.* Washington, DC: Economic Policy Institute.

Skiba, R. (2006). Discipline and disproportionality in the New IDEIA. Presented at the Annual Meeting of the Council for Exceptional Children, Salt Lake City, UT.

Steele, C. (2003). Stereotype threat and African-American student achievement. In T. Perry, C. Steele & A. G. Hilliard, III (Eds.), *Young, gifted, and Black: Promoting high achievement among African-American students* (pp. 109–130). Boston, MA: Beacon Press.

Tyson, K. (2008). Providing equal access to "gifted" education. In M. Pollock (Ed.), *Everyday antiracism: Getting real about race in school* (pp. 126–131). New York, NY: The New Press.

Watanbe, M. (2008). Tracking in the era of high-stakes state accountability reform: Case studies of classroom instruction in North Carolina. *Teachers College Record, 110*(3), 489–534.

CHAPTER 10

PATHWAYS TO TEACHING: THE PERSPECTIVES AND EXPERIENCES OF TWO BLACK MALE TEENS CONSIDERING TEACHING AS A CAREER

Kara Mitchell Viesca, Margarita Bianco and Nancy Leech

ABSTRACT

This chapter describes a precollegiate course designed to encourage high school students of color to explore teaching and presents the findings from case studies on two Black male students enrolled in the course who are now preparing to pursue a career in teaching. The research questions guiding the two case studies include: (a) What factors influence Black males to consider teaching? (b) What roles do race, ethnicity, and school experiences play in Black males' exploration of teaching? and (c) What aspects of the course are most influential in Black males' exploration of teaching and related fields? The results of these case studies expose the complexity of effective recruitment of Black male teachers. The insights

Black Male Teachers: Diversifying the United States' Teacher Workforce
Advances in Race and Ethnicity in Education, Volume 1, 133–149
Copyright © 2013 by Emerald Group Publishing Limited
All rights of reproduction in any form reserved
ISSN: 2051-2317/doi:10.1108/S2051-2317(2013)0000001014

provided by these two teens can provide substantial guidance for the
improvement of educational policy and practice in order to increase the
recruitment and retention of Black male teachers.

The need for Black male teachers in our public schools is clear – and urgent (Bianco, Leech, & Mitchell, 2011). National data reveal the gross under-representation of Black males in preservice teacher preparation programs (Lewis, 2006) and in our public school classrooms. However, the pathway to teaching for Black males is directly influenced by the number of Black males who graduate from high school and go on to college. In fact, a recent study found that nationwide only 47% of Black males graduate from high school and far too many are ending up in a pipeline to prison (Schott Foundation, 2010). Brown and Butty (1999) describe it this way:

> The relationship between African American students and African American male teachers is a symbiotic one – that is, the number of African American males who go into teaching is influenced by the number of African American males who attend college, which is in turn influenced by the number of African American high school graduates and so on. Unfortunately, the pipeline that moves African American students from public school to public school teaching is a leaky one. (p. 281)

Thus, any discussion of the underrepresentation of Black male teachers must first acknowledge how the public school system has failed the very population we need most in our classrooms. Researchers have consistently exposed systemic issues perpetuating low achievement for Black males, especially those from high poverty areas (Berliner, 2006; Schott Foundation, 2009). Further, Toldson (2011) examined the dramatic extent to which violence and unhelpful behavior management policies in schools are affecting the education of young Black males and their opportunities to learn. Based on these studies, it is evident that there is a substantial need for concern regarding the education of young Black males, as well the dearth in the number of Black males who choose a career in teaching.

In order to combat these issues surrounding academic achievement as well as establish a pathway into teaching for young Black males and other students of color, the Pathways2Teaching (P2T) program has been created through a school district/university partnership. Centered on a precollegiate, concurrent enrollment course titled "Introduction to Urban Education," P2T strives to encourage students of color to explore teaching and related fields as well as engage in critical examinations of issues of educational justice. Through this course, students are supported in high levels of academic development and college preparedness.

P2T was launched during the 2010–2011 academic school year with 33 students participating. The course was composed entirely of Black and Latino students with 9 boys and 19 girls. The focus of the research for the current chapter is on two of the young Black males enrolled in the course and their perspectives regarding teaching as a career; their perspectives provide valuable insights into how more Black males might be recruited into teaching. Interestingly, to date, K-12 student perspectives are rarely utilized in educational improvement efforts (Cook-Sather, 2002). However, research on utilizing student perspectives in school reform and improvement has consistently shown the value of such practices (Fielding, 2001; Kane & Maw, 2005; Wood, 2003). In fact, as Rudduck and Flutter (2000) argue, "To manage school improvement we need to look at schools from the pupils' perspective and that means tuning in to their experiences and views and creating a new order of experience for them as active participants" (p. 75). Thus, this chapter focuses on the experiences and perspectives of these two young Black males who participated in the P2T program and are now considering careers in education.

To contextualize the case studies, an overview of the course and the principles guiding its development and implementation will be discussed. Then the research methods for this study will be described and the overall findings of this investigation will be presented.

INTRODUCTION TO URBAN EDUCATION/PATHWAYS2TEACHING

In response to an urgent need to increase the representation of teachers of color in the teacher pipeline (Achinstein & Ogawa, 2011), university faculty partnered with a large urban school district to create and pilot the concurrent enrollment course, "Introduction to Urban Education." The purpose of the course is twofold: (a) to encourage high school students to consider teaching and related fields as viable and important career choices; (b) and to provide students with "college knowledge" (Smith, 2009). That is, students gain an appreciation of the importance of academic success, are provided with supports and mentors to achieve greater educational success, and gain an understanding of how to navigate college, scholarship search, and application process. The design of the course was informed by the literature on high school teacher pipeline programs (Clewell, Dark, Davis-George, Forcier, & Manes, 2000; Torres, Santos,

Table 1. Guiding Principles and Examples of Implementation for the
Introduction to Urban Education Course.

Guiding Principle	Examples
Increase high school students' awareness of the teaching profession as a viable career choice and an opportunity to engage in educational justice.	• Through readings, class discussions, and hands-on field experiences, high school students are reminded of the important role teachers, and especially teachers of color, play in the lives of children to promote educational justice. • One major component of the course is a fieldwork project where the high school students engage in teaching practices through tutoring elementary aged students from their community.
Include all interested 11th and 12th grade students in the course regardless of prior coursework or grade point average (GPA).	• In an effort to expand the traditionally targeted populations for grow-your-own-teacher programs (e.g., teacher cadet), inclusion of all students exhibiting any interest in the course was fundamental to stretching the reach current teacher recruitment efforts employ. • Full inclusion provides students who may be traditionally left out of high level learning opportunities with motivating, rigorous, academic engagement opportunities while also bringing their voices and perspectives into the learning process of the entire course community.
Utilize critical pedagogy and critical theory to provide student access to emancipatory knowledge.	• Developing an overarching critical lens on the hegemonic norms that perpetuate inequity in our society engages students in higher order thinking and application opportunities where they learn to proactively advocate for themselves as well as agitate the inequitable status quo. • Through the explicit introduction of Critical Race Theory (Crenshaw, 1988; Ladson-Billings & Tate, 1995) and the act of challenging majoritarian stories (Love, 2004) through counter-narrative writing (Duncan-Andrade, 2007; Su, 2007) students are encouraged to develop critical lenses on educational, cultural, and linguistic practices that label, sort, marginalize, and oppress.
Prepare students for college through challenging course curriculum that earns students three university course credits.	• The curriculum of the course focuses on sociological issues related to urban schools, communities, and teaching. • Through self-selected research projects, students in the course critically examine and present the results of their research publically regarding current education

Table 1. (*Continued*)

Guiding Principle	Examples
	issues that affect their lives, their local community, and P-12 classrooms throughout the state and country.
	• In their coursework, students also analyze achievement data (local, state, and national) by gender, race, ethnicity, English language proficiency, and program type (gifted/talented, special education, honors, Advanced Placement, etc.) and use these analyses to generate questions, offer solutions, and engage in critical dialogue about educational inequalities and educational justice.
	• Further, students in the course develop stronger academic literacy skills as well as earn three university credits.
Mentor students of color with teacher candidates, graduation students, and faculty of color.	• Students are provided with opportunities to establish mentor/mentee relationships with community members, teacher candidates, master's level students, doctoral students, and faculty of color. The teacher of the course is a Black woman, the professor who collaboratively teaches the course is a Latina, and the teacher candidate who supported the course during the first year was also a Latina. Further, a nationally recognized scholar of color was invited to participate as a guest speaker via internet video conference call.
Visit local college campuses multiple times across the course of the school year.	• Campus visits coincide with various state conferences as well as teacher recruitment efforts and university-wide speaker series events.
	• Students also have the opportunity to speak with current college students from similar backgrounds to learn about the challenges and opportunities attending college provides.
	• Additionally, students have the chance to attend college courses and due to repeated visits, develop a comfort in finding their way around a college campus.
Involve community and family through culturally responsive practices that includes frequent communication, home visits, and school and community sponsored family sharing evenings.	• Regular communication between family members and the teachers of the course is fundamental and occurs regularly across the year.
	• Parents are regularly informed of the work of the class and invited to learn about it through student led presentations.

Peck, & Cortes, 2004; Vegas, Murnane, & Willett, 2001) and created around several guiding principles influenced by a commitment to educational justice and equity. Each of these guiding principles is listed in Table 1 along with examples of how they are implemented in the course.

Students who complete the course should be able to discuss why it is important for students of color to consider a career in teaching, several of the current issues of educational injustice, and potential solutions to these issues. Further, students will have developed research, writing, teaching, leadership, and presentation skills to support their continued academic success as well as to their potential future profession in education.

METHOD

This case study (Stake, 2005; Yin, 2008) focused on the following research questions: (a) What factors influence Black males to consider teaching? (b) What roles do race, ethnicity, and school experiences play in Black males' exploration of teaching? and (c) What aspects of the course are most influential in Black male students' exploration of teaching? A case study approach was appropriate as we were interested in bounding our research based on Black male students who showed interest in pursuing teaching as a career.

Participants

Two 18-year-old Black males who participated in the P2T program as high school seniors and are now considering careers in education were selected for in-depth investigation for this study. These two students were selected for this study because of their ability to provide insights into the experiences and perspectives of young Black males who have an expressed commitment to a career in education. Table 2 provides basic demographic information for each of the two participants.

Table 2. Demographic Information for the Participants.

Pseudonym	Age	GPA	Identified as Gifted?	Taking AP Classes?	1st High School Graduate in Family?
Michael	17	3.4	Yes	Yes	No
Kent	18	1.7	No	No	Yes

Data Sources

There are multiple data sources that are the foundation of this study. First, data from students' essays were utilized with particular attention to an assignment where students wrote a personal counter-narrative after an initial investigation of Critical Race Theory (CRT). Additionally, interview and survey data for Michael and Kent were also used in this analysis (described in detail in Bianco et al., 2011).

Data Analysis

The case studies presented below were conducted with what Stevenson (2004) terms an "interpretive paradigm of inquiry" which enables a focus on "the unique understandings and experiences of the individuals involved" (p. 43). Stake (2000) calls the type of study we conducted an "instrumental case study," where a case is "examined mainly to provide insight into an issue or to redraw a generalization" (p. 437). In the analysis of these two young Black males' perspectives, our interest focused on the systems and structures in which they detailed participating and how those systems appear to either support or limit the opportunities for these young Black males to consider teaching as a career.

Following Yin's (2008) suggestion to "play" with the data, this analysis was conducted through multiple, varied readings of the data over time. With each reading, extensive notes were taken, modified, reorganized, and refined in order to narrow in on the prominent themes in the data. Once completed, we conducted a thorough analysis of our notes to finalize and check the assertions and arguments that are discussed and presented below. Additionally, we cross-checked our interpretations and came to consensus as a research team regarding the assertions and themes that emerged. Finally, member checks were conducted to verify the accurate representation of our findings.

MICHAEL: "I DON'T WANT TO BE ANOTHER BLACK STATISTIC"

Michael participated in the P2T program during his senior year of high school. He entered the program with a strong GPA of around 3.4 and positive schooling experiences in his past, including being identified as Gifted and Talented in 6th grade. During middle school, he participated in a leadership class where the students who had been identified as Gifted and Talented would meet together and help make decisions and plans for the school. In high school, he continued to get involved in activities at school, in the local church and other community organizations that provided him with leadership opportunities. Four major themes emerged from Michael's data including: leadership, race, schooling, and public speaking. Each of these is delineated below.

Theme #1: Leadership

It appears that Michael's sense of leadership had a significant effect on him considering a career in education. He feels a strong sense of himself and believes that he is capable of achieving difficult goals. Michael also feels proud of his actions in situations where he knows he could have behaved poorly. For example, about an incident he felt was racist at school he reflected, "When I talked to [an administrator] him and two other guys were like amazed by the way I handled myself because racism is a big thing and everyone was expecting a Black [name of high school] kid to go off and blow things out of proportion, but I didn't." He wants to be a school counselor or a principal because he loves public speaking and feels confident in his ability to be a leader. Overall, Michael's positive schooling experiences, involvement in church, constructive leadership opportunities, and strong sense of self appear to be major factors in his consideration of and dedication to a career in education.

Theme #2: Race

It appears that race has also played a motivating factor in Michael's exploration of teaching. A consistent theme across Michael's data is his sense of being different. In an interview he said, "I don't want to be another Black statistic: in a gang, dead, in jail. I want to be one of the ones people talk about as being successful." Michael discussed having friends and family members in jail and credited some of the issues these loved ones faced to negative peer pressure. Based on this experience he chose to research peer pressure for his major research project in the course. He said, "I see peer pressure everywhere and am involved in a lot of great organizations that take teens away from peer pressure." It appears that his desire to be free of the labels and life-paths that have been stereotypically associated with young Black males is a motivator in his commitment to educational achievement as well as a career in education.

Theme #3: Schooling

The experiences Michael reported with his teachers across his years of schooling also appear to have a racial component as well as have influenced his desire to work in the education field. He described experiences where he felt teachers White teachers did not know what to expect from him because he is a Black male student. Yet, he explained that once they saw that he is smart and wants to succeed, they worked hard to support his success. However, he also reported instances where teachers "automatically presume that I'm going to be a gang banging jail type."

Over the years, Michael had a handful of teachers of color who he felt could relate to him and pushed him to higher levels of achievement; two factors he also discussed as important for recruiting and retaining more teachers of color. Michael felt it was important for students of color to have teachers who could relate to them, understand their needs, and maintain high expectations by pushing them to succeed. Overall, it appears that race has played a significant role in Michael's commitment to an education career in that it has motivated him to live and tell a counter-story to the negative stereotypes of Black males as well as see the need for more leadership and engagement in education by Black males.

Theme #4: Public Speaking

Michael felt that the strongest experiences he had in the class affecting his commitment to a career in education were the multiple opportunities to speak in public about the need for more teachers of color. Over the course of the school year, the students in the Introduction to Urban Education class presented their ideas and work at multiple local conferences, including a research symposium at a nearby university and a statewide teacher conference. Early in the school year Michael and his peers participated in a field trip to a teacher recruiting event where their Introduction to Urban Education teacher was scheduled as the keynote speaker. When the group arrived and realized that their teacher would be addressing the event participants, Michael specifically asked to speak in order to share his experiences in the class before his teacher gave her address. During this impromptu addition to the keynote, Michael discussed the need for more teachers of color, the powerful experiences he and his peers were having working with young students at a local elementary school, and the reason the P2T program is good for him and his peers. He said, "I think this class is good for us at [name of high school] because we are always the underdogs in [name of the state]."

While the first three themes appeared to contribute to Michael's commitment to a career in education, the opportunity he had to share this information in various public forums proved even more powerful. He said,

> For me, it was speaking in front of people and really expressing how I feel without being held back. When you can do that and people can see your point of view, you can make the world better and the teaching field better.

It appears that the leadership and public speaking opportunities the class afforded Michael built on those from his past and showed him how to channel the skills and passion he has into fighting for educational justice through his future career in education.

KENT: "BECAUSE I'M IN FOSTER CARE, I DON'T REALLY GET TO CELEBRATE ANYTHING"

Kent was also a senior while participating in the P2T project. However, unlike Michael, he did not come into P2T with a solid GPA (it was below 2.0) or positive schooling experiences. These factors most likely would have excluded Kent from a teacher-recruitment program without an expressed commitment to complete inclusion. Kent spent all of his teenage years in the foster care system; since the time he was in middle school he had been placed with five different foster families. Each placement meant a different school and often there were substantial breaks between living with the different families when he would live in the family crisis center. Overall, he missed over two years of schooling, had no contact with his biological parents, and did not have strong relationships with teachers or peers. In fact, until he joined the P2T program, he had not seriously considered going to college or a career in education. His primary focus was leaving the foster care system, living independently, and figuring out how he would take care of himself after graduation.

Theme #1: Foster Care

A major factor in Kent's life is his participation in the foster care system. Before he joined the P2T program, he was very secretive about being in foster care and never shared this information with his peers or teachers because he felt shame associated with his foster status. However, through his work in P2T, he became a highly vocal advocate for improved schooling opportunities for foster care children. He shared his story in various forums, including a research symposium at a local university, and focused his class research project on learning about what teachers know and do not know in terms of supporting students in the foster care system. His research, conducted collaboratively with several peers and a course instructor, exposed how little teachers know about students in the foster care system and how infrequently the topic is addressed in teacher preparation. Kent described his commitment to improving educational opportunity for students in foster care saying, "Being a young African American male, I've experienced the foster care system and I feel there were not enough supports or knowledge about foster children's well-being in schools."

Overall, Kent's participation in foster care was a challenging and difficult aspect of his life. He attributes his academic gaps and low GPA to long periods of time in the family crisis center without a "real teacher" or access to classroom learning. Kent also felt that the lack of consistency with school placements and multiple foster homes contributed to his poor school performance.

The inconsistency of Kent's life not only impacted his school performance but also his sense of belonging – to family, community, and any traditions. Kent reflected on this and stated, "Because I'm in foster care, I don't really get to celebrate anything." However, through positive learning experiences in the P2T program, it appears that Kent decided to use his difficult life experiences as a motivating factor in planning for a career in education with the specific intent of reaching out to other children in the foster system and to informing teachers about the needs of children in a broken system.

Theme #2: Race

For Kent, his connection to his own racial background is complex. Because of his foster status he never learned of his own family's ancestral history. Further, because of multiple foster homes, Kent did not have any connection to family celebrations or participate in meaningful cultural traditions. For these reasons Kent felt a sense of disconnect with his own identity at home and at school.

Kent attended multiple schools with students from all different racial backgrounds. He described instances when he attended predominately White schools where he felt singled out and treated unfairly. He described one situation where a teacher accused him of cheating saying, "He was a White teacher so he was just being protective of his White students and wanted to make me look bad." Along these lines, Kent sees race as a reason for educational inequity. He felt that the racial imbalance in the teaching field might be deliberate: "I believe they want to keep the teaching field White, their own color ... I think they want to have the advantage of teaching all the kids lower standards." He then went on to discuss how predominantly White schools achieve at higher levels than predominantly Black schools. However, the predominantly Black schools have mostly White teachers. He questioned why they "don't show a higher level of teaching to the students here?" For Kent, the opportunity to help students have a better education than he has had, especially students in foster care, is a strong motivating factor to become a teacher. Therefore, these issues around race play a role in his commitment as well.

However, it appears that race has also, like with Michael, played a motivating role to be different.

Theme #3: Schooling

The high school teacher working in the P2T program recruited Kent into the course and he quickly became interested in discussing educational inequities and exploring a career in teaching. The opportunity P2T provided him to work with younger students and see the joy of their learning as well as their progress proved powerful in his decision to focus on teaching as a career. He also greatly benefited from the regular campus visits as well as interactions with college professors. In fact, Kent now plans to not only become a teacher, but also a teacher educator. He wants to research issues around education for students in the foster care system and plans to get a PhD one day. The P2T program had a powerful effect on Kent applying to college, planning to attend college in the fall, and seeking a career in education.

Without the P2T program and the Introduction to Urban Education course, Kent would not at all be considering a career in teaching. Before his participation in the program he had never been encouraged to attend college or consider teaching as a profession. He also had very few teachers of color over the course of his schooling and had mostly negative experiences in school. One of the reasons he felt that more students of color do not consider a career in teaching is because, "No one ever tells them about how great it is to be a teacher. It's always the negative side about it. It's always the work is too hard and it never stops even if I leave the school and I don't get paid enough for what I do, so you shouldn't do this." Once he joined the P2T program, had some positive teaching experiences himself, learned about the need for more teachers of color, and realized he could bring a unique voice to the field, he became extremely committed and motivated to become a teacher and eventually a teacher educator. P2T successfully provided Kent with the kind of experiences he needed to both go to college and begin to plan for a career in education. In fact, it appears that through participating in P2T and having such positive learning experiences in the program, Kent substantially altered his life path.

CROSS-CASE ANALYSIS OF THE CASE STUDIES: MOTIVATORS TO BECOME A TEACHER

Despite the substantial differences between Kent and Michael, there are some similarities. Interestingly, neither Michael nor Kent spoke much about gender issues in terms of teaching and a career in education and it did not emerge as a major theme across either of their cases. However, Michael did mention that one way to encourage more Black males to become teachers would be to let them know, "that it's a two way job. Meaning it's a male and a female job and both can be very successful in teaching." Across all of the data collected for both Michael and Kent, this was the only mention of teaching as a female profession and it potentially being a barrier for Black males consideration of careers in teaching.

Another similarity was in terms of the participants' discussion regarding race. Like Michael, Kent also sees himself as set apart from his peers. He discussed deliberately choosing not to hang out with other Black students as he did not want to get "caught up in the drama or jail." While both young men have come from different family backgrounds and had substantially varying schooling experiences, they both see the labels put on Black males as very negative and position themselves as different. Kent even described those labels saying, "They don't see you doing anything else besides being a criminal." In this way, race is a motivator for both of them to live in contrast to the negative stereotypic perceptions and be something different, like an educator.

Another common theme that emerged in the case analysis of both Kent and Michael is the power of schooling experiences. While Michael had a history of positive schooling experiences and was identified as gifted and talented, Kent had a history of negative experiences colored with multiple transitions and numerous challenges. However, both of them benefited from participating in the P2T program. For Michael, being in P2T supported him on a path toward college, a path that he was already on. However, the P2T program may have helped Michael on his pathway to teaching by providing him with opportunities to explore his strengths in this area. Kent's experience in P2T appears to have substantially altered his life path and opened significant opportunities for him in terms of college and career. Therefore, it appears that strong schooling experiences, like those provided in the P2T program, can have a positive effect in recruiting Black males into teaching, even those who may have struggled in school.

CONCLUSION

This study utilizes the perspectives of Black male teens to explore the issues surrounding the dearth of Black males who consider a career in teaching. Several themes emerged as factors influencing these two young Black males in planning for a career in education including schooling experiences, race, and other personal elements such as leadership skills, public speaking opportunities, and foster care. Their perspectives provide useful insights into the experiences of young Black males and what might recruit more Black males into teaching. The results also show the power of excellent learning opportunities provided in schools to support leadership development in young Black males as well as to encourage Black teens to plan for a career in education. The P2T program appears to have continued to support a student already on a path to leadership in education as well as changed the education and career path of a student who had struggled in school. Therefore, the potential effect of P2T and programs like it could substantially improve the pipeline into teaching that currently exists for young Black males.

However, the results of this study also show the powerful effect of stereotypes and cultural myths regarding young Black males and how these issues influence Black male teens perceptions of the world and opportunities available to them. While both of the case study participants proactively positioned themselves in contrast to the negative stereotypes they described as prominent about young Black males, it is troubling that these young men found positive identities by positioning themselves as *different* from their peers. Further investigation into the role these negative labels, stereotypes, cultural myths, or majoritarian stories (Love, 2004) are playing on the educational outcomes and opportunities for young Black males is warranted, along with a focus of their impact on Black male teens perceptions of teaching as a career. While the P2T program holds great promise to increase the number of students of color, particularly Black males, entering teaching, it appears that issues of racialization in society and through educational practices also need to be addressed across the educational pipeline in order to substantially increase the students of color who choose teaching as a career.

CASE ANALYSIS

In this chapter, we learned about Michael and Kent as well as their perspectives as they consider teaching as a career. Several salient themes emerged from these case studies that play a role in both of their decisions to pursue careers in education. For both Michael and Kent race and schooling emerged as common themes that affected their desire to consider teaching as a career. But they each had very different interests and life experiences that affected their commitment to education as well. For Michael this was leadership and public speaking and for Kent his experiences in foster care proved salient. In considering the similarities and differences between these two Black teens, it appears that the P2T program was a positive learning experience that provided assistance to both teens in choosing to pursue a career in education.

The findings around race that emerged, while not surprising, are troubling. It appears that Black male teens today face substantial issues around the negative stereotypes associated with that population, particularly around criminal, drug, and gang activity. Michael and Kent both proactively distanced themselves from these negative images of Black teens and developed positive identities that included an interest in education as a career.

Overall, with concerted effort and positive learning opportunities, programs like P2T can be successful in supporting Black male teen's exploration of and commitment to a career in education. More learning opportunities like P2T should be created in schools across the country to encourage students of color, particularly Black males, to pursue a career in education.

DISCUSSION QUESTIONS

1. What can we do in schools and communities to challenge the negative stereotypes about Black male teens?
2. In what ways might teachers, principals, and other education stakeholders be unknowingly perpetuating these stereotypes to and about Black males teens?
3. What kind of positive learning experiences in school, like those in the Pathways2Teaching program could be utilized to better encourage Black male teens to pursue a career in education?
4. How can teachers create curricula that allows students to explore and share their perspectives on educational inequities they have experienced?
5. How could more partnerships between school districts and teacher preparation programs be developed to create more Pathways2Teaching for Black males?
6. How could we encourage more Black males to consider a career in education?
7. This is a case study of only two participants, therefore, what might be some other barriers and possibilities to encouraging Black male teens into a career in education?

REFERENCES

Achinstein, B., & Ogawa, R. T. (2011). *Change(d) agents: New teachers of color in urban schools.* New York, NY: Teachers College Press.
Berliner, D. C. (2006). Our impoverished view of educational research. *Teachers College Record, 108*(6), 949–995. Retrieved from http://dx.doi.org/10.1111/j.1467-9620.2006.00682.x
Bianco, M., Leech, N., & Mitchell, K. (2011). Pathways to teaching: African American male teens explore urban education. *The Journal of Negro Education, 80*(3), 368–383.
Brown, J., & Butty, J. (1999). Factors that influence African-American male teachers' educational and career aspirations: Implications for school district recruitment and retention efforts. *Journal of Negro Education, 68*, 280–292.
Clewell, B. C., Dark, K., Davis-George, T., Forcier, L., & Manes, S. (2000). *Literature review on teacher recruitment programs.* Washington, DC: The Urban Institute for the Department of Education, Planning Evaluation Service.
Cook-Sather, A. (2002). Authorizing students' perspectives: Toward trust, dialogue, and change in education. *Educational Researcher, 31*(4), 3–14.
Crenshaw, K. W. (1988). Race, reform, and retrenchment: Transformation and legitimation in antidiscrimination law. *Harvard Law Review, 101*(7), 1331–1387.
Duncan-Andrade, J. M. R. (2007). Urban youth and the counter-narrative on inequality. *Transforming Anthropology, 15*(1), 26–37.

Fielding, M. (2001). Students as radical agents of change. *Journal of Educational Change*, *2*(2), 123–141.

Kane, R. G., & Maw, N. (2005). Making sense of learning at secondary school: Involving students to improve teaching practice. *Cambridge Journal of Education*, *35*(3), 311–322. doi: 10.1080/03057640500319024

Ladson-Billings, G., & Tate, W. F. (1995). Toward a critical race theory of education. *Teachers College Record*, *97*(1), 47–68.

Lewis, C. W. (2006). African American male teachers in public schools: An examination of three urban school districts. *Teachers College Record*, *108*, 224–245. doi: 10.1111/j.1467-9620.2006.00650.x

Love, B. J. (2004). Brown plus 50 counter-storytelling: A critical race theory analysis of the "majoritarian achievement gap" story. *Equity & Excellence in Education*, *37*(3), 227–246.

Rudduck, J., & Flutter, J. (2000). Pupil participation and pupil perspective: 'Carving a new order of experience'. *Cambridge Journal of Education*, *30*(1), 75–89.

Schott Foundation for Public Education. (2009). *Lost opportunity: A 50 state report on the opportunity to learn in America*. Retrieved from http://www.otlstatereport.org/

Schott Foundation for Public Education. (2010). *Yes we can: The Schott 50 state report on public education and Black males 2010*. Retrieved from http://blackboysreport.org/

Smith, M. J. (2009). Right directions, wrong maps: Understanding the involvement of low-SES African American parents to enlist them as partners in college choice. *Education and Urban Society*, *41*(2), 171–196.

Stake, R. E. (2000). Case studies. In N. K. Denzin & Y. S. Lincoln (Eds.), *Handbook of qualitative research* (2nd edn., pp. 435–454). Thousand Oaks, CA: Sage.

Stake, R. E. (2005). *Multiple case study analysis*. New York, NY: Guilford.

Stevenson, R. B. (2004). Constructing knowledge of educational practices from case studies. *Environmental Education Research*, *10*(1), 39–51. doi: 10.1080/1135046203200173698

Su, C. (2007). Cracking silent codes: Critical race theory and education organizing. *Discourse: Studies in the Cultural Politics of Education*, *28*(4), 531–548.

Toldson, I. A. (2011). *Breaking barriers 2: Plotting the path away from juvenile detention and toward academic success for school-age African American males*. Washington, DC: Congressional Black Caucus Foundation.

Torres, J., Santos, J., Peck, N., & Cortes, L. (2004). *Minority teacher recruitment, development and retention*. Providence, RI: Brown University.

Vegas, E., Murnane, R. J., & Willett, J. B. (2001). From high school to teaching: Many steps, who makes it? *Teachers College Record*, *103*, 427–449. doi: 10.1111/0161-4681.00121

Wood, E. (2003). The power of pupil perspectives in evidence-based practice: The case of gender and underachievement. *Research Papers in Education*, *18*(4), 365–383. doi: 10.1080/0267152032000176864

Yin, R. K. (2008). *Case study research: Design and methods* (4th edn.). Thousand Oaks, CA: Sage.

CHAPTER 11

A CALL FOR AFRICAN AMERICAN MALE TEACHERS: THE SUPERMEN EXPECTED TO SOLVE THE PROBLEMS OF LOW-PERFORMING SCHOOLS

Vivian Gunn Morris and Curtis L. Morris

ABSTRACT

In segregated elementary and high schools, African American male teachers played the role of mentor in the lives of African American male students which included serving as role model, authority figure, counselor, emotional and academic supporter, encourager, and community activist. The seven men interviewed for this study believed that African American male teachers can serve these same roles in today's schools as they assist African American males and other students of color in navigating through the sometime difficult maze of what it takes to successfully complete high school and postsecondary degrees. Factors are also noted that may encourage or discourage African American males' entry into the teaching profession.

Black Male Teachers: Diversifying the United States' Teacher Workforce
Advances in Race and Ethnicity in Education, Volume 1, 151–165
ISSN: 2051-2317/doi:10.1108/S2051-2317(2013)0000001015

CHAPTER OVERVIEW

This chapter presents the successful roles played by African American male teachers during the legal segregation and early desegregation periods in the life of a southern school community and builds on the lessons learned as we attempt to recruit and retain more African American males into the teaching profession today. The study reported in this chapter was guided by three major questions: (1) what were the successful roles played by African American male teachers during the legal segregation period in the United States? (2) How did the role(s) of African American male teachers change during the desegregation period? and (3) What impact did African American male students believe that African American male teachers made on their school lives and career choices?

This chapter begins with this chapter overview, an introduction that outlines some of the concerns from the related literature about the need for African American male teachers in P-12 schools, and the research questions explored. Second, methods and procedures used in the study and a historical view of African American male teachers during the U.S. segregation period are presented. The next section of the chapter includes changes in roles of African American male teachers following the *Brown* decision and closes with factors that may encourage or discourage African American males' entry into the teaching profession today, future research recommended, and a case study analysis with discussion questions.

INTRODUCTION: THE NEED FOR AFRICAN AMERICAN MALES AS P-12 TEACHERS IN U.S. PUBLIC SCHOOLS – WHO'S CALLING AND WHY?

Despite what we see in the daily electronic and print media, there is considerable talent among young men in African American communities that can be harnessed for service in professions in addition to the entertainment and sports industries in the United States. What if we began searching for and nurturing talent for the teaching profession (and other professions as well) in the same manner as we do for football and basketball in African American communities? Are there recruitment strategies that we can learn from successful coaches of college and university sports?

Why are so few African American males choosing teaching as a profession in the 21st century? Noguera (2008) reminds us that public schools have an important role to play in determining what happens to African American males in our nation. He states that:

> The trouble with Black boys is that most never have a chance to be thought of as potentially smart and talented or to demonstrate talents in science, music, or literature. The trouble with Black boys is that too often they are placed in schools where their needs for nurturing, support, and loving discipline are not met. Instead, they are labeled, shunned, and treated in ways that create and reinforce an inevitable cycle of failure. (p. xxi)

The recent call for the need of African American male teachers in P-12 teachers has been highlighted by Secretary of Education Arne Duncan via the national press with visits to Historically Black Colleges and Universities (HBCUs) to encourage African American males to choose teaching as a profession. Scholars, primarily African American, have been calling for the critical need of African American male teachers especially since the humiliation experienced when they lost their jobs or teacher-principals were demoted following the 1954 *Brown* decision when many white school boards were forced to desegregate schools (Morris & Morris, 2002b; Pitts, 2005). While effective African American male teachers are very essential, they cannot single-handedly solve the myriad problems experienced by many African American school-age boys. The educational pipeline through which potential African American male teachers emerge is fraught with leaks all along the way. Many arrive at the schoolhouse door already at risk because of pervasive poverty, inadequate health care, and gaps in early childhood development. As they continue through the school years they experience inequitable educational opportunities, abuse and neglect, unmet mental and emotional problems, substance abuse, and an ineffective justice system (Alexander, 2010; Children's Defense Fund, 2008; Morris, 2008).

Lynn (2009) noted, in a case study of an African American male teacher, that African American male teachers in elementary, middle school, high school, college, and peers in his professional life played important roles in his development and decision to become a teacher. A survey of high school seniors revealed that 74% of the seniors surveyed had never had anyone discuss with them teaching as a career option (Hopkins, 1989).

Irvine (1989) asserted that African American teachers are needed as mentors rather than as role models because teachers fall short of students' perceptions of familial and celebrity role models. She states that:

> Mentors are advocate teachers who help black students manipulate the school's culture, which is often contradictory and antithetical to their own. They serve as the voice for black students when communicating with fellow teachers and administrators; when

providing information about opportunities for advancement and enrichment; and when
serving as counselors, advisors, and parent figures. (p. 53)

Cooper and Jordan (2003) describe some distinct advantages that African
American male teachers may have in educating African American boys
which include:

modeling appropriate behavior, strategic use of shared knowledge, and in some cases,
common social experiences. The rapport that Black male teachers establish with Black
male students through their common cultural heritage can be maintained in the face of
social class differences. Therefore, in addition to raising the overall quality of the school
through comprehensive reform, the value-added dimension of being exposed to good
teachers, who are Black males, might be a factor in raising the success rates of Black
male students. (p. 391)

What are some other compelling reasons for having African American
males and other teachers of color as members of the current teacher
workforce? African American boys need to see successful teachers in schools
who look like them as evidence that they can succeed and should strive to
succeed (Loehr, 1988). The Carnegie Forum Taskforce made a compelling
statement regarding the effects of the absence of minority teachers on
children's learning environment:

The race and background of their teachers tell them something about authority and
power in contemporary America. These messages influence children's attitudes toward
school, their academic accomplishments and their views of their own and others'
intrinsic worth. The views they form in school about justice and fairness also influence
their future citizenship. (Smith, 1989, p. 12)

Smith noted that perhaps the most serious consequence of an education
without teachers of color is the "hidden curriculum."

White and non-white children alike will not see minority adults in professional roles at
school but in the roles of bus driver, custodian, groundskeeper, and cafeteria worker.
The daily, unspoken messages that our society is stratified by race and class distinctions
will be transmitted much more forcefully than the message that a democratic society
offers hope through its promise of equity. (Smith, 1989, p. 12)

METHOD AND PROCEDURES

Description of Participants

The data used in this chapter were part of a larger case study of a southern
African American school community, Trenholm High School, Tuscumbia,
Alabama, conducted over a period of years by the authors (Morris & Morris,

2000, 2002a, 2002b, 2005). Participants in the original study included former students, teachers, administrators, and parents who completed a questionnaire related to the quality of education at the previously segregated African American school and the desegregated school in their community. For this chapter, seven individual interviews were conducted in 2011 with African American males from this same school community related to the roles that African American male teachers played in their personal and professional lives, benefits of having African American male teachers in 21st century classrooms, their beliefs about why so few African American males are choosing teaching as a profession today, and their beliefs about factors that might influence African American males to enter the current and future teaching force.

Six of the respondents graduated from Trenholm, the segregated African American school and one was a teacher at both Trenholm and Deshler (the desegregated high school) where all students began attending following the closing of Trenholm in 1969. The six interviewees who hold college degrees all began their college work at HBCUs in the southeastern U.S. and completed advanced degrees at various predominately white colleges and universities throughout the country. At the time of the 2011 interviews, all had retired from their first major careers. Careers or positions held by respondents included: high school teacher, college/university teacher, program coordinator at community college, assistants to college or university presidents, central office administrator in school district, executive in nonprofit organizations, county government director, legislative director for U.S. Senator, funeral director, laborer in aluminum plant, and officers in the U.S. armed forces. Many of their children, grandchildren, and other family members attended schools in the same community. See Table 1 for additional details.

Procedures

Data sources from the original study included interviews, focus groups, school board minutes, school year books, local newspapers, student handbooks, principal questionnaires, and accreditation reports which served as background information for this chapter. In addition, seven new interviews were conducted with African American males who were teachers or students in this school community. Triangulation of data from interviews, school boards minutes, and local newspapers was employed to formulate final themes for this study.

Table 1.   Description of Interviewees.

Name	Degrees	Years of Teaching and/or School Adm.	Age Range
Dean	Ed.S.	19	>80
Erin	M.S.	0	>70
Leonard	M.S.	34	<70
Leroi	M.S.	14	>70
Manual	M.S.	14	>70
Wilson	H.S.	0	<70
Wellington	Ed.S.	44	>80

Age range = 68–84 years; range of years of graduation from Trenholm is 1944–1960.
Pseudonyms are used to ensure confidentiality.

HISTORICAL VIEW OF AFRICAN AMERICAN MALE TEACHERS DURING THE U.S. SEGREGATION PERIOD

The same year that the Compromise of 1877 passed, marking the end of Reconstruction in the South and the withdrawal of federal troops (Woodward, 2002), the African American citizens of Tuscumbia established the Osborne Colored Academy for its children (An Honor, 1877; Morris & Morris, 2000). Woodward noted that with the withdrawal of troops, the Negro was abandoned as a ward of the nation which essentially gave up on ensuring the civil and political equality of formerly enslaved people, and left the disposition of their rights to southern whites. This situation has some similar marks of what happened following the passage of the *Brown Decisions* in 1954 and 1955. The same school boards that operated separate but unequal schools for African American children for decades were assigned the legal responsibility by the courts to develop desegregation plans for unitary school systems (Hendrie, 2000).

African American Male Teacher-Principals in the Trenholm School Community

Local newspaper articles from 1870 through the 1890s revealed that schools for African Americans in Tuscumbia were headed by a male teacher-principal, and one to two female teaching assistants (Morris & Morris, 2000).

Gradually, other male teachers were added to the faculty with a high of eight males in the 1963–1964 academic year. By this time, male teachers comprised about 1/3 of the total faculty of 22–24 members for grades 1–12. Male teachers taught a variety of subjects in grades 7–12, that is, science, social studies, mathematics, automotive mechanics, physical education, foreign languages, and served in the roles of librarian, coach, guidance counselor, and band director (Trenholm School, 1981).

Early Teacher-Principals that Influenced Trenholm High School Programs and Personnel

William Hooper Councill and George Washington Trenholm were two teacher-principals and later college presidents who had a significant, long-term impact on the education of African Americans in Tuscumbia. W. H. Councill, President of the now Alabama A & M University in Huntsville, Alabama, from 1906 to 1975, was a frequent speaker at the Tuscumbia Colored Public School, beginning in the early 1880s. The patterns that Dr. Councill established were followed by principals and the community in Tuscumbia and throughout North Alabama (Morrison, 1994).

In addition to serving as principal of the Tuscumbia Colored Pubic School from 1896 to 1916, G. W. Trenholm was an active educational, religious, and political leader within the local, state, and national communities. He held state offices in educational organizations and provided professional development for educators at the local, state, and national levels. Mr. Trenholm was president of the now Alabama State University from 1920 to 1925. Many teachers and principals at Trenholm High School completed their teaching and administrative training at the college where he was president (Morris & Morris, 2000).

AFRICAN AMERICAN MALE TEACHERS AT TRENHOLM

The interviewees noted that African American male teachers played six different roles that had an impact on their personal and professional lives, that is, role model, authority figure, counselor, emotional and academic supporter, encourager, and community activist. The three teachers identified by male graduates, spent all or nearly all of their teaching careers in this school community where they taught at both the segregated African

American school, and the desegregated school, that is, Fred Johnson, Charles S. Mahorney, and John W. Winston.

Fred Johnson joined the Trenholm faculty in 1950 as a mathematics teacher. He later served as guidance counselor and the last principal of the segregated school from 1967 to 1969. He became assistant principal at Deshler, the desegregated high school, in fall 1969 and was principal from 1973 to 1979 when he retired (Morris & Morris, 2000).

Charles Mahorney was hired as coach and teacher of health and physical education in 1949 and spent the next 19 years as head coach for football, basketball, and track and field for both boys and girls at Trenholm. He was named Coach of the Year five times by the North Alabama High School Athletic Association. When Trenholm closed, he went to Deshler where he served as assistant football coach and head basketball coach until he retired in 1982 (Grand Marshall, 1990; Morris & Morris, 2000; Trenholm School, 1981).

John Winston joined the faculty at Trenholm in 1951 where he was the band director, choir director, and teacher of social studies. When Trenholm closed in 1969, he was offered the position of assistant band director at Deshler, but chose rather to be a full-time social sciences teacher and head of that department. Mr. Winston retired in 2003 (Morris & Morris, 2000).

Roles Played by African American Male Teachers

Role Model

As role models, former students noted that male teachers "dressed very nicely," were good speakers, smart, demanding, and prepared them well for specific vocations.

Authority Figure

As authority figures, their teachers were very disciplined, expected, and demanded good disciple among students, and knew their subject-matter well. All were family men whose children attended school in the community as well.

Counselor

Interviewees noted that they could usually go to the male teachers with their problems and they seemed to understand. These teachers had personal concern for the educational, physical, and spiritual welfare of their students.

Emotional and Academic Supporter
Students noted that their African American male teachers taught them practical lessons. They expressed a love for their teachers because they taught them how to study, to do homework, and how to keep moving forward both emotionally and academically. They viewed their teachers as good helpers and loving professionals.

Encourager
Interviewees reported that their teachers and other African American men in their community were very encouraging in their pursuit of further education and careers. One interviewee noted that he was especially encouraged by a number of male teachers throughout his life that encouraged him to choose teaching as a lifetime career, that is, a principal who rented a room in his home, another with whom he rode to school with during his high school years, and several principals with whom he engaged in conversations during his college years.

Community Activist
African American male teachers at Trenholm were actively involved in the school community as volunteers that furthered their efforts to bring about social, political, and economic changes in their community. They served as Boy Scout leaders, organizers of Saturday tutoring programs, and as leaders in local churches. These same teachers were members of social and civic clubs that provided social and recreational outlets for adults and children in a segregated community (Morris & Morris, 2000).

AFRICAN AMERICAN MALE TEACHER AND DESEGREGATED SCHOOLS FOLLOWING THE 1954 *BROWN* DECISION AND BEYOND

Changes in Roles

With the closing of Trenholm in 1969, African American teachers were demoted and displaced as they were in other southern school districts (Tillman, 2004). No African American teachers in Tuscumbia lost their jobs, but most experienced significant changes in their new positions. For example, changes in roles of the three teachers in this study included: Fred Johnson, principal at Trenholm for two years, became assistant principal at

Table 2. Total Number and Percentage of Students Enrolled in Tuscumbia City Schools as Compared to Faculty and Administrators by Subgroups, 2010–2011 Academic Year.

Subgroup Total	Total Students	% of Students	Total Faculty	% of Faculty
African American	613	35	10	8
White	1116	64	113	92
Other	23	1	0	0

Source: Tuscumbia City Schools.

Deshler; Charles Mahorney, head coach for all sports at Trenholm for 19 years, became assistant football coach and head basketball coach at Deshler; and John Winston, band director at Trenholm for 18 years, was offered the job of assistant band director, but chose instead to become a full-time teacher in the social sciences (Morris & Morris, 2000).

Current Presence of African American Male Teachers in Local School Community

In 1963–1964, there were 24 African American teachers employed by the Tuscumbia City Schools, all at Trenholm, 8 were African American males. During the 2010–2011 academic year, a total of 10 African Americans were employed in the 4 schools in Tuscumbia, 2 were males. Table 2 highlights demographics for the district. African American students enrolled in the four Tuscumbia City Schools could very likely attend P-12 in this school district without ever having an African American teacher and neither will any other student.

FACTORS THAT MAY ENCOURAGE OR DISCOURAGE AFRICAN AMERICAN MALES' ENTRY TO THE TEACHING PROFESSION TODAY

The reasons noted by the respondents in this study regarding the factors that might encourage or discourage entry of African American males into the teaching profession are echoed by many researchers and practitioners in educational literature, that is, income and prestige, job opportunities in other professions, working conditions, recruiting strategies, and beliefs and hiring practices of school districts (Alexander, 2010; Duncan, 2011; King,

1993; Noguera, 2008). Integrated into this discussion are some recommendations of practices that may assist school districts in recruiting African American male teachers and other teachers of color to ensure a diverse teacher workforce for students enrolled in their schools.

Income and Prestige

Respondents noted that the average beginning salary of $32,000–35,000 and a top figure of less than $100,000 at retirement (unless you are a top administrator) are just inadequate to meet the growing needs of many families. And often in this country, prestige is associated with higher incomes. Respondents believed that higher salaries would likely attract more African American males to the teaching profession.

Job Opportunities in Other Professions

Following the passage of the 1964 Civil Rights Act, job opportunities for African American male college graduates expanded to many professions they had desired during the segregation period but were outright denied or had limited opportunities, so they chose teaching in segregated schools instead. Respondents reported that because of the higher salaries and prestige associated with other professions, fewer African American males are choosing to join the teacher workforce.

Working Conditions

Too often, African American males are hired to teach in schools that exhibit poor teaching and learning conditions. In addition to having an unsafe and disorderly school environment, these schools may also have inappropriate teaching assignments, unmanageable workloads, lack of resources with which to teach, and lack of advice and support from principals and colleagues. If schools districts want to retain effective African American male and other teachers for all children, schools must make teaching assignments in subject areas in which they are prepared, maintain manageable workloads, make available sufficient resources with which to teach, principal and colleagues assist in maintaining stable and orderly work environments, and provide a high quality induction and mentoring program that assists in teacher practice (Johnson, 2004).

Recruiting Strategies, Beliefs, and Hiring Practices

The recruitment of African American male teachers should begin as early as elementary school (and continued throughout middle, high school, and college) with encouragement from parents, teachers, and counselors in school environments where the students' needs for nurturing, support, and loving discipline are met. In addition, school districts should make strategic recruiting visits to HBCUs and other universities that graduate large number of students of color in their teacher preparation programs. And once African American males apply for teaching positions, their applications should be fairly considered. It may be necessary to provide appropriate professional development experiences for district personnel who are involved in the hiring process in order for African American males to be seriously considered for teaching positions. Beliefs and attitudes about African American males that may serve as barriers in hiring African American males as teachers and therefore must be confronted in professional development experiences for faculty and staff in local school districts. Noguera (2008) stated that black men have "been regarded as a menace to innocents (particularly white women) and a potential danger to the social order. They are a threat that must be policed, controlled, and contained" (p. xi).

RECOMMENDATIONS FOR FUTURE RESEARCH

Millions of school-age African American boys and girls are enrolled in low-performing schools in small towns, rural, and suburban districts throughout this country that are not taught by a diverse teaching force (Feistritzer, 2011; Miretzky & Stevens, 2012). However, these school districts are often ignored in the discussion of the need for a diverse teacher workforce in favor of large urban school districts. Are the findings from this small southern town, that is, representation of African American males and other teachers of color, mirrored in other areas of the country? What do the recruitment plans of these school districts reflect in terms of seeking out additional men and women teachers of color to their ranks? Do these school districts actively reach out to HBCUs and other colleges and universities who graduate large numbers of teacher education students of color? What is the relationship between the teaching performed by highly effective African American males and the educational outcomes of African American boys and other children of color, that is, standardized test scores, retention and high school graduation rates, and attendance at postsecondary institutions?

These are a few of the questions that require additional research if we are to diversify our teaching ranks throughout this nation.

CASE STUDY ANALYSIS AND DISCUSSION QUESTIONS

Case Study Description

Leon, an African American male, is a first year 5th grade teacher in a small city in the southeastern U.S. He grew up in the northeast and completed his teacher preparation program at a predominately white college in the northeast. He responded to the call for African American male teachers by accepting this teaching position. Robert, the African American principal of three years at Trenton Middle School, which serves children in grades 5–8, was extremely pleased to hire Leon. The school has 325 children enrolled and consists of 60% white children and 40% African American. Robert, the principal, is responsible for mentoring and evaluating all teachers in his school building.

Leon is responsible for teaching all core subjects for the 25 students enrolled in his self-contained classroom. Robert has observed Leon twice this semester and his post-conferences included recommendations for improving his teaching. In this third month of the school year and during the third observation, there were a number of issues that concerns him. First, all of the African American boys were sitting at the back of the room and their recent report cards show that the majority of the boys earned Ds or Fs on their report cards. They are generally quiet during class time. Leon's first conference with the parents of the African American boys did not go very well, he is unfamiliar with the families of the children, and during this last observation, it took nearly five minutes of instructional time to get the students' attention.

Discussion Questions

- In a post-conference, what might be some areas that need attention that would assist Leon in being more successful with the African American boys?

- What are some strategies that Robert could suggest that would assist Leon in familiarizing himself with the students and their families?

- How should Robert structure this post-conference with Leon so that he will not be discouraged as a teacher, yet assist him in moving his professional practice forward?

- If you chose to discuss three areas for corrective action, what would be the priority areas?

REFERENCES

Alexander, M. (2010). *The new Jim Crow: Mass incarceration in the age of colorblindness.* New York, NY: The New Press.

An honor worthily bestowed. (1877, July 13). *North Alabamian.*

Children's Defense Fund. (2008). *Cradle to prison pipeline.* Retrieved from http://www.childrens defense.org/child-research-data-publications/data/cradle-prison-pipeline-disussion-guide-08.html

Cooper, R., & Jordan, W. J. (2003). Cultural issues in comprehensive school reform. *Urban Education, 38*(4), 380–396. doi: 10.1177/0042085903254967

Feistritzer, E. C. (2011). *Profile of teachers in the U.S. 2011.* National Center for Education Information. Retrieved from http://www.ncei.com/Profile_Teachers_US_2011.pdf

Grand Marshall: Mr. Charles Mahorney. (1990). *Trenholm High School Reunion 1990* (p. 11). Tuscumbia, AL: Trenholm High School Reunion Committee.

Hendrie, C. (2000). In black and white. In *Education week staff, lessons of a century: A nation's schools come of age* (pp. 62–74). Bethesda, MD: Editorial Projects in Education.

Hopkins, P. (1989, January). Against the odds: Recruiting minority faculty and staff. Paper presented at the annual meeting of the Southwest Educational Research Association, Houston, TX. Retrieved from http://eric.ed.gov/PDFS/ED306685.pdf

Irvine, J. J. (1989). Beyond role models: An examination of cultural influences on the pedagogical perspectives of Black teachers. *Peabody Journal of Education, 66*(4), 51–63. Retrieved from http://www.jstor.org/stable/1492713

Johnson, S. M., & The Project on the Next Generation of Teachers. (2004). *Finders and keepers: Helping new teachers survive and thrive in our schools.* San Francisco, CA: Jossey-Bass.

King, S. H. (1993). Why did we choose teaching careers and what will enable us to stay? Insights from one cohort of the African American teaching pool. *The Journal of Negro Education, 62*(4), 475–492. Retrieved from http://www.jstor.org/stable/2295518

Loehr, P. (1988). The 'urgent need' for minority teachers. *Education Week,* October, p. 32.

Lynn, M. (2009). Dancing between two worlds: A portrait of the life of a black male teacher in South Central LA. *International Journal of Qualitative Studies in Education, 19*(2), 221–242. doi: 10.1080/09518390600576111

Miretzky, D., & Stevens, S. (2012). How does location impact meaning and opportunity? Rural schools and the NCATE diversity standard. *Teachers College Record, 114*(5). Retrieved from http://www.tcrecord.org, ID Number: 16325.

Morris, J. (2008). Research, ideology, and the Brown decision: Counter-narratives to the historical and contemporary representation of black schooling. *Teachers College Record, 110*(4), 713–732.

Morris, V. G., & Morris, C. L. (2000). *Creating caring and nurturing educational environments for African American children.* Westport, CT: Bergin & Garvey, an imprint of Greenwood Publishing Group, Inc.

Morris, V. G., & Morris, C. L. (2002a). Caring – The missing C in teacher education: Lessons learned from a segregated African American school. *Journal of Teacher Education, 53*(2), 120–123.

Morris, V. G., & Morris, C. L. (2002b). *The price they paid: Desegregation in an African American community.* New York, NY: Teachers College Press, Columbia University.

Morris, V. G., & Morris, C. L. (2005). Before Brown, after Brown: What has changed for African American children? *University of Florida Journal of Law and Public Policy, 16*(2), 215–232.

Morrison, R. D. (1994). *History of Alabama A&M University 1875–1992.* Huntsville, AL: Golden Rule Printers.

Noguera, P. A. (2008). *The trouble with Black boys ... and other reflections on race, equity, and the future of public education.* San Francisco, CA: Jossey-Bass.

Pitts, L. (2005). Fighting for children's rights: Lessons from the civil rights movement. *University of Florida Journal of Law and Public Policy, 16*(2), 337–360.

Smith, G. P. (1989). Increasing the number of minority teachers: Recommendations for a call to action. Paper prepared for the Quality Education for Minorities Project, Massachusetts Institute of Technology, Cambridge, MA.

Tillman, L. C. (2004). African American principals and the legacy of Brown. *American Educational Research Association, 28*, 101–146. Retrieved from http://www.jstor.org/stable/3568137

Trenholm school. (1981). *Trenholm school faculty list: 1907–1968.* Tuscumbia, AL: Tuscumbia City Schools.

Woodward, C. V. (2002). *The strange career of Jim Crow: A commemorative edition.* New York, NY: Oxford University Press.

CHAPTER 12

BEING BLACK, BEING MALE, AND CHOOSING TO TEACH IN THE 21ST CENTURY: UNDERSTANDING MY ROLE, EMBRACING MY CALL

Chezare A. Warren

ABSTRACT

Teaching has been a passion of mine from an early age. Making the decision to teach was challenging enough without the hardships of completing my degree as a race and gender minority in the elementary education program at a predominately White institution. Nor was I prepared to manage the many challenges associated with transition into the teaching profession. This chapter is a memoir of a few significant lessons learned during my teacher preparation and early professional teaching practice. Specific recommendations are made to support Black males' ability to: build and cultivate professional relationships with school stakeholders; capitalize on the range of professional opportunities available in the field of education; and sustain an impactful career in K-12 teaching. Finally, this narrative is revelation of the personal and professional perspectives useful to individual(s) desiring to better recruit, retain, prepare, support, and nurture Black males aspiring to teach.

Black Male Teachers: Diversifying the United States' Teacher Workforce
Advances in Race and Ethnicity in Education, Volume 1, 167–182
ISSN: 2051-2317/doi:10.1108/S2051-2317(2013)0000001016

"You know you're too smart to teach!" ... "The children these days are horrible, you sure you want to be a teacher?" ... "Teachers don't make much money ... You need to become a doctor or a lawyer ... ." These sentiments crowd my psyche as I stepped onto the campus of my state's flagship public institution of higher education. Excited to escape the fast pace of city life, I began anew at a large, predominately White university in the middle of nowhere. Still, I was perplexed by the notion of true success. I contemplated what success really meant and how one knew when he or she had actually attained it. Being accepted into a highly selective university was by most people's standard, an extraordinary accomplishment given my socioeconomic background. The problem was that I simply wasn't prepared for the social, intellectual, and cultural challenges this new, unfamiliar space would pose.

The thoughts of my family, former teachers, and close friends followed me as I registered for my first college courses. At 18 years old I was immediately struck with what I thought at the time to be an immensely important decision. Anxiously, I pondered how my major would set the trajectory for my professional career and inevitably shape the quality of my adult life. I vacillated, "Should I do what I feel or what I know?" I recognized the power and privilege of becoming a teacher, but the lack of Black male teacher exemplars in my own schooling experiences and the advice from those I respected to abstain from becoming a teacher weighed heavily on my mind. The lessons I learned both as an education student at a predominately White institution (PWI) and as teacher in an urban school setting cohere to frame the significance of this chapter to 21st century teaching.

The pages to follow are a memoir of my early years as a preservice teacher and professional educator. My story is a counternarrative (Delgado & Stefancic, 2001; Solorzano & Yosso, 2002, 2009) to the dominant perspectives of what it takes not only to survive, but also thrive in the teaching profession as a gender and race minority. The chapter includes important benchmarks in my development as an effective educator as well as recommendations of interest to other brothers seriously considering a career in teaching. My intention by telling *my* side of the story is to buttress efforts to recruit, retain, and equip Black males for work in the schools and communities that need them most. Even though I write this chapter to Black males, it isn't written solely for Black males. It is also written to provide first-person insight to university faculty and staff, school leaders, and education policy makers at-large. By sharing my experiences I hope to shed light on how stakeholders in a range of education institutions can better support and nurture Black male talent. I call attention to the personal considerations and private conversations guiding my career. My story is one of many that exist among an isolated cohort of Black males persisting in an increasingly White and female dominated profession.

HUMBLE BEGINNINGS

The son of working class parents, I spent the majority of my childhood living with just my mother and younger sister. I had occasional access to my father and I wouldn't say by any stretch that he was a deadbeat dad. However, I desired more of his presence in my life during the times that mattered most, like buying a car or choosing a partner. The pivotal moments that shaped my masculinity and influenced my various social and cultural perspectives commenced absent of his fatherly wisdom and guidance. This is a matter I still regret.

I grew up modestly – few designer labels and little money for CDs, posters, or other pop-culture relics kids buy to boost their popularity in school. I made due with my Goosebump books, Saturday morning NBC cartoons, and the Cosby show (I had a huge crush on Rudy). When my overprotective mother let me out to play, I enjoyed trading baseball cards and riding my bike near the lake with the White, Asian, African, and Indian kids in my north side neighborhood. My mother's job was situated on the margins of the far southwest side of the city. We finally settled down my sophomore year of high school on the South side, where for the first time I attended a predominately Black neighborhood school.

I knew I would be a teacher at 7 or 8 years old when the babysitter praised me for successfully corralling the toddlers long enough to sing the entire A, B, C song. In 5th grade I remember sitting in an area of the coat closet that I officially sanctioned as my office. I moved two or three other desks into the closet and the classmates punished for misbehavior became my students. I graded papers, gave out awards, and mimicked the practices of teachers who taught me. I felt strongly that my gift of gab and attention to detail made me a viable candidate for a career as a teacher. Consequently, loss of the Golden Apple Scholarship – a selective preservice teacher preparation enrichment program – and the adamant request of a mentor teacher to find a more "lucrative" career, stirred in me a serious sense of doubt. I left for college very unsure of myself. I didn't know what I wanted to do with my life anymore. I would spend the first couple of years of college searching and sorting out various academic options before settling.

UNDERGRADUATE YEARS

Matriculation to the University meant new people, new experiences, and a fresh opportunity to be the guy I wanted to be for the first time without pressure of performing to please those around me. I left the drama, negativity, and poverty of my upbringing behind. I was proud to be an example that my family could glean from. I took a music class on Monday, an ultra boring history and rhetoric course on Tuesday and Thursday, and I can't forget the overwhelming and intimidating Anthropology course held in Washington Hall on Monday, Wednesday, and Friday afternoons. After I almost failed this 500-person lecture-discussion course, I made a pact with God that if the University invited me back, I would try harder and do better. I kept that promise, though the journey was quite tumultuous.

Summer after my freshmen year of college, I boarded a plane alone for the first time to spend the entire summer, getting paid next to nothing, teaching Black and Latino students from the 3rd ward of Houston, TX. The summer teaching internship allowed me to get experience teaching, writing, and implementing a math and music curriculum of my choice to gifted students from lower-resourced neighborhoods of a major U.S. city. As nervous as I was to be so far from home, I knew I would never discover my full potential until I changed contexts and did something uncomfortable. It turned out to be a truly rewarding summer.

By the beginning of sophomore year, I still wasn't 100% sure teaching was in my future. Anxious to have no regrets, I set up a meeting with a tenured African American professor in the college of education at The University, I'll call Professor Violet. I don't remember the details of that initial conversation, but I left feeling more confident and more assured than I had felt in a long time. Professor Violet was one of the first individuals to look me straight in the eye and assuage my fear of becoming a teacher. She astutely assessed my character, recognized my talent, named my potential, and articulated exactly what I needed to hear at that moment. Professor Violet pledged her support and became a mentor of mine from that day to the present. The meeting with Professor Violet coupled with my teaching experience in Houston the summer before was all the confirmation I needed. Teaching was not just a choice, but a calling. That day, I finally embraced it.

I began my junior year as one Black man among what seemed to be a sea of White female preservice teachers in the first full cohort orientation session. Many of my classmates hailed from many different suburban and rural townships in my home state. Most flaunted privileged upbringings. Several of my classmates had never interacted with a person of color, let alone a Black man, prior to having class with me. I don't know if it was my physical stature or my silence that intimidated them more. I'm a naturally outgoing, extroverted personality, but there was something about the space that felt so alienating. Many of my classmates were pleasant, but I noticed how some would avoid me if they could. Early interactions with my new White colleagues made me very self-conscious and insecure about how I presented myself.

Many of these young White female preservice teachers acted as if anything falling outside of their cultural norms was deficient. I didn't perceive them to be intentionally bad people, but they had never been in a position to be corrected, especially by a person of color. There were times when I had to speak up and I remember several of my colleagues being visibly frustrated with my counterargument to a flippant remark made in class. "Race shouldn't matter ... kids are kids and they just need to work hard." These colorblind perspectives were regularly transmitted in class-room discussion, validated by the Euro-dominant theories posited in textbooks and further supported by lectures rendered by tenured White professors with little teaching experience in urban contexts. My classmate's superior perspectives and misguided assertions about people of color and impoverished communities were reinforced time and again regularly denigrating my own lived experiences. This made many of the courses I was required to take as an Elementary Education major highly contentious. I was the *other* in a room full of White faces.

I relished the opportunity to work alone in each University course that I took in the elementary education program. When I was forced to do group work (which was often) my contributions were routinely overlooked for someone else's idea. In the advanced mathematics methods course, we were forced to complete the homework as a group. I sat on one end of the table alongside the only other two Black people in my cohort while my three White female colleagues sat on the opposite end of the roundtable huddled together. Each group member did the week's reading. Then the group was tasked with answering the 25 or so questions assigned each week in class together. Each group member (six of us total) earned an identical grade for the homework assignment. The expectation was that we complete it collaboratively. After about 5 weeks of being outright ignored, I stopped talking altogether. I earned a minor in math, so I understood the work. I listened attentively while working out the problems alone. I had no qualms taking the A for *our* homework. The next thing I knew, the teaching assistant (TA) accused me of being an isolationist and demanded I complete the next homework assignment alone for a separate grade from the group.

I had to complete an assignment meant for six people by myself. I was given the same amount of time as the group to complete the assignment. What's worse is that the TA never asked my side of the story. She assumed I had been freeloading off of the group and without ever inquiring about the details of the conflict. I was left having to once again defend and prove my competence.

This experience was the final straw for me. It was the catalyst for a new internal compulsion I had to be better than the best. Perfection was the standard. I tirelessly scrutinized the grades I received. I became ultra-critical of my work, how I spoke, what I wore, and calculated every interaction with my instructors and classmates. I examined syllabi and rehearsed the directions to class projects and assignments over and over to ensure I didn't miss a beat. My family socialized me as a child to remain silent when you didn't know something or when you didn't trust the persons you were engaged with. Keen observation became a priority as I negotiated various exchanges with classmates and faculty. I became hyperaware of my behavior in front of them. I felt like I was constantly on stage as I lamented how these White women would judge Black boys like me who they would potentially teach someday. I wanted those boys to have an advantage and hopefully dodge being so grossly misunderstood as I had been. I believed that I was an example, much like Barack Obama is, useful for shifting people's schema for what a Black man is capable of accomplishing. I refused to give these White female teachers another reason why Black kids were deficient. It is a tension I carried into my professional career.

Not only did I complete the homework assignment, I earned a higher score on it than the group. I felt good about the accomplishment, but I was still upset about being unnecessarily ostracized. I harbored this frustration with the TA and my White female group mates the remainder of the semester. As I reflect on that time, the frustration I felt is common among Black students in similar situations on predominately White campuses. Scholars term it racial microaggression and racial battle fatigue (see Smith, Allen, & Danley, 2007; Solorzano, Ceja, & Yosso, 2000). Both constructs characterize the intellectual, emotional, and physical responses to the negative racialized experiences had by people of color, particularly Black males. The TA never attempted to confirm the accusations of my group mates. She simply acquiesced to their request to rectify the problem they were having with my perceived lack of participation. I rejoined the group, but unfortunately very little changed about our interaction.

When asked why we wanted to become teachers by the only Black professor I had as an undergrad, many of my classmates echoed "I just love children" and "I really want to help those poor kids" and "its such a good mommy job." Here I am agonizing over a decision to teach, waging war with my will and the wishes of my loved ones while many of my classmates are agreeing that teaching is a good mommy job? It was disconcerting to think that any one of these young women could possibly end up teaching students of color. After all, White women dominate the teaching workforce (U.S. Bureau of Labor, 2008a, 2008b) — a fact reflected in the demographic of my graduating cohort.

My academic performance by senior year became less about being intellectually excellent and more about shifting the perspective many of these privileged White women held of people of color. I became determined to be the social, cultural, and intellectual contradiction. I spoke up more, smiled more, gave off good energy, and networked profusely. These were my colleagues and I knew that any effort to help them better prepare to teach "Other People's Children" (Delpit, 1995) began with their having a real life model that they could talk to and relate with.

In retrospect, the teacher education program I attended at the University trained me to teach, but not to be a teacher. Teaching requires that one understands how to critique his or her own practice in such a way that children stay central to the work in a culture of school reform that puts adults at the center. I find that being a good teacher versus simply teaching well, includes learning how to consistently and meaningfully negotiate human interaction with youth so that *they* feel affirmed, cared for, and inspired. Technical skills such as how to write a lesson plan mean very little to a child labeled by the institution as "at-risk" and uneducable. My training didn't account for the uniqueness of Black, poor, or urban youth. I learned very little of African American history and the contributions of people representing the African Diaspora, but this is the demographic I taught.

THE EARLY YEARS …

I jumped through every hoop of the teacher credentialing process, met every requirement, and passed every test (and there were many high-stakes tests). The challenges of my undergrad were now behind me and I was finally a teacher. My first job out of college was to prepare the first graduating class at BEST academy to be highly competitive for the city's selective enrollment high schools. It was a charter school and we had a lot to prove. The school sat in the heart of the west side of Chicago. I was the school's first 7th grade math teacher. In Chicago, 7th grade test scores were used by the top high schools to determine eligibility. Teaching comes with a number of unknowns and this teaching job was no exception. After the 2-week training, the students would sit in front of me and their success (or failure) now rested on my shoulders.

One afternoon as I sulked, rather defeated in my classroom, the principal, a dark-haired White gentleman I'll call Mr. O walked in and closed the door. He looked me in the eye and said, "If these students don't make at least two years gain in math this year, it is your fault." Up to this point I had been working 12, 13, and 14 hours a day just to keep up. The anal retentiveness I had developed as an undergrad found its way into my teaching career. I spent countless hours planning, keeping my classroom work current, and tutoring students. The school day began at 7:30 am and ended at 5:00 pm for students. Two years academic growth in a year for a stellar, veteran teacher is almost impossible and by most accounts highly unreasonable. I refused to complain. I gave everything I had with little thanks and what I felt at the time to be few rewards.

By November, I was at my wit's end. I was constantly ridiculed by who should have been my biggest support. Mr. O rarely had kind or encouraging words. He spent little time as a classroom teacher but had what I perceived to be a passion for urban school reform. Accordingly, he wanted results by any means necessary. I was pushing as hard as I could with few favorable outcomes. Mr. O seldom entertained my request to engage students with new, innovative activities I had recently read about. He maintained control of every aspect of my instructional practice. Mr. O sat in my classroom 3 or 4 days a week typing feverishly on his laptop as I taught. "Line your desks up like this ... You shouldn't do this activity because its too audacious a task for you ... Stand here when you talk ... There is too much noise in your class, the kids can't be learning" are the types of comments he made in passing. I lost pieces of my personality with each passing day. I had little time for recreation or friends anymore which meant I had no balance. I was under an extraordinary amount of pressure to perform.

When I returned to work the Monday after Thanksgiving break, I opened the door to my classroom to find that it wasn't my classroom anymore. I was optimistic to make improvements to my instruction to find that my posters and materials had been stuffed in a box thrown in the corner of the room. To make matters worse, some other person's decorations and name was on *my* white board. It was like someone punched me in the stomach. I was overwhelmed with emotion, sick at the thought that I could be so easily replaced without any prior warning. Eager to figure out what was going on, I sat quietly with my class at the Monday morning all-school meeting.

Mr. O began the meeting by reading a letter out loud to be sent home to parents alerting them of a few personnel adjustments. The letter read something close to the following:

> "We've had some changes in our school's teaching assignments to ensure greater instructional effectiveness ...
> Ms. Rankin will be the new 6th grade reading teacher
> Mr. Johnson will transition to the 5th grade math vacancy
> Mrs. Perry will now teach 5th grade reading
> Mr. Warren will be the assistant to the 7th grade teacher." (Names have been changed)

No warning, no meeting, no anything. He had made his decision without preparing any of the teachers for the drastic changes. While the changes he proposed were to take place following the holiday break, he felt the need to make the change to my teaching assignment effective immediately. Keep in mind that I was the only professional Black male on staff. The school was 100% Black students and the one professional role model they had was publicly demoted. I lost authority, credibility, and respect with the students in a matter of minutes.

I didn't know how to handle this devastating sense of failure. Once again, I was left questioning whether becoming a teacher was the right decision. I had been asking myself all school year did I make a mistake. Should I have listened and done something else? I began thinking about an immediate career change. I was at a crossroads. I had to make another important life decision. The reality at the moment was that I was no longer a real teacher anymore. To make a long story short, Mr. O eventually released me out of my contract the following Friday with 2 months full pay and benefits. He called me into his office and said, "This is just not a good fit." What should've been a sad time was the most liberating. I posted my resume on Monday, interviewed for an 8th grade position on Wednesday, picked up my teacher editions for that position on Friday, and began teaching the following Monday. One door closing was the precursor to a better door being opened. Being let go from BEST (with pay no less) marked a significant turning point on my journey. I learned many new skills at BEST that served me well in this new position in a rougher, more disorganized school.

I made a significant discovery while reflecting on the experience I had at BEST academy. That is, I wanted so badly to be accepted and approved by Mr. O that I allowed him to strip away the parts of my character that made me a good teacher. Administrators don't always know how to develop capacity in their teachers without pressuring them to change who they are.

Some will demand teachers conform to narrow perspectives of what a good teacher looks like and can accomplish. Teaching is deeply personal work requiring one's ability to be vulnerable and open to sudden change. Teachers can't do that if they are constantly torn down, berated, or unsupported. Like students, teachers need care, they need support. The only way teachers can focus their attention on fully caring for students and attending to the work of providing high-quality educational experiences for youth is if they have an equally supportive administrator.

The school where I began teaching after my tenure at BEST had a different set of challenges. The students were much more misbehaved. The new school didn't have the modicum of parental involvement that BEST boasted. Nor did I have access to the many resources provided to me at BEST. Nonetheless, it was the optimal teaching situation. I grew tremendously, both personally and professionally. I walked into a situation where I was the students' fifth teacher in 4 months of school. The principal at the new school took one look at my resume and said, "Look, I know you're smart, but can you teach? These 8th graders need a strong Black male teacher who can teach." A little taken aback by the principal's forthrightness, I accepted the job. My students soared academically. It was a challenging year given the circumstances, but the difference in this school versus BEST was that the principal demonstrated her trust in my ability by treating me as a professional. She released me to do what I thought best for the students based on my professional judgment. She supported my endeavors with relevant professional development experiences and resources when she could. She asked what I needed and did her best to ensure I had the support. The administrator regularly communicated care in a way I understood it. As a result, I was motivated to work hard not to let her down.

When you make important decisions about your career, recognize your worth and the many talents you bring to the table. Interview the school. Learn the community and talk to the teachers working in that building. Every situation you encounter, individual you meet, and obstacle you overcome is meant to teach you something as you prepare for the next level of promotion. When you're done complaining and/or beating yourself up, be determined to persevere. One of your greatest feats as a teacher will be to show up every day optimistic for the change you can make in a young person's life. From that day to the present, I've had a very fulfilling career as a teacher and school administrator. I've developed an extensive professional network that continues to serve me well in every professional endeavor I undertake. Had I quit BEST, I am sure that I would never have fully embraced my call; which I am positive would mean an empty and unfulfilled existence.

EMBRACING THE CALL ...

Embracing the call to teach is acceptance of the nobility associated with a life full of service to others. The commentary up to this point was meant to lay the groundwork for a deeper discussion of what it takes to embrace the call and prepare for a challenging, but rewarding career as a classroom teacher. My story nuances the consequences and benefits of a vocation desperate for *any* teacher committed to doing what it takes to improve failing schools. The problem of Black males' under representation in the teaching profession is exacerbated when those who do pursue a teaching career as continually abused, marginalized and mistreated. In addition to the anecdotes for success I've already shared, the four recommendations to follow have helped me sustain a prosperous career in education. If I was giving advice to Black males considering teaching and those mentoring them, this is what I would say.

PERSEVERE

Like teaching, perseverance is a choice. It is a personal quality that is highly understated. I have yet to hear of a methods course that explicitly emphasizes this important character trait. Teaching is one of, if not the most, challenging of careers. Half the battle is showing up every day with intention of making each new day count for the youth sitting in front of you.

Attending a PWI was not difficult because of the rigorous academic expectations. On the contrary, it was the lack of support from instructors and the Eurocentric curriculum that lacked cultural relevance. The cultural insensitivity of my classmates and the deficit perspectives many of them employed to make judgments about people of color. The social context was one that impeded difficult conversations around matters of race and class in shaping how one experiences school. These were issues out of my control. What was in my control was how I responded to it all. I showed up to class earlier, provided sharper, more critical interpretations of texts, and gave impeccable presentations. This is your responsibility. Perseverance is never about getting revenge or stepping on the people who've abused you (though those things may be motivation). You must practice humility and be gracious at all times. Your professional *success* will always be the best recompense.

FIND A MENTOR/ALLY

Professor Violet was the first person who pushed my thinking about the benefits and difficulties of becoming a teacher. Identify an individual who engages you on *your* terms. True allies and mentors want to learn from you just as much as they want to teach you. The support they offer should align with your needs and less their personal agenda. Professor Violet was straightforward, honest, and caring. Your mentor should be attentive to your various concerns.

Mentors do more than provide guidance. He or she is an advocate as well. Your mentor/ally may be an individual with significant experience in the field who can show you the ropes. He or she should offer you sound advice and share opportunities with you that will mature you professionally. This person should have a track record of trustworthiness. A mentor can come in multiple forms – race, gender, or class status doesn't matter. What does matter is that the mentor makes a commitment to you to support your progress despite the sacrifice.

DO THE WORK

Being Black, male, and choosing to teach in the 21st century sometimes means doing the work that no one else wants to do. The work may be coaching the failing basketball team or serving as the faculty sponsor for a controversial student organization. The work may be as simple as making yourself available and visible at community events and after-hour school functions. Community members and parents alike want to get to know you and support your efforts to educate their children. This is not to say that you should stress yourself out trying to fill every void the school has. Choose how you engage, but DO engage.

Do not be covertly coerced to become the face of diversity for your teacher education program, school, or school district (unless you really want to). Your primary role is to be an effective educator and that must remain central to your participation in the institution. When your activities detract you from being an excellent teacher, then it is okay to respectfully decline. I insist that as a Black male teacher, you have an obligation to have your voice be heard. Sit on the local school council and attend the parent advisory board meetings. The relationships you develop as a result of your participation will take you a long way as you progress throughout your career. Also, don't wait until graduation time to professionally prepare to teach. Get active in the local schools where your university is located. Become a mentor or tutor and build networks wherever you go. I got my first job because I attended job fairs 2 years before I graduated. Create opportunities, take initiative, and nurture professional relationships with individuals of influence on your campus.

BE WHO YOU ARE

There are true rewards in your ability to acknowledge the uncomfortable parts of who you are and be willing to change. Students are like a mirror; they show you everything about yourself that you would rather not see. They expose the quirky, seemingly embarrassing aspects of your identity. The sooner you come to terms with all of who you are, the better apt you will be to communicate and respond to the developing personalities of your students. Whether you are the most athletic or you lack physical dexterity, embrace every facet of your personhood. Believe it or not there are great benefits to being uniquely you. The courage to do so will inspire your students in many ways. They need to see that all Black men are not the same. There is considerable diversity among us.

Mr. O taught me that I am really good at being myself, but not so good at being someone else. I took every unsolicited suggestion he offered against my better judgment. As a result, both my students and I suffered. Mr. O got me to give up control and that is when I failed. Students appreciate honesty and vulnerability. Modeling these qualities gives them permission to be who they are. Be critical of the suggestions and criticisms others offer you for how to modify your practice. Put your best foot forward but speak up when you are being stretched too far. Your teaching practice will improve over time as your teacher identity develops and matures.

CONCLUSION

Education needs more Black male professors, school board members, administrators, and advocates in positions of influence speaking on behalf of young people everywhere. Bold initiatives to recruit Black men to teach, like the appeal of U.S. Secretary of Education Arne Duncan to the men of Morehouse College in 2011, are admirable. Still, without the proper training Black men who are unprepared to tackle the challenge of teaching in the 21st century stand to do the same, if not worse damage to Black and Latino youth. My narrative has been shaped by the lives of young people I've had the privilege of teaching and the plight of those I will never meet. Black males must understand their role of advocacy, critical engagement, and concomitant problem solving. He must embrace the call to speak up for the underserved students and families who may never have a seat at the tables of privilege where he has been afforded access. The education community must come together now to make the profession a place where Black men can be successful. The future of our schools rely on it.

CASE ANALYSIS

Reggie is a talented leader. He is an all-star college athlete and a gifted writer. His classmates call on him regularly to be the cooperative group leader, but Reggie would rather just contribute. Reggie enjoys school, but he is not the most exceptional student. He does what he has to do to get by, but he most enjoys playing sports. Many big name universities recruited Reggie to play ball for them. Reggie's high school coach thinks that he has the talent to possibly go pro, but isn't sure that he can compete against the other very talented ball players his age. Nonetheless, Reggie is a starting player at his university.

Additionally, Reggie has always enjoyed working with children. He enjoyed growing up in the city for all there is to do, but Reggie equally loved going to work as a camp counselor in rural Michigan every summer. The camp was specifically designed for inner-city youth and was sponsored by Reggie's church. He considered becoming a teacher, but he loves sports and dreamed of playing professionally, which made summer camp the perfect retreat every summer.

Now Reggie is nearing the end of his sophomore year and he must choose a major. There is also major buzz that upon graduation Reggie can be drafted to play professionally. He knows that if he pursues a teaching degree, it will make playing sports very challenging because of the significant time commitments he would have to give the two activities. Reggie has to decide whether he will apply to the Education major or if he will reside to pursuing a less time-intensive, less rigorous program of study. He went to visit an advisor in the college of education to explain his situation and weigh his options.

Using the case analysis, answer the questions:

(1) If you were Reggie's coach, what would you advise Reggie in making his decision? From your experience, how do you believe the coach in this vignette would really advise Reggie?
(2) What should Reggie be doing to prepare for his meeting? What other considerations should he make in helping him determine whether or not he should pursue a teaching career?
(3) What are the benefits for Reggie if he pursues the education major? What are the challenges?
(4) If you were the academic advisor, what would you say to Reggie to help him make his decision? What considerations should you take when deciding how to advise Reggie so that he makes the BEST decision he can for himself?
(5) As an academic advisor with the goal of recruiting individuals BEST suited to teach, what other information do you think is important to know about Reggie? What questions would you ask him and why?
(6) What other individuals should Reggie seek out to help him make an informed decision about becoming a teacher and why? If Reggie came to you, what advice would you give him to help him make his decision without showing a bias to one choice or the other? How would you talk about both the challenges and the benefits to being a Black male teacher?
(7) If you had 60 seconds to convince Reggie that he SHOULD pursue a career as a teacher, what argument would you make?

ACKNOWLEDGMENT

The author would like to thank Jean Johnson for critical feedback of this manuscript in preparation of this chapter for submission.

REFERENCES

Delgado, R., & Stefancic, J. (2001). *Critical race theory: An introduction.* New York, NY: New York University Press.
Delpit, L. (1995). *Other people's children.* New York, NY: New Press.

Smith, W. A., Allen, W. R., & Danley, L. L. (2007). Assume the position ... You fit the description. Psychosocial experiences and racial battle fatigue among African-American male college students. *American Behavioral Scientist, 51*(4), 551–578.

Solorzano, D. G., Ceja, M., & Yosso, T. J. (2000). Critical race theory, racial microaggressions, and campus racial climate: The experiences of African-American college students. *The Journal of Negro Education, 69*(1/2), 60–73.

Solorzano, D., & Yosso, T. J. (2002). A critical race counter-story of race, racism, and affirmative action. *Equity and Excellence in Education, 35*(2), 155–168.

Solorzano, D. G., & Yosso, T. J. (2009). Critical race methodology: Counter-storytelling as an analytical framework for educational research. In E. Taylor, D. Gillborn & G. Ladson-Billings (Eds.), *Foundations of critical race theory in education* (pp. 131–147). New York, NY: Routledge.

U.S. Bureau of Labor. (2008a). Employment by detailed occupation, sex, race, and Hispanic ethnicity, 2008 annual averages. Retrieved from http://www.bls.gov/cps/. Accessed on August 2, 2009.

U.S. Bureau of Labor. (2008b). Labor force characteristics by race and ethnicity, 2007. Publication No. 1005. Retrieved from http://www.bls.gov/cps/. Accessed on August 2, 2009.

SECTION III
THE VOICES OF CURRENT
BLACK TEACHERS

CHAPTER 13

THEY DESERVE IT

Justin Newell

ABSTRACT

After 10 years of teaching, my feelings, and opinions are based on experiences in the classroom and my own life. By no means am I an expert with immense amount of statistics and graphs. I teach from the heart and in these pages, I wrote from the heart. I have had the privilege of working with hundreds of children in three different school districts. These districts had varying demographics, but in each the black or African American population was a significant number. I currently teach in a city that has been ranked among some of the worst in the country in terms of both crime and education and academic performance. However, each child that walks through my classroom door is as precious as any other on the planet. They deserve my best!

At the end of my high school graduation ceremony on that muggy June 1997 day, I had a basic framework of an idea of how my future would look. In the fall, I would head off to Wesley College in Dover, Delaware. I'd graduate in four years with my Bachelor's Degree in Physical Education. I would land a job at my alma mater, Glassboro High School in Glassboro, New Jersey. During the day I'd roll balls out to the students or be "steady pitcher" during kick ball and softball games in school, and then I would coach football during the fall evenings. Later on in each year, I would coach

Black Male Teachers: Diversifying the United States' Teacher Workforce
Advances in Race and Ethnicity in Education, Volume 1, 185–192
Copyright © 2013 by Emerald Group Publishing Limited
All rights of reproduction in any form reserved
ISSN: 2051-2317/doi:10.1108/S2051-2317(2013)0000001017

baseball during the spring evenings. Being a creature of habit that likes to stay in my own comfort zone, I figured I would gladly and snugly fit into the eventual rut that this future life could bring. Both my perspective and prediction were wrong on many levels. One misconception was my idea of what a Physical Education teacher or a teacher of any subject actually does on the job wasn't doing good teachers any justice.

Another wrong assumption was I hadn't yet realized that I wasn't always in control of my own stages of my life. God's hand gracefully, omnisciently, and sometimes humorously lines up the events in my life, and He has His way whether I recognize it or not. Who I am now is totally different than who I imagined I would become while standing in my high school parking lot looking out over the football field where I had graduated moments earlier. Sixteen years later, I am humbled by the challenge yet proud of the profession as an educator. I am both fearless and terrified about the idea that the future of my students is many times in my hands. I want to be the best teacher I can be for each student who enters the threshold of our classroom. Currently, I take immense pride in being a 5th grade teacher at LEAP University Charter School in Camden, New Jersey. I am entering my 11th year as a teacher, and every time I boastfully mislead myself into believing that my handle on this profession is extra solid, I get a reminder that isn't always gentle that there is and always will be room to get better!

When I was younger, I wanted to be something. I guess I basically needed confidence. My parents were divorced, and my dad wasn't consistently in my life. We went through times of poverty. There were also times of lacking supervision at home because my mom ended up becoming a night-shift nurse. So my older sister and I were left at home alone many nights.

Growing up in that environment didn't lead to much authentic confidence building. So surviving as a student was good enough for me at the time.

The picture of that version of me is why I became an elementary school teacher. I knew there were so many students with similar backgrounds and academic circumstances. I wanted to be the one to tap into their potential, and let them see that their futures are without bounds. I don't want my students to ever feel like I felt ... lacking confidence, second-guessing them-selves academically, and being satisfied with "getting by." Judging by my experience as a student and later a teacher, many black students in similar environments and circumstances share a similar outlook. I wanted (and still want) to be a difference maker for such students.

After student teaching in the 4th through 6th grade setting, I realized that this age range might be my wheelhouse as a teacher because of the vibe and energy that this group brings in the classroom every day. I currently teach Language Arts and Social Studies. I have taught these two subjects for the majority of my 11-year career. This is very different than what I thought I would be doing, but the agent of change from me majoring in Physical Education to Elementary Education was a teacher! Dr. Sturgis was a very nice man at Wesley College. He was my professor for several classes including *The Methods of Teaching Social Studies* and *Teaching Reading in the Content Areas*. He pulled me aside right before winter break of my junior year and told me, "If you stick with PE, you will come out of college as a dime a dozen ... If you were an elementary teacher, as a black or minority MALE, you will be able to write your own ticket! Justin, you are smart enough to do it!" He told me to take my time over winter break, consider his words, and let him know if I wanted to change my major. I was about 5 days into my break when I left him a message on his voicemail, which he later returned. He told me he'd handle the paperwork, and we'd check my scheduler for any necessary changes. It might be easy to overlook Dr. Sturgis' influence or involvement. However, to me, it was monumental. It also is a confirming moment of God's involvement in my life. He used Dr. Sturgis as an instrument in my life. For that I am extremely thankful to both! This taught me a lesson about teaching that I feel all teachers need. As his student, Dr. Sturgis showed me he believed in me. In spite of his experience as a professor and the hundreds of potential teachers he taught to be professionals, he thought I was good enough to be one of them! Every student needs that same belief whether they are 3 or 40!

"... but I still love ya, baby!" Famous words by Mrs. Legis, my 11th grade history teacher. She could spend 20 minutes tearing into us about talking, or being off task, or being lazy. She was very patient with us until she started to give us a speech. At the end of her soapbox speech, she'd conclude by saying, "I still love you!" This is the only time I can remember those words from a teacher. I remember them more than any other words said in any other class. Mrs. Legis taught my mother, my father, all of my aunts and uncles, my sister, and me. I don't know if my family or any of my classmates see Mrs. Legis the same as I. I've even had the honor of being colleagues with Mrs. Legis in my teaching career. It's hard to tell me that God's hand wasn't involved in that! Mrs. Legis is still teaching, and I hope she still tells her students that she loves them! Because of her, I use those words with mine!

Mrs. Melvin, Mr. Barry, and Mrs. Legis had different styles, different approaches, and they taught in different buildings. Ironically they all taught me social studies, one of the subjects I now teach. They also all shared a desire to tell us there was a future for us. They told us we were preparing ourselves for what was to come.

Professors from college honestly changed me as a man. Dr. Sturgis helped navigate my path and helped me get into my specific subjects and grade level. However, there were some that literally changed my view of the world around me, they taught me how to be professional, and developed my understanding of being a lifelong learner. It just so happens that none of them are minorities. Looking back, they knew that their jobs were to prepare us for the world that was coming in the very near future. I stumbled upon my college because my buddy went there a year before me to be a gym teacher and a football player. As mentioned before, that was my initial blueprint too. He ended up leaving after 2 years, but I stayed, and looking back now, I'm so blessed to have attended Wesley College. My education professors especially were way ahead of the game. I still go to professional developments where what is presented is being given as new and a best practice, but I learned it in college 12 years ago. Eight A.M. Mondays, Wednesdays, and Fridays, I had Dr. Angst for Sociology. His passion for the subject, his organization, his classroom disposition, and his 8 A.M. energy were admirable. He connected both Sociology and Geography during a different semester to my other understanding of Social Studies.

"You're one of the smartest students who ever walked through the doors in this building, Justin, but you are satisfied with doing the bare minimum to get by." Dr. Pat, one of my education professors said these words to me and made me step up my game! I didn't realize I had slipped back into survival mode during Methods of Teaching. Yet Dr. Pat called me on it. I'm so thankful she did. Plus I couldn't believe she saw me as one of the smartest students to come through her doors. Looking back now, that probably was Hollywood talk to get me to buy into what she was saying, but I bought it. That semester seemed so overwhelming at the time. Her words coupled with my stubborn drive helped me get better as a student and ultimately as a future teacher. Wesley College truly helped make me the man and teacher I am. Dr. Petzer, Dr. Fole, helped continue to expand my mind to literature. Dr. Roberts published my writing that I've since shared with my students. The list continues, and so does my gratitude!

I've been pretty fortunate and blessed to have the educational channels that I did. I can't say the same for many of my peers and friends simply because I don't know the extent of all of their experiences. I have several friends who have felt like some teachers were biased to say the least toward nonminority students. Yet I've also had teachers and have worked with colleagues who have poured their hearts upon all of their students regardless of their cultural background or ethnicity.

Young black males need to see constant and consistent reminders that there are minority men who are educated, hard workers, and believe in the students. When I was in 7th grade, about a dozen and a half of my friends and I was called down to the auditorium. There waiting for us was a very large man flanked by about 10 college students. Our principal told us that we were selected to be part of a mentoring program being carried out by Mr. William H. Myers, a professor and dean at Rowan University. The Alpha Phi Alpha fraternity developed a program called "Gentlemen by Choice." They ended up staying with us and following up with us until we graduated high school. There were about 20 total members of GBC, and 18 of us graduated from college. They took us to see entrepreneurs, architects, engineers, doctors, physical therapists, and many other professionals. They invested time in us, and told us that we could be whatever we wanted. The great part of their experimental mentoring was it worked! We needed to hear that we could accomplish our goals and reach our dreams. It built up our self-image and efficacy. Some of us weren't exposed to black professionals and entrepreneurs before. This experience and exposure to black professionals for most of us was mind broadening.

Black male teachers can have immense effects on black male students (and all of their students). Sometimes, I spend more time with my students throughout the day than their parents do. I take that concept seriously! I want them to understand that I am there for them and I want them to understand some ideas in that time with me besides the content I am responsible for teaching them. Here are three such ideas:

(1) I want to reinforce the idea that there are educated, hard working men, who look like them, and come from backgrounds similar to their own that can and will succeed. Just like Mr. Young, Mr. Myers, and Gentlemen By Choice, for me seeing that example can be paradigm shifting for a young man.
(2) Based on my experience, another concept young black males need is a vested interest in them as a student, as a person, not just as a number on a teacher's roster. Students need to know they aren't just a warm behind in a seat that needs to follow the way the teacher operates or else he is a nuisance. He needs to know he is allowed to be safe, strong, and free. He can attack the world, his dreams, and his goals with conviction and

determination with the confidence to succeed. I personally approach the classroom with the understanding that these young people are people first and my pupils second. I want my students to see it in my eyes that I believe in them and I know they can be whomever and whatever they want to be!

(3) I've also realized in my experience that when students surround themselves with positive like-minded friends and peers, they end up lining themselves up with a great support group. It seems like peers have a more powerful influence than parents at times. It appears that peers shape and shift the way parts of a population can think. In any groups it seems like acceptable ideas and concepts are unofficially developed. They seem to informally come up with norms such as working hard, seeking success, and trying their best. The norms from the wrong peer group could be negative and limiting toward a young man's potential. My friends and peers that were recommended and accepted into Gentlemen By Choice fed off one another and emulated and duplicated each other's success. I've witnessed students in my school environments do the same thing. While teaching at Thomas E. Bowe School in Glassboro, New Jersey, I had a group of young black boys in my class that were self-motivated. Most of them lived in circumstances very similar to mine at their age. In that peer group, there were such qualities as outstanding athleticism, some exceptional musical talent, academic understanding, and boundless potential. This particular group of boys seemed to innately see forms of these qualities in each other and they pushed each other. It was a beautiful thing to see, and I was proud to be their teacher.

As a black teacher, I want to foster skills and qualities like those exhibited in that 6th grade class at Thomas E. Bowe School. However, if a sense of community and togetherness can be developed by a group of peers in a class, positive results can be infectious and spread throughout the classroom and beyond. These boys and all of their school community can benefit. Moreover, characteristics, habits, and routines can be developed that these students can adopt and improve upon throughout their lives ultimately contributing to their individual success.

Based upon my experience, there are five practical strategies for teachers and parents I'd like to share. I've seen them work in my life. I try to instill or apply them throughout all of my students. They are just based upon what I've seen as an educator and experienced as a student in my personal journey.

FIVE PRACTICAL STRATEGIES FOR
TEACHERS AND PARENTS

(1) *Regardless of your role in a young person's life, stress the importance of reading!*

If research is correct students especially those who are minorities or are in low-income households who don't grasp solid reading skills by the end of 1st grade will have the same problem by the end of 4th (Juels, 1988). When would this trend reverse itself? It won't! However, our males need to know that reading affects their futures in many aspects.

(2) *Edify areas of strength and fortify areas of weakness!*

It is common sense to know that all students and learners have potential and can learn. It may go without saying, but students need to know there are areas and skills that may come naturally to them or that they are inclined to be successful in as well as areas that need extra practice or particular attention to make up for deficiencies. Weak areas especially need to be identified and addressed while areas of strength are being identified and built upon as foundational supports for their learning.

(3) *There is nothing wrong with saying "I love you!"*

Mrs. Legis, my 11th grade History teacher instilled this in me as her student and a teacher. In my experience, I've found when my students know I love them, they know it is safe to learn, explore, and take chances with me. These words coming from a teacher made me feel like someone believed in me and knew I could accomplish good things. I was worth investing in, and therefore made me want to show her she was right for putting that investment in me. I want my students to feel that same investment in them. It's three small words, but their affect can be profound upon a student's learning.

(4) *Discipline is a sign of love, not meanness!*

I have made the mistake and seen the mistake made by others of trying to be "the cool teacher." My thinking was based upon a line thought that went something like this: "*If they see I'm cool, they'll work, and try their best for me.*" How wrong I was! If I am too lax in my consistency and my expectations for them, why would they push themselves harder than me when my role is the authority in the room? There is a difference between being authoritative and an authoritarian. It seems as though when children know that rules are there for their benefit, they are easier to adhere to for the student. In my opinion and experience, setting ground rules and expectations along with consequences for breaking rules plus having them buy into them seems to lead to more cooperation between the child and the adult regardless of role.

(5) *Seconds or minutes of consistent organization can help prevent endless "straightening" or "reorganizing binges."*

I have my students keep binders for my school subjects. Many of my students find it hard to stay organized. It is just a personal preference and observation, but organizing their binders, their school work, their desks, or even their rooms at home carry over into having an easier handle on an organized life. I give my students binder checks that count as a grade. When I announce an upcoming binder check, after the collective gasp, many students pull out a waded, collection of papers resembling a bird nest. They try to organize them on the spot and it resembles a major home renovation ... total breakdown and rebuild! If this organization (simply putting a sheet of paper inside the rings of their binder instead of cramming it in an available pocket inside the binder) were just habitual and consistently applied, it would develop the habit of the process and keep their belongings and thoughts organized. I am convinced that this organization can help with success at school. The loss of materials, papers, important documents, and homework can't and won't happen if this were followed through.

I'm not the best teacher to ever stand in front of a classroom of young faces charged with assignment of disseminating information and sharing life lessons. I know there are many teachers whose school bag I couldn't even carry. My strength as a teacher lies in my willingness to share my heart, life, and passions with my students. I continuously want to get better for me, but more importantly, I want them to come to school every day expecting me to teach them something new. I am there on their behalf, and I want them to have my best. They deserve it!

REFERENCE

Juel, C. (1988). Learning to read and write: A longitudinal study of 54 children from first through fourth grades. *Journal of Educational Psychology*, *80*(4), 437–447.

CHAPTER 14

OPPORTUNITIES TO DIE FOR

Jamil Alhassan

ABSTRACT

My chapter includes a discussion of various elements throughout my life that were very influential for the attainment of a successful education that I believe can also help other Black male students receive a successful education. The chapter begins with an explanation of why I became a teacher and my passions to enhance the education of Black male students with the use of the same influential elements that enhanced my education. The influential elements I highlighted are opportunity and exposure, discipline and accountability, recognition, and mentorship. I compared and contrasted the effects of these elements on my life with others who lacked these same elements, and provided examples of what I observe today as an educator in reference to these elements. I further speak about how I have implemented these elements in my classroom and in my interactions with young Black males today. Finally, I provide possible solutions to reshape the image and education of Black male students and create a positive impact on future generations. When a Black male student has an exemplar of an educated professional to emulate they can gain motivation to strive for academic greatness that will bring them true greatness rather than fighting and dying in the streets over false opportunities. Ultimately, Black male students will strive for academic greatness, which is truly ... an opportunity to die for.

Black Male Teachers: Diversifying the United States' Teacher Workforce
Advances in Race and Ethnicity in Education, Volume 1, 193–204
Copyright © 2013 by Emerald Group Publishing Limited
All rights of reproduction in any form reserved
ISSN: 2051-2317/doi:10.1108/S2051-2317(2013)0000001018

WHY I BECAME A TEACHER

It's a war zone outside with many Black male victims. Our youth are misguided casualties in this war and blinded by ignorance. I became a teacher to change the game and bring this war from the streets onto the battlefield of the mind. In my classroom I have an opportunity to drop grenades of knowledge and shoot bullets of wisdom.

I became a teacher because I believe the best way to empower and inspire young people is to teach and expose them to the possibilities and advantages education can warrant. For me, education was a ticket to a better life, away from the slums of my southwest Philly neighborhood and the vacancy of a father-figure. Throughout my life, I have been granted numerous opportunities and blessings that I can trace to an educational attribute or achievement. For most inner city Black males, such opportunities are scarce and realities are harsh.

Provided with opportunities, I felt obligated to provide opportunities for others. My passion for science and educating others led me to join Teach For America. As a high school Biology teacher my goal is to not only teach science, but also to serve as an example of how to transcend beyond the plight of difficult circumstances through the use of the benefits and possibilities provided by education. As I reflect back on my educational experience there are five fundamental factors that I believe were essential to my success: exposure, discipline and accountability, recognition, mentorship, and most importantly, opportunities.

MY EXPERIENCES AS A BLACK MALE GRADE SCHOOL STUDENT

Growing up in inner city Philadelphia, I had limited access to adequate education. I went to Samuel B. Huey Elementary School, a predominantly African American school that often struggles to meet state standards. Although the student population was mostly African American, most of the teachers were White women; it was difficult to relate to any of my teachers. Despite race and gender my first grade teacher, Ms. Hollam, played a pivotal role in my life by granting me an opportunity to enhance my education.

Opportunity

Ms. Hollam, a small Caucasian woman, inspired me to excel academically because of her dedication and commitment toward student achievement.

She noticed that I was a bright student, who liked to learn and frequently volunteered in class. At a time when the wealth of my ambition was confounded by the poverty of my circumstance, Ms. Hollam, like all great teachers, looked beyond the symptoms of my situation. Ms. Hollam helped me gain admittance into the Mentally Gifted (MG) program, a program that ultimately changed the trajectory of my life. After being admitted to the MG program, my journey began and, as my mother once said, I was now "on the fast track to success." The MG program consisted of an advanced enrichment curriculum that supplemented the school's regular classroom curriculum in order to further develop advanced cognitive skills.

Most importantly, the MG program provided its students with an opportunity to experience things outside of the classroom that they would not have traditionally been exposed to. Through this program, I was selected to attend Conwell Middle Magnet School – the second best public school in Philadelphia. Transitioning from elementary school to Conwell Middle Magnet School was the first time that I was exposed to an educational environment rich with students from various backgrounds and cultures. In addition, I was afforded numerous opportunities at Conwell that would not have been possible otherwise. By going to a unique and diverse school I was afforded opportunities to prestigious programs such as the John Hopkins CTY program for talented youth.

However, opportunities like mine were uncommon to the majority of other students in Philadelphia. In Philadelphia, a student's residence determined the school he or she attended. Being that a majority of the poorly performing schools existed in predominantly Black neighborhoods, most Black students were confined to such schools and continually matriculated into similar caliber high schools. Sayre Middle School, the middle school designated for my neighborhood, is ranked as one of the lowest performing middle schools in the city.

In addition to the lack of equal education in impoverished neighbor-hoods, the schools' lack of diversity limited its students' perspectives on the world beyond their neighborhood. I remember my neighborhood friends, including my younger brother, would always discuss the problems at their schools such as the fights and lack of discipline. It seemed the expectation of these students were to get into altercations and nonsense rather than focus on their education. Where the highlight of my day was learning a new fact or a debate over a topic in class, my neighborhood friends' high-lights revolved around competitions with girls, money, fights, or sports. Education, academic opportunity, and advancement were not a priority to the predominantly Black neighborhood schools, and as a result, were not a priority to the schools' students.

After middle school, I matriculated into Central High School. Although I was now attending the second best high school in the city, the majority of my neighborhood friends attended Bartram High School, a low performing institution that was predominately Black. At Central High I was among some of the most talented, diverse, and intelligent students in the city of Philadelphia.

Soon after I started at Central, I realized that Black students that were seen as intelligent were offered far greater opportunities than Black students who weren't seen as high achieving. Unfortunately compared to middle school, I was no longer fully focused on my academics and became complacent in school as the harsh realities of my home circumstances became more apparent. As a teenager living in a single parent household in a bad neighborhood, I was plagued with problems outside of my academics. When I was in tenth grade, my mother fell ill and lost her job at Temple University. This loss crippled my family, especially since my mother's salary was the only financial support we had.

As the oldest male in the house, I took on the responsibility as the "man of the house," attempting to be a father-figure for my younger brother while trying to find ways to help my mother with the bills. Quickly my responsibilities flipped and providing for my family and making it safely in the streets took precedence over my education. This dilemma plagued a lot of my peers in my neighborhood, with many of them dropping out of school and turning to the streets to provide for themselves and their families. Although some tried to stay away from the streets and find jobs, many of them were unsuccessful.

However, once again, my academic background would present an opportunity that would have been unavailable to many of my peers. One week after I turned 16, I applied for my first job at a KFC restaurant. My boss saw that I went to Central and hired me on the spot. My boss knew that Central was a well-recognized school and assumed Central students would be better employees than other high school students. Within three months of working at KFC and through the recommendation of a classmate, I was offered another position at an Old Navy clothing store. I was then able to work two jobs simultaneously throughout the remainder of high school.

Despite all of my academic abilities I was still a regular Black student from southwest Philadelphia who shared the blight of my peers. In my opinion, the one defining factor between the trajectory of my life and the typical Black student was that I had opportunities that they couldn't even fathom.

Exposure

I was exposed to an enriched curriculum in my MG program in elementary school, which enhanced my learning by sharpening my reading and critical thinking skills. Further, the MG program gave me the opportunity to work with computers even though I didn't have one at home. I was also able to go on educational field trips that exposed me to tools and things that were important to the world that were created through subjects like science. I vividly remember during elementary school I was fascinated with Ben Franklin's story of developing electricity, and wanted to learn how to create such innovations myself.

At Central High School I was exposed to a diverse community and upper level course work. Central offered classes such as Psychology, Anatomy, Advanced Geometry, AP Physics, and Calculus that challenged my intellect. Compared to my neighborhood high school that the majority of Black males attended, such high-level courses were often inaccessible if not absent. I believe that without exposure to rigorous classes most students are unable to comprehend complex concepts. Being exposed to rigorous courses before college is one of the key reasons for my success and progression in college. Of the Black males who graduate high school in Philadelphia, about 25% of them are reading on grade level.

Accountability/Discipline

I was also a successful student because I was disciplined and held accountable for my actions and the actions of others. Ever since elementary school my mother made sure my sibling and I were disciplined to focus on our academics. My mother always made me get my schoolwork done before I could play with my brother or friends. My mother also took an active role in my education and would come to my school if there were any issues with my behavior. I became used to the routine of completing my school assignments and my positive behavior stemmed from not wanting to be subject to my mother's corrective actions.

My success in school eventually transformed into a personal responsibility. I was accountable for my grades and susceptible to losing certain privileges if I did not take care of my academic responsibilities. My schoolwork came before anything else. I think this element of discipline and accountability was very important to my success because it helped me keep my focus on my academics and encouraged me to value education.

My educational success was important to my mother, and I was determined to set, meet, and exceed expectations. Many of my friends in my neighborhood were not provided with a model of accountability and discipline. Most of my friends were allowed to do as they pleased because their parents were preoccupied or indifferent to their academic success. The norms to many families were to spend time in jail with the expectations being set very low. I believe that without a sense of urgency or discipline to excel academically, more of our youth are vulnerable to life sidetracking their academics.

Recognition

Another important element that motivated me to excel was being recognized for my hard work and academic performances. Recognition for my academics allowed me to be aware of my achievements and confirmed my capabilities of academic achievement. This recognition started in first grade when I was first put in the MG program. That recognition sparked a passion inside of me that gave me the will to continuously apply myself in school.

Based on my experience, many students are unaware of their gifts because they have never been applauded for their achievements. I received numerous awards growing up that recognized my scholastic and leadership commitments. Communities are a good place to provide such recognition and give ownership to the student. When I was in fifth grade, I entered an essay contest to write an essay to the Philadelphia mayor about my ideas to change and positively transform my community. Among the many applicants, I was selected and invited by the mayor to read my essay at a banquet and receive an award that recognized my ideas of leadership and community service. Recognition by a man of such stature made me realize that I had a voice and perspective that people cared about and valued. Receiving praise for my thoughts, actions, and aspirations reinforced my hunger for scholastic success and motivated me to steadily improve.

I believe that confidence in academic ability is a quality that is missing among most Black males. Without the reinforcement or initial recognition of a child's capabilities, the child may have less confidence in their abilities or set low expectations for themselves. Many students are uninterested in the classroom because they don't feel like an integral part of the classroom because they are often ignored for their work and contributions. The recognition many Blacks males see is due to athletic abilities and musical talents rather than academic success. Without confidence or the recognition of certain capabilities, more of our talented youth will fall by the wayside or be consumed by their environment because they are unaware of their ability to excel beyond their neighborhood circumstance. Students must be recognized for their academics and positive contributions to society, so that they are motivated to continue this and set higher expectations for themselves. With the image of the Black male being recognized as an athlete, thug, or criminal, less Black males inherently associate themselves with academic achievement.

Mentoring

Another important element to my success as a student was mentorship. A mentor can serve as a guide and potential benchmark for a student to gauge how much or how little they want to accomplish. As a child I considered my family doctor, Dr. Whitney, as a mentor and role model. Dr. Whitney helped me keep my focus on my academics and all the possibilities they could afford me. In Dr. Whitney, I saw a vision of uncommon success that could be attained by a man of my circumstance. As an African American man passionately serving our community, Dr. Whitney inspired me to use my love of science to do the same. Having this mentor strengthened my passion for medicine because I was provided an open line of communication to ask questions about medicine and learn the necessary steps to pursue it. Hailing from Central High School himself, Dr. Whitney was the one who recommended Central to me.

My friends didn't have such accomplished mentors like Dr. Whitney. Many of them viewed older relatives and neighborhood guys as mentors and aspired to be like these people who were often uneducated and committing crimes. Without real examples of success, students will not aspire for more. I believe positive mentors for Black males is most essential for the proper development of the Black male in order for him to focus and have his priorities in order.

THREE THINGS BLACK MALE STUDENTS NEED TO BE SUCCESSFUL IN SCHOOL

From my former experiences as a student and from my current experiences as a teacher I am able to assess what Black male students need to be successful in school and ultimately in life. Now, as a high school Biology teacher for Teach for America in Camden, NJ, I am able to use the strategies that were beneficial to my life and implement them in the classroom for the benefit of my students. Black male students need mentorship, opportunities, exposure, discipline, and recognition.

Black male teachers can be critical in addressing Black male education because we can mentor and provide our students opportunities to enhance their academic abilities and expose them to the benefits of a great education. By creating a strong classroom structure, culture, and setting high expectations, students are challenged to adhere to this framework and will be recognized for their accomplishments and as well as disciplined for their transgressions. I have outlined these strategies for teachers and parents to support Black males in school.

FIVE PRACTICAL STRATEGIES FOR TEACHERS AND PARENTS TO SUPPORT BLACK LEARNERS

Five practical strategies that I've employed in my interactions with my students to help Black male students facilitate their personal and academic growths are: providing opportunities, increasing exposure, facilitating mentorship, instilling discipline, and giving recognition. These five elements were influential in my life and when applied to my classroom have been influential to my student's lives. I provided opportunities and exposure for my students both inside and outside of the classroom. In my classroom, students have multiple opportunities to engage and earn points in class to enhance their grades.

Providing Opportunities

One opportunity that a lot of my students loved was to teach or lead the class. I give students the opportunity to lead a lesson or explain concepts to the class in exchange for participation points. Black males often are not glorified for speaking up in class, but I've noticed that when they are comfortable and given a chance to express themselves they jump at the opportunity. Giving a Black male, or female student an opportunity to lead a class instills confidence in them and fosters leadership, which is a necessary trait for all students.

Increasing Exposure

I have also found that exposure to college and seeing an actual college degree provides further motivation for my students. I have invited my professional and college friends to school to speak to my students about higher education and the possibilities it can grant them. The exposure to Black college educated students opened their minds to ideas of college and professional careers. I believe that the ability to interact and engage with others who are just a few years older than them and being able to relate to them allows my students to visualize themselves accomplishing such feats. Many of these students do not know anyone like them who has completed college or a professional education. The exposure to Black college educated young adults has caused my students to have a hunger for the world beyond their individual neighborhoods.

Exposure to resources outside of the classroom is another pivotal aspect of students' development. I have given my students information about scholarships, colleges, and job opportunities that they have now pursued. Further, I took my students to the Annual Black Male Youth Development Symposium at Arcadia University to expose them to a culturally relevant event that was centered on the overall development of the young Black male. At the symposium students were able to attend and participate in development workshops.

Teachers and parents should provide Black students opportunities and exposure to college, professional careers, and educational activities so that the students are always focusing on a positive goal geared toward educational enhancement. In order for a Black student to emulate success they must be exposed to success and given opportunities to become successful.

Facilitating Mentorship

The third strategy that works in my classroom and also fosters personal growth, is facilitating mentorship opportunities. Mentorship is very important to the development of Black students because they are able to learn and grow from other individuals. Being a Black male teacher, I use my time outside of class to personally get to know my Black male students. I develop relationships with my students and offer advice on subjects inside and outside the classroom that builds a respect between us. This relationship makes my students more willing to pay attention in class and heed my messages.

I also believe that Black male students mentoring each other will allow them to learn how to positively interact with others and ensure each other's success. A sense of brotherhood and cohesiveness is missing between many Black males. If teachers and parents became or provided mentors for Black students, I believe that more of them would aspire for academic achievement.

Instilling Discipline

A fourth strategy that I find crucial for the development of a Black male student is instilling discipline and setting expectations. From my experiences, Black male students lack self-discipline and setting high expectations. In my class, students are expected to achieve at least an 80% class average. When students misbehave they lose points from their average, serve detentions, have parent teacher conferences, and are excluded from certain fun activities.

Students are held accountable for all their work and actions, and if problems occur we have meetings after class to address those problems. In order to hold students accountable for their assignments, I create contracts with students stating that they must complete their work by certain dates for partial credit or will fail that assignment. By correcting the actions of our students and refocusing them on academic success, they will develop their own self-discipline to behave accordingly and complete tasks. With distractions being great and opportunities for success being scarce, self-discipline is most necessary.

Giving Recognition

The fifth strategy that was helpful in my success and that I employ in the classroom is recognition. While I was a student, being recognized for my academic success and abilities made me feel important and motivated me to continue to excel. From my experiences I've noticed that all students, especially Black male students, like to be recognized for their hard work and talent. I recognize my students for their academic achievement and engagement in class. In my class I have a wall of achievement where I post color coded degrees for each student that receives an 80% or higher on a major class assignment. Students receive a Bachelor degree for 80–89% achievement, a Master's degree for 90–94% achievement, and a Ph.D.

degree for 95% or more. By creating this degree system students develop a sense of pride for their work and are motivated to earn another degree.

Aside from this, there is a weekly SWAG shout-out wall with students' names posted for students who participate the most and add to the positive culture of the classroom. In my room, SWAG stands for Students Will Achieve Greatness. It is important students feel their work and presence are appreciated so they continue to excel. I like to call home and compliment parents on what their students did in class that day. Rarely are phone calls home to parents of Black male students, phone calls of positivity or recognition. By teachers and parents recognizing Black males for their accomplishments and attempts for success, more Black males will aspire to be successful.

FINAL REMARKS

My recommendation and hopes for the education of Black males is that they are exposed to a better quality education system geared toward their personal and academic success. I believe many institutions that a majority of Black males attend are inadequate in resources and information as compared to their White counterparts. Education should be comprehensive and equal at every school regardless of the school's location or population.

In today's society, people are successful because of their education, opportunities, exposure, and sometimes by default of their family wealth or status. However, a lot of our youth possess the same qualities, but are unsuccessful, because they lack opportunity, or are blinded by the default of their reality. As publicized and perpetuated on television, the image of the Black male is a superior athlete or glorified criminal. Seldom if not never, are there a plethora of images depicting the Black male as a distinguished, charismatic, scholar, or professional. We must fill the void of Black male professionals and expose the youth to the truth, and instill a broader perspective of success. If Black male students continue to follow negative stereotypes they will continually be misguided and fall behind in progression. My mission, our mission, and the mission of future black male teachers, must be to change the perception of a Black male so that our students can no longer be confined to the stereotypes but instead see an image of success that can become the new default.

Teaching our youth is a most necessary essential, but it takes a certain person to teach them, to be mentally far from the hood but understand the streets. Black male students need to be mentored and exposed to the importance of education at an early age. By hiring more Black male teachers, Black male students will see their reflection as an intelligent professional. A majority of Black male students are unable to relate to their instructors and feel disconnected from the classroom, which propagates the continual disinterest in academic achievement. With more Black male teachers, Black male students can relate more and feel comfortable in school. By being able to relate to their teachers, the students are more prone to pay attention and apply the advice given by their teachers. With a Black male teacher, a Black male student has an exemplar of an educated professional to emulate and will strive for academic greatness which is ultimately an opportunity to die for!

CHAPTER 15

BEYOND PAYING LIP SERVICE TO DIVERSITY: STRATEGIES FOR RECRUITING, TRAINING, AND RETAINING BLACK MALE TEACHERS

Khary Golden

ABSTRACT

The concept of diversity in education is often a starting point for dialogue regarding the persistent achievement gap in American classrooms. However, simply advocating for diversity without recommending or adopting strategies to achieve diversity does not necessarily create the forum for fruitful dialogue. Various educational institutions and organizations pay lip service to the concept of diversity without actually engaging in practices to increase diversity. The state of education in our nation's most impoverished and marginalized communities can be affectively addressed through various strategies, including increasing diversity among our teaching force. Nevertheless, even organizations like Teach for America, *who recognize the importance of bringing diversity to the classroom, struggle to recruit, train, and retain African-American and Latino male teachers. This is truly a troubling circumstance because*

Black Male Teachers: Diversifying the United States' Teacher Workforce
Advances in Race and Ethnicity in Education, Volume 1, 205–217
Copyright © 2013 by Emerald Group Publishing Limited
All rights of reproduction in any form reserved
ISSN: 2051-2317/doi:10.1108/S2051-2317(2013)0000001019

*educating our African-American and Latino male students have proven to
be a task that we as a nation are wholly inept and dreadfully incapable of
accomplishing. If we are to provide better educational services for our
most at-risk populations of students, we as a society must no longer
simply pay lip service to diversity. We must devise complex strategies to
bring diversity into our nation's classrooms in order to diversity our
teacher workforce, and more effectively recruit, train, and retain African-
American and Latino male teachers.*

My decision to become an educator was solidified at a time when I was
much less concerned with the broader issues facing our black community,
and more concerned with simply making it through life unscathed. I was
sitting in a college classroom when I first heard what would become the
incredibly popular adage in intellectual social science circles, that there are
more black men in prison cells than in college classrooms. I did not doubt
the accuracy of the statistic, but my eyes still scanned slowly across each
student I sat amongst in my predominantly Caucasian *Intro to Afro-
American History* course. After my eyes confirmed what I already knew in
my head and heart to be true, my eyes rested on the reflection of a confused
young black man staring back from my laptop screen. Contemplating the
gravity of the moment, I reasoned that up to that point I had never
considered myself special in any conceivable way, but in that moment I felt a
spotlight shining onto my desire for what so many take for granted – a
normal life.

After transferring from Morehouse to Rutgers University – Camden,
I had slowly begun to give up on my visions of grandeur. No longer did
I want to become president or CEO of a Fortune 500 company, and I scoffed
at pursuing a career as a professional athlete or entertainer. I simply wanted
to not become a failure. I wanted to escape the seemingly inescapable force
that deterred young black males from making it out of the community in
which I was raised. I wanted to never become my father, who missed my
childhood while tiptoeing the thin line between functioning addict and
homeless vagrant. He had become a nameless and faceless victim of the crack
epidemic. As my professor recited this statistic once again for emphasis,
anxiety set in. It felt like some unseen force had transformed what
I considered normal into something obtuse. How audacious could I have
been to think I could escape the inescapable, achieve the impossible, and
outrun statistics that say I should not even have been where I was on that

very day? Though I was confident in my ability to overcome the obstacles in my path, this uncomfortable truth made me question everything I had ever thought about myself. I had spent so much time trying not to become a product of my environment that I had lost touch with everything I wanted to become as a person. I had spent my entire life being the "smart black kid," and yet I now felt like everything I worked for was a façade.

Whatever meager success I achieved would be a drop in the bucket in the grand scheme of things. Knowing that so many black males, who could have been the "smart black kid," were instead convicted felons was enough to make me denounce our system of education and capitalism. I felt I was at the crossroads that other black males had come to, whether to play within the confines of the game and accept the arbitrary nature of my existence and environment, or to reject the game I had been forced to play and live outside the contexts of larger society. I almost felt justified walking out of the classroom if for no other reason than to protest the egregious unfairness and unlevel playing field that characterized my existence.

Yet I was far past that fateful crossroad separating black males into two distinct categories of students and prisoners. I had made the decision to never become the latter, but I refused to believe I was in any way better than the millions of black males in prison. This realization was what initially encouraged me to enter the field of urban education to provide dynamic educational experiences for the marginalized black males in Camden, NJ. I became an educator because though I accepted the stark realities of this statistic, I rejected the notion that our next generation of black male learners is intellectually inferior. I work in the trenches of the fight to educate our black males because at a young age I knew black males were more engaged and motivated when taught by black males.

MY EXPERIENCES AS A BLACK MALE
GRADE-SCHOOL STUDENT

Hearing that statistic did not make me feel particularly uncomfortable or upset. However, it did make me much more cognizant of exactly what it meant to be a black male, and exactly how my unforgivably black skin tone related to my potential for future success. Since I was a grade-school student, I had become accustomed to being the "smart black kid," in both classrooms of all white students and all black students. I was an outsider in both. My black classmates could not fathom why I so wholeheartedly believed education was the key to success, while my white classmates knew even if I worked hard, their distinct resource advantages would never allow me to compete. I became more aware of my place in the world and more cognizant of the plight of black males. Most importantly, this statistic made me reflect on my experiences as a student.

I had never felt part of a community in the sense of shared responsibility or interwoven destiny. As a grade-school student, I felt like a man on an island surrounded by a sea of chaos. While my white teachers and black and brown classmates struggled to understand why they could not understand each other, I soaked up whatever learning was left before the teacher became frustrated into apathy. I now feel the burden of being a black male much more acutely, and I shoulder broken dreams of those who never made it past the crossroads. This statistic was an incredible interruption in my life. I realized my sense of normalcy had been warped by the nature of my aspirations. I was no longer a black kid with a dream; I was an anomaly, an outlier, and an inconvenient truth. What that inconvenient truth was or would become escaped me.

As a grade-school student I ignored the distinct differences between my classmates and me, but on that day I reflected on the collected minutiae of my life, and exactly what needs to be done to fix this broken system of education. I reflected on what had allowed me to escape the grips of the poverty cycle. I was insulted at the notion that my meager ambitions of things like middle class success, gainful employment, home ownership, and general happiness were outlandish for the average person that looked like me and came from where I came from. That statistic made me finally realize how far this population was marginalized to the edges of society and away from the American Dream.

Personally, this statistic would become the catchall cause, motivation, and inspiration for everything I sought to accomplish academically and professionally. It proved to be a wake-up call and a call to action. This statistic proved to me that the plight of black males in this country had reached epidemic level proportions, and no further studies were needed to confirm my belief. I reasoned in my young mind that the average black male was being subjected to conditions arguably worse than chattel slavery. For the first time in my life I felt like this entire undertaking of trying to achieve the American Dream, for me, was indeed something very special. I envisioned former friends and classmates, and I shuddered to think that while I was on one side of this statistic, inevitably some were on the other. I wanted to tell my formers friends and classmates, more concerned with sport statistics than math equations, the ramifications of their actions.

For as long as I can remember, all I ever wanted to be was normal, and I thank my mother for being honest enough to tell me that life had so much more to offer than what we could afford. As a single mother of three, living in the heart of the Whitman Park neighborhood of Camden during the last throws of the crack epidemic, she was outspoken in denouncing the deplorable conditions throughout the city. Whether it was the failing school district or the open air drug markets across the street from our house, she never held her tongue in encouraging my older sister and me to strive for better than what she was able to provide my family. Working in a low-paying service industry job after having never attended college, my mother insulated my siblings and me from the indolence and inaction that begets the poverty cycle. Her expectations were clear and the formula seemed easy enough; working hard in school would pave the way for future success.

With an older brother already in law school it was an easy sell, and my older sister and I easily outpaced our classmates. Looking back, I view my formative years in elementary school as the foundation and driving force behind our academic and professional success, each of us achieving an undergraduate and post-grad degree. My teachers were the conduit for my success, and they kept me engaged and challenged me to always reach beyond what I would typically think of myself as capable of accomplishing. My experiences as a black grade-school student are what have shaped my perspective of what black males require to succeed in our nation's classrooms.

THREE THINGS BLACK MALE STUDENTS NEED TO BE SUCCESSFUL IN SCHOOL

My sixth grade science teacher in particular had the most profound impact on my life. His name was Mr. Ward, and it was the first time I had ever seen a black man in a tie that was not a deacon at my church. In many ways he was everything that I hoped to become, as a man and as an intellectual. Aside from being the first black male I had encountered in the classroom, he was the one positive black male role model in my life up to that point. It seemed very anecdotal at the time, but even though I had always been a competitive student, he was the first reason I ever had to be excited about learning. Being the "smart black kid" became a good thing. He invigorated my interest in math and science, and he helped me to become a self-motivated and dedicated student. He would be the last African-American male teacher I would have until I enrolled as a freshman at Morehouse College in the fall of 2002. I spent the intermittent six years searching for that same confidence and spark that I felt in Mr. Ward's classroom, and the choice to attend Morehouse was an attempt to find validation as a young black intellectual. What I found at the HBCU of my dreams was not the bastion of forward-thinking progressivism that I had envisioned, but it did help me to realize that I was not alone. I was surrounded by thousands of other "smart black kids," and this utopian cocoon of black intellectualism almost made me think that I had achieved normalcy, despite the fact that even with an academic scholarship I could not afford to finish my undergraduate studies there.

Though my journey through education was not a straight line, I was able to make a conscious decision at a very early age to succeed, regardless of my circumstance. I attribute a great deal of this conscious decision to Mr. Ward, and it would be very easy to say that what every black male student needs is his own personal Mr. Ward, a dynamic educator that is willing to go the extra mile to raise expectations, inside and outside of the classroom. Yet, the reality of the situation in urban centers like Camden, Philadelphia, New York, and Detroit is that my experiences as a student are atypical. I was able to effectively reverse the poverty cycle in one generation with the help of a dedicated single parent and a dynamic sixth grade science teacher. Though my fiancée and I, a third grade charter school teacher and high school guidance counselor respectively, do not yet have children, when we do they will be equipped with optimal parent support and preparation for success in higher education and the competitive global marketplace. Their success will not be an anomaly. Their future will not depend on thin hopes that a single mother will keep them afloat until Superman arrives in the form of a dynamic educator.

There are so many African-American men from inner city communities just like the one in which I was raised, whose lives are on an entirely different trajectory. Profound and impactful figures like my science teacher Mr. Ward are few and far in between, and it seems as though our nation's public schools have given up on the idea of enlisting highly qualified black males in classrooms to address the problem of the achievement gap. Black males in this nation's most impoverished communities have grown wholly incapable of envisioning their long-term academic and professional success, and I attribute a great deal of this to the lack of positive role models who understand the obstacles they face in their communities, the challenges they face in the classroom, and the uncommon path they will need to walk in order to avoid a life of criminality and joblessness, which has become the status quo for black males. For these reasons, the three most important things black males need to be successful in school are:

1. aggressive and relentless parental support, from pre-K to higher education,
2. a dynamic young educator who can empathize and sympathize with their circumstances, while educating, engaging, inspiring, and raising expectations,
3. the audacity of hope, the wherewithal to understand that education is their top and only priority as a student, and the courage to dream.

FIVE PRACTICAL STRATEGIES FOR TEACHERS AND PARENTS TO SUPPORT BLACK LEARNERS

1. *Forget everything you thought you knew about young black males. Get back to basics.*

I have invested my time and energy to sell a dream to black males in my community. This is a dream, which I gave up very long ago, that continues to haunt me as I navigate the widening of my own spectrum for potential success. The dream of Dr. Martin Luther King Jr., that one day I would be judged solely on the content of my character and not on the color of my skin, my affinity for hip-hop culture, or my ethnic sounding name. As I strive each day to ascend the corporate ladder I still encounter the type of close-minded individuals that are generally shocked by my confidence, overly impressed with my eloquence, and wholly taken aback by my unforgivable blackness. I went from being the "smart black kid" in my grad school courses to the "smart black kid" in the conference room. Though I have grown used to the shock and awe that ensues after I speak truth to power, my white counterparts have not gotten used to the sound of an educated black man. If my self-perception were a reflection of society's expectations for me as a young black male, I would never have dreamed of achieving success, and I would not be equipped to encourage other black males to dream big. I never allow public perception or conventional wisdom to shape what I believe my students to be capable of achieving. Championing the cause of young black males in education, I have had to adopt the basic principle that our democracy and meritocracy has been founded on; all things are possible through hard work and self-determination, regardless of the circumstances.

As the Director of College Access for the LEAP Academy Charter High School in Camden, NJ, I assist students who otherwise would never contemplate making the transition from high school to higher education. The success of my students is a constant reminder of the social change created by manifesting opportunities for renewal and empowerment, and I know that through our shared experiences I am able to help my students envision their own success through the obstacles I have overcome in my life. I am a firm believer that solutions to our myriad of social issues can only be found in uplifting the next generation of thinkers, inventors, activists, and innovators. Perhaps my confidence in the virtue of children is just a way of subconsciously accepting my own personal stake and responsibility in our calamitous world community, kicking the can down the road for our children and grandchildren to address. The generations of my parents and grandparents ascribed to Dr. King's pointed last words in his infamous Mountaintop Speech, "I may not get there with you ..." suggesting the inevitability of our impending victory against racial discrimination, sub-jugation, and oppression. Yet at the turn of the century, a generation of young black males was and continues to be mired in a calculated onslaught, fully funded by the multibillion dollar prison industrial complex.

Not even the election of the first black president could recapture the optimism dripping from the lips of Dr. King mere hours before his assassination. Resembling slavery only more nefarious, with elements of Jim Crow but more thoroughly institutionalized and proliferated throughout society by mass media, the genocide of black males is more prevalent in my mind than any of our nation's many ills. With two degrees and a director's position I am far removed from handcuffs and felony charges, and yet this new Jim Crow handcuffs my faith in progressivism and positive social change. This perception prevents many teachers and parents from doing everything in their capacity to save our black males, and even the most well-intentioned educators are paralyzed into action when considering the image of the uncontrollable, unteachable, and unruly black male. This image is more than just an antiquated minstrel. It has become the defining question of the next generation: are black men more suited for the Oval Office or an eight-by-ten jail cell. I refuse to believe that black males are inherently inferior or intellectually challenged, and I am vocal with the students I work with in encouraging them to ignore the lowered expectations society has set for them. I urge these students to forget everything they have ever been told about what they are capable of accomplishing, and I make it a point to tell them that if I could overcome everything in my life to become normal, so could they. I do not mince words when telling them that their communities are the antithesis of normalcy, and when their eyes become open to the endless dynamic possibilities for success through education they are no longer handcuffed by history.

2. *Encourage young black males to envision success, regardless of their circumstances.*

If a black male, regardless of the nature of his environment or the circumstance of his upbringing, is able to envision success, he is capable of achieving success. In assessing the likelihood that our black males will overcome the tremendous obstacles in their path, it is imperative that one understands the tools at their disposal. In this new "post-racial" society, where supposedly any underprivileged youth can achieve greatness, comprehensive and compulsory public education is the tool for any aspiring and ambitious student. Public education has always been the great equalizer in this nation, our nation's schools are supposed to be the level playing field that feeds our great democracy and capitalist economy. Yet, coming on the heels of an economic slowdown only rivaled by the Great Depression, we as a society have reverted back to a sense of rugged individualism and a "pull yourself up by the bootstraps" mentality that can be wholly unrealistic for an inner-city youth attending a high school that has devolved into a dropout factory. This is why it is imperative for black men to envision success. Political infighting and inefficiency in education will continue, and until solutions are developed for this broken system, black men must take it upon themselves to envision success.

At a time when it would seem most critical to ensure the quality of instruction in our public schools, politicians on both sides of the aisle have advocated for the proliferation of school choice, ignoring the millions of students that have yet to make the jump to a charter school. These politicians have effectively given up on fixing the one institution that is supposed to foster entrepreneurship, innovation, and upward social mobility. Though I work in a charter school and advocate for school choice in communities with failing public schools, I am not under the illusion that charter schools are the one-size-fits-all remedy to a desperately broken system. I always advise the graduating seniors whom I assist in the high school to higher education transition process that education is the best and most reliable "hustle" in the world today.

Grandiose dreams of success in the NBA or as a movie star are merely pipe dreams when considering the bevy of studies that have been conducted linking higher education attainment to increased quality of life standards. Facts and figures and theory versus practice mean absolutely nothing to a black male living in the inner city, subjected to a dysfunctional home and dysfunctional school. Pulling oneself up by the bootstraps is no easy task for a black male when perpetual failure is the modus operandi of their environment. Dreams of ascending to greatness become meaningless when you are only concerned with fulfilling the physiological needs on the lowest level of Maslow's hierarchy. Self-actualization, as a black male in the inner city, can become wholly nonexistent, especially when the only models for success are contrived images of super-rich and hyper-sexualized hip-hop artists. We as a nation have created a generation of black males that have lost any semblance of reality and upward social mobility. They live in households and communities where drug-fueled violence, lack of parental engagement, and a warped sense of what it means to be a man are ever-present. Repairing the families that have been ripped apart by poverty, welfare dependence, and the crack epidemic is a gargantuan task in and of itself, but fixing this nation's schools is a fight that should not have progressed to a point of such utter desperation. Nevertheless, the first step is for black males to make overwhelming changes to the way they approach education, and teachers and parents can support black males by encouraging them to envision success.

3. *Diversity is more than a buzzword. Educate black males with black males.*

Schools have failed black males in the worse possible way. Failure and distrust is reciprocal, as the schools have lost confidence in the ability of black males to learn, and black males have given up on the ability of schools to teach them. The social contract has been fractured, and only a revolutionary approach to repair this relationship will suffice. Yet I do not suggest overhauling the infrastructure of education. There are a myriad of common sense strategies, though the simplicity of these strategies is belied by the stubbornness of policymakers who adopt them. Experts have spent decades prescribing the next cosmetic appendage for schools; seemingly insistent on outsmarting themselves instead simply aggressively recruiting, training, and retaining more black male teachers. Organizations like *Teach for America* (*TFA*) seek to raise the bar of teacher quality by seeking highly qualified undergraduate candidates. They send the best and the brightest into the inner-city schools to save impoverished and embattled minorities, and yet they do not think enough of their black and brown pupils than to do anything more than pay tacit lip service to diversity. In championing "The Importance of Diversity," *TFA* expounds:

> We believe in the power of diversity ... It will take a movement of leaders who are diverse in every respect for our country to reach the day when all children are able to attain an excellent education. Having a diverse corps not only enables us to have a bigger impact on the students we teach, but ensures we don't limit the voices and ideas our alumni bring to the table as leaders working to close the achievement gap ... We place particular emphasis on recruiting individuals who share the racial or socio-economic backgrounds of the students we teach, 90% of whom are African American or Latino.

TFA has become synonymous with a recent heightened intellectual approach to public education, that is, stick an Ivy League grad in front of a class of inner-city students and wait for magic to happen. The hypocrisy in this logic model is so astoundingly insulting that it is a wonder there has not been an even greater backlash. Listed prominently next to this tacit lip service on the *TFA* diversity page is a graphic explaining among 2012 corps members, 60% were Caucasian while a mere 13% were African-American and 10% were Latino. Let's deconstruct this clouded and dysfunctional picture.

4. *Develop new strategies for recruiting, retaining, and training black male teachers.*

TFA works to reverse the achievement gap and prepare minority students for higher education. *TFA* believes in the "power of diversity" and places "particular emphasis on recruiting individuals who share the racial or socioeconomic backgrounds" of their students, who are overwhelmingly black and Latino. Yet this renowned, multimillion dollar organization is clueless when it comes to recruiting candidates that are a living testament to their work. Founded over two decades ago, *TFA* has not been able to bring about enough positive change in impoverished classrooms to create a pipeline of candidates to draw from. Instead of recruiting relentlessly on the campuses of Howard, Morehouse, Spelman, *TFA* scours the Harvard, Yale, and Princeton. Instead of boosting the self-esteem of students by finding positive black and brown role models, *TFA* seeks to boost its own prestige by hiring the best and the brightest and the whitest. *TFA* wants to close the achievement gap, without investing in a product of its own labor.

TFA believes the achievement gap to be so profound that it even lists reasons for why it struggles to develop a diverse corps, claiming there are far too few qualified minority applicants from the most prestigious colleges and universities. If *TFA* is fully aware that the achievement gap prevents the

overwhelming majority of blacks from attending highly selective institutions, and admission to these institutions is more a product of access than
aptitude, why would it not take tangible steps to refine its strategy? Why not
recruit on the campus of North Carolina A&T instead of NYU, or
Grambling instead of Georgetown, or Fisk instead of Fordham? The
hypocrisy is stunning, but it is not isolated to organizations like *TFA*.
Schools struggle to "control" black males in the classroom, yet view black
males as being capable or qualified enough to hire. Black male attainment
lags behind white counterparts, but policymakers refuse to make the
decision to aggressively recruit and retain black male teachers. Policymakers
outsmart themselves, pay lip service to diversity, and black males languish in
the margins.

5. *Change the narrative of success and failure in our urban communities.*

The fact that the education industry continues to ignore the common
sense approach of aggressively recruiting, training, and retaining black
male teachers calls into question whether policymakers and dedicated
educators truly want to improve an admittedly broken system. In the city
of Camden, home to arguably the worst schools in the state of New Jersey,
the failure of the public school system has been so egregious and doggedly
consistent that Governor Chris Christie recently pushed for and passed the
Urban Hope Act, which would bring additional charter schools to New
Jersey's most impoverished areas. The charter schools that will be founded
in Camden in the months and years to come will join an already crowded
swath of charter and alternative schools leeching students from the two
dying public high schools left in the city. The school system in the city of
Camden had become synonymous with the narrative of failure, leaving
public perception of this system stained with the indelible mark of
ineffectiveness, mismanagement, and being an inexcusable waste of public
funding. Regardless of any small pockets of success or incremental
improvement, the narrative of failure in the city of Camden is what drives
politics and politicos. This narrative of failure is what has convinced
Governor Christie that the public schools in the city of Camden are the
problem and their slow demise is the solution. This narrative of failure is
what drives public perception and media coverage, and it is the lynchpin in
the groundswell of support for the privatization of education through
school choices. Education management organizations, with no proven
history of long-term success or effectiveness could potentially benefit from
countless dollars in federal funding, without explicating exactly how their
approach will be any different than the public schools. It seems as though

we as a society have given up on fixing our public schools, instead opting to spread out the severity of the problem. I shudder to think where we will be as a nation if the great experiment with school choice proves less than effective.

I know the narrative of failure is what has co-opted public perception, but each time I help black male transition into higher education brings this fight back into focus. I recently assisted one of my black male students gain acceptance to and enroll at Cornell University, revitalizing my commitment to uplifting black males. I know in viewing me as a role model, he was able to overcome any doubt that he could achieve greatness. However, if there is not a concerted effort to get more African-American teachers into urban classrooms, the achievement gap will widen. Policymakers must stop paying lip service to diversity, and start aggressively recruiting, training, and retaining teachers of color, because without this strategy black males will never envision success and outrun statistics.

CHAPTER 16

CHOOSING DISCIPLESHIP OVER THE VEIL

Randy R. Miller Sr.

ABSTRACT

Teachers are more than just instructors. Teachers are counselors and mentors; teachers guide students and prepare them for the world. Part of that preparation includes being transparent about the challenges that await them in addition encouraging students that they are capable in overcoming them all. Preparing students in that way requires teachers understand both the socioeconomic and sociohistorical psychology of their students, which impact their experiences and circumstances. For African American male students, an African American male teacher provides a natural harmony of understanding these very experiences and circumstances. This is not to say that only an African American male can teach African American male students, rather the unique experiences central to the Black male experience in America require educators who desire to speak of those experiences in the classroom in an attempt to both equip students with the necessary academic and interpersonal skills for their success in life. In the case of the African American male teacher, he not only can speak to the Black male experience in America, he lives it daily. This testimonial is from an African American male teacher who believes that as an African

Black Male Teachers: Diversifying the United States' Teacher Workforce
Advances in Race and Ethnicity in Education, Volume 1, 219–231
ISSN: 2051-2317/doi:10.1108/S2051-2317(2013)0000001020

*American male who teaches, he has the unique opportunity to mentor
and disciple his Black male students through honesty and transparency
rather than through "protecting" them from the realities that await
them.*

I do not pretend to be a divine man, but I do believe in divine guidance, divine power,
and in the fulfillment of divine prophecy. I am not educated nor am I an expert in any
particular field. But I am sincere and my sincerity is my credentials. (Malcolm X, A
Declaration of Independence, March 12, 1964)

Schools do not educate people ... societies do.

Institutions are a part of systems and systems, the simple and the
complex, make up societies. The fate of people is measured by the fate of
their society – as the society goes, so do the people. Societies are always
moving and evolving; human beings evolve with society. Thus, human
beings are educated and socialized for the sole purpose of survival within
our environment. An education doesn't end when one has either received or
has given instruction. Instructions are like seeds planted in the soil; when
planted, seeds don't just remain in the ground but they grow into a plant
that serves a purpose within society. Instructions do the same thing ... they
grow within the human vessel purposed to carry out a purpose within
society in order to keep the society moving.

The reason why many of our K-12 public schools are failing our
students is because the "instructions" we provide are not consistent with
the instructions our students are receiving from society. Whether or not
we agree with the progression of society is another discussion for another
day. Because schools are organisms that despise change and are hesitant
to adapt and society is always evolving and continuously adapting,
schools are being left behind and so are millions of students. Combine
that with the impact that our country's history of racial prejudice and
discrimination has had on the shaping of our current dispensation; is it
any wonder why educators are having a hard time "instructing" African
American students, specifically Black males? Schools aren't speaking the
language Black male students speak and without knowing their language,
there is no way you can communicate with them. When you leave someone in an environment surrounded by people he/she cannot communicate
with, that person has to figure everything out the hard way. For Black
males, learning the hard way often ends up costing them their lives in
some form or fashion.

WHY I BECAME A TEACHER

As a father, I am a teacher to my son. The lessons that I will teach him aren't from textbooks or worksheets. These lessons come from life experiences and the gained knowledge of my interactions within my environment. The tests he will receive will not be essay questions or multiple choices to be scanned through a machine. The tests in his life will be given by society, where he will have to make decisions that will shape the course of his future. His success or failure will depend heavily on what he has learned from me based on what he's been instructed and what he's seen me do. I know that my son has a chance to make successful choices because he will have access; access to the opportunity of hearing my instructions. It will be completely up to him to take my instructions and put them to good use. If I were not in the picture, he would not have access to me or my instruction; I know that without his father in his life, my son's growth and maturation would be different. To instruct my son is my obligation and is a service to my community, humanity, and to my God. To instruct the sons and daughters of others is the same obligation and service to the same constituency; this is why I am a teacher.

There are various reasons why I could teach history as a discipline, yet my reason for teaching it is because I believe that lying to students does them harm. To discard the importance of history is to deny one the opportunity for defining his/her identity. Many of our Black male students, and urban students in general, are unaware of who they are because they have no frame of reference when it comes to their history. What they know is what they've been told by society. To teach history accurately, is to teach truth. To teach truth is to create thinkers and thinkers determine the order and progression of society. In the community where I teach, the natural order is social, economic, intellectual, and spiritual devastation and where there is devastation within a community, there is money to be made by ones looking to exploit the people. I teach history as a means of equipping students with the weapons of knowledge, wisdom, and understanding. For me, teaching history is to assist with constructing identity.

GRADE SCHOOL EXPERIENCES

Looking back on my education, I can honestly say that it was good enough, but it could have been better. There are two things that stand out when I think back to grade school: (1) there was hardly any adult in authority that looked like me or could culturally relate to me and (2) learning wasn't fun rather it was a job. With that being said, I pained my way through elementary, middle, and high school and once I got to college, I was okay. Once in college, I was exposed to knowledge that helped me piece together my identity and the meaning of my grade school and high school experiences. I was able to ask questions of my professors freely and not feel like I was speaking another language. I came to realize that learning, reading, and writing was not just fun, but the key to functioning in society. I'd often wonder to myself why grade school wasn't college; a place with teachers of color teaching me things I actually don't mind reading about, writing about, and learning about?

The very first teacher I ever had was an African American woman; that was in kindergarten. There was another African American woman in second grade and between second grade and college I didn't see another African American teacher. I never had an African American male as a teacher or administrator of any sort throughout all of my K through 12 experiences. That shaped my outlook in a lot of ways about education and ultimately, the world. Regardless the subject, my teachers looked the same: always white and mostly female. The same is true for the students that I teach – I am the only Black male teacher in my building; one of four in my entire district.

When I think about my parents and their desire that I receive the best education they could provide, I thank them for their commitment to my education. I do not regret their "strategy" so to speak, however looking back, I wish they had exercised a bit more authority when it came to who educated their child. I was sent to Catholic School from preschool through twelfth grade; I received a quality education. Yet when I think back, I see a young man who could have been better prepared for the world awaiting him. I see a young man with trepidation in his face as he moves forward through his academic career. In elementary and middle school, he was comforted by the sea of familiar faces in his classrooms until he reached high school, where he looked around all of his classrooms and he saw his black skin in a sea of white faces. I see a young man who was unsure if he could compete once he reached high school. I see a young man who was taught from a perspective not similar to his own and for a few years, that young man struggled. I had no clear cut understanding on my own identity. I knew that I was a young Black man. I understood that doing well in school was imperative. Yet I really was unsure of who I was. That is not to say that having Black teachers or teachers of diverse ethnicities would have prevented me from feeling that way. Maybe if I had been taught by individuals who looked and thought liked me; people who were raised in similar homes with similar values and similar outlooks on life, and to have had those perspectives as a resource when there were questions to be asked and concerns to be addressed, it is very possible that my confidence in my own ability would have been reassured in a way I could have better identified with.

It's deeper than not learning the truth about history, the untold truth about the history of African Americans in America or the ways in which society has failed African Americans and other racial minorities. I was never really understood; my teachers didn't know what to do with me. As a kid, I was labeled as "rambunctious," "extremely loquacious," and someone to be both "controlled" and "managed." Does that sound like most kids? I suppose it does. But as an adult and an educator, I know those are also code words, especially when referring to male students, both Black and Hispanic. As an adolescent however, I had no clue of the various motivations behind the treatment of myself and my peers; all motivations and intentions behind the behavior of the adults in charge, most of whom were white, was veiled behind the overly emphasized emotions of compassion and sympathy. That veil prevented me from seeing what was actually behind it – the truth. Not that I would have been able to understand all things at such a young age, but when presented with information, we can begin to inquire and engage in the beginning stages of critical thinking. I was never given the opportunity; and so initially, I believed in what I call, "the veil."

When I entered high school, the veil slowly began to be removed. In grade school, I went to school with African Americans and Hispanics. I had a schedule of six to eight different classes with different teachers. None of whom were where I was from, none of whom knew of the experiences I've had to that point or the experiences that I would have as a Black man. I can say with certainty that many of them didn't care about me being a Black male – not because they were evil, but because they didn't believe race was of any significance. "The veil" was in place in high school to do the same thing it did in grade school; mask intentions and motivations which inspired actions and behaviors as care, concern, and compassion. But the difference was the variable that was in place that wasn't there in grade school ... white students. I grew angry. Race became a bit more apparent to me. My young mind was maturing and it could begin to handle certain truths, although I did not always process them the best. I rebelled in my own way by not investing in the school or the people who supposedly cared about me. I became cold.

I wasn't overtly mean to people, specifically to white people, yet I did not allow myself to get invested in meaningful relationships with the white students at my school. Quite honestly, I believed that the people were fakes. I let instances of what I perceived to be assumption based on my ethnicity stop me from engaging in the community of my school. One such instance was one morning during my sophomore year. I happened to be walking to the cafeteria and I saw a contemporary of mine, a Puerto Rican gentleman, standing at the door. He and I greeted with the customary "urban" handshake. As we were at the point of unclasping our hands, a gentleman by the name of Mr. Rocks takes both of our clasped hands and pulls them apart to see if there is anything one of us was passing along to the other sneakily. In plain words, he assumed our handshake to be a drug transaction. He said, very nonchalantly, *"How you doing fellas, just checking for funny business, it's been happening around here lately there ... okay, seems good, have a good one fellas alright? Yes."* Alright???

This man comes to us saying all of this with this suspicious sounding laugh and forced smile on his face to make us feel comfortable while suspecting our handshake, which was not a "regular" shake but rather an "urban" handshake, was masking a drug deal. I felt violated. As an adult educator looking back on this experience, I can recognize his perspective ... Mr. Rocks was the Dean of Students: he was the "disciplinarian" of the school. His job was to keep order. That is what he was paid to do. But he also maintained "the veil." It was at that point that I became aware of the veil, although I wasn't sure exactly what the veil was. I wasn't sure how to deal with it. At that point, education became synonymous with a lie – society dictated our behaviors in that building, intended and unintended. Society was the teacher and the system of education was a living contradiction. Along with the archaic nature of the lessons and the teachers, I was unfortunately distracted from even caring about my "education." Fear, of my parents and from becoming a failure, was my only motivation.

When it came to the classroom, the various lessons and the various instructors ... many were horrible. Society is always moving; knowledge is always growing and so society evolves with the new knowledge. I never picked up a book for casual reading. I never believed that you could honestly read a book for enjoyment, let alone to actually read to learn something. The periodic table never got me excited. Dissecting insects and animals are things I did when I played outside growing up. Numbers and formulas were of no interest to me, and so I wondered why in the world I was being taught this mess? Why was everything such a complex and difficult process? What is wrong with me that I don't understand these teachers? Now I realize that many of those teachers weren't good; the truth is that many of them were below average (that is being very gracious). Neither were their lessons any good; they were irrelevant. What was relevant in my life was rap music, the internet, Napster, and burnable CDs. My hormones were relevant ... I don't care about Rogers and Hammerstein; teach me how Swiss Beats makes this song sound so hot.

My teachers didn't speak my language. They weren't saying the same things the society, that we all lived in, were saying. It's bad enough that these people didn't look like me, talk like me, valued what I valued, or understood why I was the way I was. What made things worse is that they bored the hell out of me. Society was telling me that cash ruled everything around me; maybe Rza or Method Man should have taught me that lesson on capitalism. When a conversation started getting racial, teachers got uneasy and shifted the discussion. The most folks talked about regarding cell phones and technology was that electronic equipment was banned from usage. Rap music was not considered on par with the sonnets of Shakespeare; the stories of Jay-Z, Biggie Smalls, or Nas weren't held with the same esteem as those of Milton, Dante, or Homer. I love "classic" literature, but that wasn't the only literature ever written. Looking back, I can't blame my teachers; they were middle aged, suburban, and white ... they couldn't relate to me nor did they really want to try. The majority of those teachers came to school to teach and go home. I wasn't the first Black male student to go through that and unfortunately, I won't be the last.

THREE THINGS BLACK MALE STUDENTS NEED TO BE SUCCESSFUL IN SCHOOL

There are various "solutions" for engaging and motivating the Black male student; issues of student motivation and student achievement when it comes to Black male students, and urban students in general, are hot button issues in education, where educators and pseudo-educators alike seek to find creative answers to address them. I subscribe to a more pragmatic approach to teaching students of color. There is no full proof way of reaching and teaching young people regardless of the race of the teacher. The Black teacher shares some of the same challenges as the white teacher. Each student is their own person with their own set of circumstances to be accounted for. With that said, there are three things that Black male students need in order to be successful; Black male students need (1) validation, (2) transparency, and (3) relevant experiences.

First, Black male students need to be validated. Black male students need to know that they are not dismissed; that their experiences, point of view, and values are highly regarded and understood. This does not mean that everything they may believe is correct. In fact, most young people have ideas that evolve and change over time – many of those ideas change because they were incorrect in the first place. The important thing is that we hear Black male students and allow them the safety of being heard. It is not enough to be able to pronounce the names of your students or have a few friends that are African American ... An educator needs to see these young men for who they are. The colorblind mantra sounds very nice and makes Americans feel like everyone gets a fair opportunity to be successful regardless of skin color; however the history has proved that to be untrue. When we are colorblind, we don't see color; when we don't see the "color" of an individual, we fail to account for the various characteristics, culture, and experiences that have shaped the totality of that individual up to that point. All human beings want to be validated. When validated, students are now not overly concerned with being heard; they can actually focus on hearing others. When they are hearing, they are learning.

Second, Black male students need honesty and transparency; simply put, you must remove the veil. Don't feel sorry for Black male students; they do not need your sympathy. Don't "protect" them by overemphasizing that they follow the rules or by passing them along when things seem too tough for them to accomplish due to additional challenges they may have. Never say that your rational for "protecting" them is that you care for them. That is an excuse. Your job is not to protect them in that way. You can best protect them by preparing them. That is what schools are designed to do: teach, inform, and prepare. Preparation means honest and transparent dialogue on what they should expect when they leave the comfort of school and home for the real world ... such discussions and classroom lessons are for all ages. It is never too early for a young Black man to learn about the truth of what society thinks of him, what awaits him in society, and the tools necessary to be successful. Masking the truth in an attempt to protect him will do the opposite.

Lastly, Black male students need relevant experiences in order to be successful in school and ultimately in life. A class project regarding presidential elections; whether it is a mathematics lesson on probability or a history lesson on the Electoral College may or may not be relevant to a Black male student. Not that all the students in a given class are all Black males, but if the majority of students are, let's not kid ourselves; most students will not be excited ... initially. Relevance is not simply the topic that you teach, but is also the very specific connections that you make between the topic and real life circumstances. That lesson on the Electoral College, regardless of the content focus, must be connected to the experiences of the Black male student if the instructor wants to reach him. For some, earning money is a priority; for others self-expression. If this sounds familiar, then it's because many youth of different backgrounds share similar priorities. The difference is that Black male students may exhibit these priorities in ways that for those not like him are either not use to or uncomfortable with. Making lessons relevant would mean that a teacher may have to step out of his or her comfort zone to create a lesson relevant to the Black male dynamic. When you give more to any project or assignment, you get more out of it. You cannot expect to get the maximum out of Black male students when you give them minimal, even if you think you are giving your best; the terms best and maximum mean different things to different people. When given lessons that are relevant to his experiences, the Black male student can relate, he can understand, and he can internalize your instruction. That is when you know learning took place.

FIVE PRACTICAL STRATEGIES FOR TEACHERS AND PARENTS TO SUPPORT BLACK LEARNERS

There are a number of strategies that teachers and parents can employ to support their Black male students and all Black students. Here are five practical tips for parents and teachers of Black student(s): (1) know your audience, (2) be concerned about the people your students will become, (3) speak their language of technology, (4) tap into their "hustlers" spirit, and (5) adopt a project-based approach to your lessons and/or major units.

In order to be effective in the classroom, regardless of your racial makeup, you've got to know who you are trying to reach and you must know what makes them tick. You have to know what circumstances and events helped to shape the people you are teaching. When you know who they are; when you understand how they've become the folks they have become, you understand their habits, their behaviors, and their ways. The likelihood of you "criminalizing" their behavior and mindsets as well as marginalizing those students personally will be minimal. Not that those certain behaviors are to be tolerated or celebrated, but rather they are understood and handled in a way that seeks to work through those behaviors and mindsets in love. In addition to knowing your audience, you must know yourself. Maybe you didn't grow up in an urban neighborhood. Maybe you didn't grow up with the same set of circumstances as many of your students. Maybe you had two parents, violence was something you never had to live with and drug addiction has never hit your immediate family. Pain and suffering is not a prerequisite for teaching urban students. However, when you recognize your experiences in addition to the experiences of your students, you can begin to measure how much of your perspective to add to a conversation or a lesson. You begin to measure how much of your students perspective to account for when teaching, instructing, and disciplining.

Another strategy that will help you with male students of color is to focus on developing the type of people they will become rather than focusing simply on the "goals" of getting a job that pays well. Once you know your audience, you become aware of what makes them tick. You are aware of the language society speaks to them; you understand the images and the messages they are inundated with on a daily basis. Many of the messages that Black males students receive, all students in fact, are ones of materialism, consumerism, and self-indulgence. Rarely do commercials, advertisements, and products tell people to be the best person they can be. Society equates being your best self with how much money you have and how much you possess. When teaching and instructing, focus on imparting lessons and skills that will create better people rather than simply a skilled workforce. Black male students need to know that they have the capacity to do good in their communities and in the world because they are good people, despite what society says about them. When you invest in the lives of these individuals, you will gain their admiration, loyalty, and most important, their trust. When you gain the trust of a Black male student, you can begin to instruct, cultivate, and develop them. Trust enables you the ability to not simply speak their language, but actually translate your message so that they can hear and understand it. One of the best ways of translating into a language Black male students understand is by incorporating technology in your speech.

No matter the race or socioeconomic status, most students, if not all students have some piece of technology on their person: ipad, iphone, or an android which does everything under the sun from playing music to getting online. We often penalize our students for using electronics while in class and yes, cell phones are a distraction and do students use them for social networking and texting, of course they do. But a tool is only good for what one can use it for. We can turn electronic tools into tools designed to conduct research, connect with other individuals, and put together projects. Sure, students get side tracked, but students get side tracked whether or not there is a cell phone in front of them. In order to peak their interest, we must use the technology at our disposal to inform and instruct our students; we must speak their language. We must use blogging, cell phones, YouTube, Google Earth, and any other technology to reach our students. A 1,000-page textbook doesn't do it anymore; that is not going to stimulate most students. Use what will stimulate them in order for them to learn a lesson. Adults use the technology for research and learning. Encourage it amongst your students.

Another strategy that will gain the attention of your Black male students is to tap into the "hustlers spirit" of your students. Urban students grow up around entrepreneurs. Most times, we focus on the negative aspects of urban life without accenting the positive – that being that entrepreneurs dominate most, if not all, urban neighborhoods, both legit and illegal entrepreneurs alike. Consider where many of our black and brown children live. They live in areas where viable employment opportunities are unavailable for many due to missed educational opportunities and the lack of opportunities and resources due to the flight of jobs from the central cities. Men who have little or no education, who may have been incarcerated, are shut out from the mainstream of society when it comes to finding meaningful work that not only can provide for their families, but also can provide them with career advancement.

Women, who are often left alone to fend for themselves by their families and men they share relations with, struggle to find a way out of a hopeless situation that may involve a child or two. Go down a main thoroughfare in any neighborhood in cities like Philadelphia, Camden, Newark, or East St. Louis and you'll find at least one of these: a church, a liquor store, a corner store, a hair salon, and a drug set within a two-to-three block radius. Some may look at that scene and simply see a church, a liquor store, a corner store, a hair salon, and a drug set. What I see is four businesses and a nonprofit. Telling a kid that they come from an environment where people determine their own fate via entrepreneurial aspiration versus telling them that they come from a city of poverty, drugs, and alcohol has a lot more power.

I am a firm believer that whenever you speak or teach to a group of individuals, you must know your audience. In order to relate to them and tap into what motivates and helps them learn, you must understand the external forces that help shape the internal motivations of a child – it is about looking at one's environment to see what influences them. We can use the environment that surrounds our urban children, not just as a deterrent but also as a motivator – in a different way. We can cite the examples of entrepreneurs using their skills in positive ways to not only provide for their families but also to provide meaningful services to the community. We can also cite examples of how not to use ones entrepreneurial skills; rather than selling drugs or selling stolen and illegally produced goods, put your talents and skills to good use by creating a business that you can have pride in. We can cultivate our students by infusing strategically crafted instruction and integrate their experiences, examples, and areas of passion.

When you are able to use the language of technology to speak the entrepreneurial spirit of urban students, you can begin to apply the concept of project-based learning. Project-based learning involves critical inquiry and investigation in the attempts to problem solve real life scenarios; you're essentially teaching a concept, providing your students with a scenario and facilitating their application of the theories and concepts you've taught so that they can begin solving the issues of the given scenario. Reflection, decision making, and critical thinking all go into this type of instructional methodology. What most students are used to is a test culminating a learning cycle. All tests do is manufacture anxiety. Tests do not manufacture excitement, motivation, or ownership in one's learning of information. However if you can give a student a vehicle to apply that learning in a way that allows him or her to feel like they can do something good in this world, you will facilitate excitement within students, and motivation and ownership amongst students. It is as simple as crafting projects based on your subject area within the community of the school. This will take more work on your part that may possibly extend your teaching day and you probably will not get the financial or verbal recognition for your commitment but we didn't get into this profession to get rich or reassured. If you care about students learning, either give the students something to care about or use something they care about to engage them in your classroom instruction. Projects, not assignment to be completed on a poster board but rather initiatives collaborated on with community organizations and businesses to improve where your students live, is much more effective than simply asking a student to write a three-paragraph essay connecting a Shakespearian tragedy to a tragedy in their lives.

IN CONCLUSION

Black male teachers are a lifeline to the Black male students, the Black female students, and for all of the students under their leadership and authority. Our perspective is unique, our passion is genuine, and our desire to empower through educating is of a transformative nature. We want to serve the communities where we work, we want to invest in the lives that we touch daily ... we want to bring hope and change to the classroom and in the lives of our children. I honestly believe, and I know without a shadow of a doubt, that there is a calling on my life to teach – during this dispensation to the people of my community. I love my vocation, not because I am good at it so much, but because I love the young men and women that God has placed in my care. I love that I am able to prepare them for the challenges that my teachers unfortunately did not prepare me for. I love that I am able to use my perspective, relating it to history to challenge the status quo with my students. Education is a labor of love and an exercise in discipleship. When we love, we will disciple others and when one is a disciple, he is trained in all manners of knowledge and skill so that he or she can be effective wherever they go. In the words of the brother Malcolm X, "we cannot teach what we do not know and we cannot lead where we won't go" (Howard, 2006).

REFERENCES

Howard, G. (2006). *We can't teach what we don't know*. New York, NY: Teacher College Press.
Malcolm, X. (1994). In G. Breitman (Ed.), *Malcolm X speaks: Selected speeches and statements*. New York, NY: Grove Press.

SECTION IV
VOICES OF LEADING SCHOLARS

CHAPTER 17

AFRICAN AMERICAN MALE TEACHERS AND THE SCHOOL LEADERSHIP PIPELINE: WHY MORE OF THESE BEST AND BRIGHTEST ARE NOT PRINCIPALS AND SUPERINTENDENTS

Leslie T. Fenwick and Chike Akua

ABSTRACT

African American male teachers are the nation's most academically credentialed and professionally experienced teachers. Though less than 2 percent of the nation's teachers are African American males, these teachers are more likely than their White male and female peers to hold a master's or doctorate degree. Additionally, African American male teachers who become principals assume the position with more years of experience as a PK-12 classroom teacher than their White peers. And, those who leave the principalship to become superintendents have more years of experience as a PK-12 principal than similarly situated White peers. Why, then, are African American males underrepresented

Black Male Teachers: Diversifying the United States' Teacher Workforce
Advances in Race and Ethnicity in Education, Volume 1, 235–249
Copyright © 2013 by Emerald Group Publishing Limited
All rights of reproduction in any form reserved
ISSN: 2051-2317/doi:10.1108/S2051-2317(2013)0000001021

in critical school district policy and leadership posts such as the principalship and superintendency while lesser credentialed and experienced White males hold these posts in percentages that exceed their representation in the teacher workforce? This chapter reviews data about African American male teachers and the school leadership pipeline and proposes a series of policy recommendations to increase representation of African American males in the PK-12 teacher and school leadership workforces.

INTRODUCTION

African American male teachers are the nation's most academically credentialed and professionally experienced teachers. Though less than 2 percent of the nation's teachers are African American males, these teachers are more likely than their White male and female peers to hold a master's or doctorate degree. Additionally, African American male teachers who become principals assume the position with more years of experience as a PK-12 classroom teacher than their White peers. And, those who leave the principalship to become superintendents have more years of experience as a PK-12 principal than similarly situated White peers. Why, then, are African American males underrepresented in critical school district policy and leadership posts such as the principalship and superintendency while lesser credentialed and experienced White males hold these posts in percentages that exceed their representation in the teacher workforce?

The African American teacher shortage is not a new problem and its repercussions for the school leadership pipeline are marked. In the South, the conjoined issue of shortage and underrepresentation has its roots in the desegregation of public schools. Desegregation, while an important and necessary civil rights achievement, ushered in the unlawful firings and displacement of thousands of African American teachers and principals many of whom were males. Nearly half a century ago, these Black educators were often respected leaders in their communities and also exceptionally credentialed (equipped with undergraduate degrees in education from historically Black colleges/universities (HBCUs) and master's and doctoral degrees from the nation's research flagships such as Columbia University, New York University, The Ohio State University, and University of Iowa among others). Nonetheless, during the desegregation years many African Americans were summarily dismissed from their teacher and principal posts and replaced by lesser credentialed and experienced Whites. The nation's schools are still experiencing the fallout of this decimated pipeline. Today, slightly more than 90 percent of urban school teachers are White. In inner-city schools 73 percent of teachers are White. Additionally, nearly 70 percent of inner-city school principals are White. In 38 percent of American public schools there is not a single teacher of color on the staff. Notably, this is the most populous generation of African American children that has not been taught by an African American teacher.

Few efforts of scale have been mounted to build on existing minority teacher pipeline programs and press for greater diversity in the principalship and superintendency. Only about 16 percent of the nation's principals are educators of color. Approximately 11 percent are African American, 4 percent are Hispanic/Latino, and less than 1 percent is Asian American. The same pattern holds true for the superintendencies. Less than 3 percent of the nation's nearly 15,000 superintendents are African American.

While women – who now comprise about 35 percent of the nation's principals – have made significant gains, these gains have only occurred in the last two decades. In the 1987–1988 academic year, women comprised only 2 percent of the nation's school principals even though they make up 73 percent of the teaching force from which principals ascend. So, why does this underrepresentation of African Americans and women (of all races) persist in educational leadership?

The short answer is simply that notions about "who should lead" still tend to support White males' access to policy and leadership posts even in education, a notoriously "female friendly" profession. Despite some changes, school leadership remains nearly as monolithic as it was 40 years ago when Harry F. Walcott wrote the ethnographic study, *The Man in the Principal's Office*. In 2012, more than 80 percent of public school superintendents, school board presidents, and central office associate superintendents and directors are White males, as are nearly 60 percent of principals. Yet, White males make up less than 25 percent of the nation's teaching force and tend to be less qualified than their White female and African American male and female peers (Fenwick, 2001). These data suggest that too often African American males are passed over for principalships and superintendencies or are consigned to the ranks of coach and disciplinarian. This is disturbing because African American males also are more likely than any other demographic of graduate student taking the Graduate Record Examination (GRE) to indicate an interest in educational administration-related graduate degree programs and careers.

THE EFFECTS OF AFRICAN AMERICAN TEACHERS ON ACADEMIC OUTCOMES

Research continues to emerge about the potential of teachers of color to improve academic outcomes and school experiences for students of color. Villegas and Irvine's (2009) review of the literature concluded that several studies suggest some positive effects. In an impressive quantitative study, researchers Meier, Stewart, and England (1989) investigated the relationship between the presence of African American teachers and African American students' access to equal education. Specifically, they investigated the following question: Does having African American educators impact African American students' school success? The researchers' findings highlighted the importance of having African American teachers in desegregated schools. In school districts with large proportions of African American teachers, the researchers found the following:

- fewer African Americans were placed in special education classes;
- fewer African Americans were suspended or expelled;
- more African Americans were placed in gifted and talented programs; and
- more African Americans graduated from high school.

The authors emphatically concluded that "African American teachers are without a doubt the key" to students' academic success (p. 6).

In her study of teachers' perceptions of African American male students, Couch-Maddox (1999) found that African American teachers were more likely than their White peers to describe African American male students as "intellectually capable." The African American teachers also reported that these male students engaged in positive school behaviors such as completing homework, attending school regularly, and serving in leadership roles (Fenwick, 2001).

Clewell, Puma, and McKay (2005), using the Prospects database, raised the question: Does exposure to a same-race teacher increase the reading and mathematics achievement scores of African American and Hispanic students in elementary schools? The researchers found that Hispanic fourth- and sixth-grade students with a Hispanic teacher produced higher test score gains in math. In reading, the same effect was noted, but only in the fourth grade. The effect for African American students with African American teachers was somewhat weaker; although, fourth-grade African American students had significantly higher scores in mathematics when taught by an African American teacher (Irvine & Fenwick, 2011).

Klopfenstein (2005) reported that the enrollment of African American students in algebra II increased significantly as the percentage of mathematics teachers who were African American increased. Other researchers have found that African American teachers, when compared to their White counterparts, are more successful in increasing student scores in vocabulary and reading comprehension (Hanushek, 1992) as well as economic literacy (Evans, 1992). Ehrenberg and Brewer (1995), using an econometric model that accounted for the nonrandom nature of teacher assignment to schools, found that an increase in the percentage of African American teachers resulted in score gains on standardized tests for African American high school students (Irvine & Fenwick, 2011).

Also of note are findings that African American teachers influenced African American students' school attendance (Farkas, Grobe, Sheehan, & Shuan, 1990) and that these teachers had higher expectations for their African American students than their White counterparts did (Irvine, 1990). Other empirical works, such as a study by Hess and Leal (1997), suggested a correlation between the number of teachers of color in a district and college matriculation rates among students of color (Irvine & Fenwick, 2011).

AFRICAN AMERICAN MALES AND SCHOOL LEADERSHIP

While the literature on the effects of African American teachers is strong, less research has been conducted about African American principals' and superintendents' leadership on African American students' educational progress. Despite the dearth of literature about the effects of African American principal and superintendent leadership on African American students' educational outcomes, one case study examined this proposition in depth. *In Keeping a Close Watch: A Cultural Philosophy of School Change*, Carter and Fenwick (2001) found that a striking feature of a lauded and high-performing Atlanta, Georgia high school was the presence of African American male administrators and teachers.

Hardly a Joe Clark type, the African American principal who led the school (Dr. William Shepherd) was described by teachers as a "counselor at heart" whom "kids don't see as a jailer." He was viewed as a patriarch to students and a facilitator by faculty. Through the principalship, Dr. Shepherd took measured steps to eradicate the negative stereotypes abounding about African American men because he believed that academic and social benefits would accrue to students who experienced this exposure. Shepherd recruited many African American men (with doctoral degrees) to the high school's administrative staff and faculty. He purposely did not place these men as coaches and disciplinarians (as he had observed in many districts' schools). Rather, they were appointed as the director of technology, assistant principals, guidance counselors, and teachers. Carter and Fenwick, (2001) found that students noticed the men's presence in the school and viewed it as unusual and positive. The students articulated a profound understanding about the value of African American male principals and teachers. According to Carter and Fenwick (2001), one student leader at the high school summarized a common interview finding:

> That was one of the first things I noticed when I came here. Before, all the principals and teachers I knew were women. When I watch TV everyone says Black men are in jail, doing drugs, fighting each other. But when I come to school I see all these Black men working together, getting along, and it makes me think that maybe there are a lot of Black me doing this. (p. 21)

All children benefit from experiencing a diverse school staff because this diversity teaches children a vital lesson – the models of intellectual authority are not exclusively White. If the nation is to expand its teacher and school leadership pipelines to more broadly include African American males then we must turn to HBCUs as a resource.

THE ROLE OF HBCUS: AFRICAN AMERICAN TEACHER AND SCHOOL LEADERSHIP PIPELINE

Though HBCUs comprise only 4 percent of the nation's colleges and university, the impact of these institutions is indisputable. HBCU schools and colleges of education graduate 50 percent of African American teachers with bachelor's degrees (National Association for Equal Opportunity in Higher Education, 2008), and the United Negro College Fund reported that in 1998 more than half of all African American prospective teachers in Missouri, Maryland, Louisiana, Virginia, South Carolina, North Carolina, Delaware, Alabama, and the District of Columbia were trained at HBCUs (Freeman, 2001). In many urban and rural settings that have HBCUs, these institutions furnish high percentages of teachers to the local school district. Many HBCUs have graduate degree offerings in educational administration and also prepare significant numbers of principals for local school districts. Consequently, HBCUs have had a major role in diversifying America's mostly White teaching force (Irvine & Fenwick, 2011).

The Ready to Teach Program at Howard University shows promise as a national model for the recruitment, preparation, and placement of African American male teachers in high-need schools. The program is a collaborative effort led by the Howard University School of Education in partnership with five urban school districts: Chicago, Illinois; Clayton County, Georgia; Houston, Texas; Prince George's County, Maryland; and Washington, DC. Supported by a $2.1 million grant from the U.S. Department of Education, the program recruits African American males (and other underrepresented populations) and prepares participants through the HUSOE's teacher education program and a series of summer institutes for a career as a PK-12 teacher. In five years, Ready to Teach has produced four Teachers-of-the-Year and one nominee for the Presidential Medal for Excellence in Mathematics and Science Teaching along with several principals and central office administrators. Remarkably, during its first four years, the program had 780 competitive applicants for 80 slots.

The Howard University School of Education is also learning lessons about producing African American math and science teachers through its Excellence and Motivation in Education Research Group (EMERG) which has been conducting a mixed-method research study examining what works in producing African American science and mathematics teachers at the undergraduate level at HBCUs. The Black Excellence in Science/Mathematics Teaching (BEST) study is funded by a $1.1 million grant from the National Science Foundation. The BEST study addresses the severe shortage of African American science and mathematics teachers in the nation's schools and HBCUs' critical role in the supply and preparation of these educators. The project's director, Dr. Kimberley Freeman, situated the study in social-cognitive and ecological theories, which explain that human development and achievement result from the interaction of individuals in contexts, and how individuals understand and interpret their experiences and environments is related to their success. The BEST mixed-method study seeks to answer the research question: What individual, instructional, and institutional factors are related to success in producing science and mathematics teachers at HBCUs? More than 65 HBCU faculty and administrators and 600 HBCU students, representing 13 four-year public and private HBCUs, participated in the study which yielded three significant findings about the individual, and instructional and institutional factors affecting

African American students' interest and persistence in STEM fields. According to Freeman (2011) the following findings have emerged from BEST:

1. *Individual: Identity and motivation are essential factors in HBCU students' success.*

HBCU students' positive racial identity, in particular racial pride, is linked with greater motivation and achievement, and is nurtured in the HBCU environment. It seems as if HBCUs create a unique psychology of success in their students, which includes being proud to be Black and academically driven. When asked about the value of attending an HBCU, many students expressed sentiments about seeing Blacks as models of intellectual authority in HBCU classrooms. In addition, the study found that being a teacher is part of the occupational identity and self-concept of the African American science and mathematics teachers in the study. Many of the teachers explained that although they did not initially desire to be teachers, once they had a teaching experience, they found they loved it and never turned back.

2. *Instructional: What works is a teacher education curriculum that is interdisciplinary, practice rich, and focuses on teachers being masters of their subjects and how to teach them.*

To produce science and mathematics teachers who are highly qualified, teacher education programs need to include education in the subject areas, pedagogy, as well as educational psychology and developmental science. Moreover, science, mathematics, and education faculty must enhance their collaboration in science and mathematics teacher education. Coordinating course sequencing is necessary, but not sufficient. A more holistic, integrated, and interdisciplinary approach to science and mathematics teacher education would be beneficial. For example, science, mathematics, and education faculty should co-teach courses, engage in professional development together, establish faculty learning communities to strengthen their own teaching, and otherwise create connections across the education, science, and mathematics curricula.

In addition, early, gradually increasing and multiple clinical experiences are critical success factors in teacher education. Preservice teachers will be best prepared for the PK-12 classroom if they are involved in real classrooms and authentic teaching experiences throughout their teacher education program.

3. *Institutional: The HBCU culture works.*

HBCUs provide a nurturing, close-knit, familial, and culturally affirming environment for Black students, which is a key ingredient to their success. HBCUs have an institutional culture of community and belongingness – and this is a core part of the effectiveness of both public and private HBCUs. HBCU faculty, in particular, play critical roles in the success of HBCU students. Faculty share positive relationships with students and provide students with both academic and emotional support. Furthermore, faculty members (despite their limited resources) have high expectations of students and are committed to student success. Students know this, and this is part of the reason they chose to attend HBCUs.

RECOMMENDATIONS

The recommendations discussed in this section are directed to policymakers and organized by using a professional continuum of teacher development that includes recruitment, preparation, induction/retention, continuing professional development, and national certification. The recommendations target how policymakers can support and leverage the resources and strengths of HBCUs to expand the African American teacher, principal, and superintendent pipelines (Irvine & Fenwick, 2011).

RECRUITMENT

Provide support and incentives to HBCUs to support innovative, research-based teacher education programs and provide monies for new teacher education initiatives.

Funding from philanthropic, federal, and state sources should target colleges of education at HBCUs. HBCUs prepare the majority of the nation's African American teachers and have been involved in substantial reform efforts that inform national and regional policy and practice.

Invest in teacher recruitment efforts at middle schools with significant enrollments of students of color, as well as in high schools.

The data about the impact of precollegiate programming aimed at sparking high school students' interest in the teaching profession is promising (Darling-Hammond, Dilworth, & Bullmaster, 1996). However, middle school students might benefit from early exposure, as well. Funding for such programs should support teacher career exploration modules, formation of future teachers clubs, and future teacher magnet programs at the middle grades level.

Assist HBCUs with the recruitment of both traditional and nontraditional students for teacher education.

Recruitment sites for African American teachers include paraprofessionals in K-12 schools, community colleges, civil rights and community organizations, churches, childcare, and other social service organizations. Recruiting New Teachers (2002) identified successful programs at community colleges where large numbers of students of color matriculate, graduate, and transfer to teacher education programs at four-year institutions. Other promising recruitment strategies include district-level "grow your own" programs with tuition scholarships.

Assist HBCUs with the recruitment of African American males.

African American male teachers are underrepresented in K-12 schools. For example, in the 2001–2002 academic year, the number of African American females who earned a bachelor's degree from a HBCU was 1,355, African American males, 550. These small numbers partially explain why fewer than 2 percent of teachers are African American males (Lewis, 2006). Particular attention should be paid to not only recruiting and enrolling males at HBCUs but graduating them as well.

Create more federal scholarships, fellowships, and loan forgiveness programs to encourage African American students to pursue teaching and/or graduate study in education.

Many African American students are the first to attend college in their families. Financial assistance and other support services are rarely available to assist these students. The U.S. Department of Education should continue to use legislation like the Higher Education Act and state Teacher Quality Enhancement Grants to expand scholarships, fellowships, and loan forgiveness programs. Additional incentives for teaching in high-need schools should be implemented for African American teachers who work in critical areas like mathematics, science, ESOL, and special education (Irvine & Fenwick, 2011).

PREPARATION

Support national accreditation and ongoing assessment of teacher education programs at HBCUs.

Policymakers should support ongoing internal and external examinations of teacher education programs at HBCUs to determine if the programs are build on the institution's mission and strengths and are based on the best research on teacher preparation and development, including the areas of content knowledge, pedagogy, and pedagogical content knowledge (Shulman, 1987). Currently, there are 84 teacher education programs at HBCUs, and 62 (74 percent) are accredited by the National Council for Accreditation of Teacher Education (NCATE). The Teacher Education Accreditation Council (TEAC) currently has one school of education at an HBCU as a candidate for accreditation (TEAC, 2009).

These numbers will increase only when HBCUs are granted the resources necessary to establish and maintain a continuous culture of assessment without struggling to meet accreditation standards. Targeted resources could assist with creating an assessment infrastructure and hiring personnel dedicated to this strategic function. Further, HBCUs need additional funding for certification examination preparation and student support services like childcare, flexible scheduling, tutoring, counseling, and financial assistance (Clewell & Villegas, 2001).

Support programs that are based in sound research and positive outcomes for learners that plan, implement, and evaluate alternative routes to teaching.

More context-specific models of alternative programs for teacher education are needed. The current debate over traditional versus alternative programs is mostly directed at structural issues such as the program's duration, the degree offered, and the sponsoring institution. The extant research that looks at these structural elements is inconclusive and often contradictory. More attention has to be placed on investigating substantive and contextual issues like the quality of the admissions process, curriculum, the fieldwork, and the social and institutional context (Zeichner & Conklin, 2008). HBCUs are excellent sites for investigating this multilayered approach in teacher education.

Develop a statewide strategy for eliminating racial disparities in pass rates on teacher licensure exams and advocate for the development of new assessment measures that do not maintain or exacerbate existing racial disparities.

One major barrier to producing more African American teachers is the requirement to demonstrate proficiency in basic skills by passing a single measure of teacher competence: a standardized test. With teacher shortages in every state and dwindling enrollments in teacher preparation programs, the nation can ill afford to use standardized tests to screen out individuals who have expressed an interest in becoming a teacher and possess other requisite abilities (Irvine & Fenwick, 2011).

INDUCTION/RETENTION

Support teacher education programs built on university–school district collaborations that focus on the induction and retention of novice teachers.

The data discussed in this chapter pinpoint the severity of the attrition problem in schools that serve some African American students. Induction and mentoring programs for beginning teachers show promise in rectifying this situation. Evidence from the National Center for Education Statistics' Schools and Staffing Survey suggests that participation in comprehensive induction programs can cut attrition in half (American Association of State Colleges and Universities, 2006). Strong (2006) conducted studies at the New Teacher Center and found a relationship between induction support and student achievement. These studies suggest that beginning teachers who receive comprehensive induction support for two years are more likely to have classes that achieve reading gains than those who do not receive this support. Additionally data from the New Teacher Center study found that 88 percent of teachers were still in education six years after participating in a mentoring program (Irvine & Fenwick, 2011).

CONTINUING PROFESSIONAL DEVELOPMENT

HBCUs and school districts should provide collaborative school-based professional development programs for novice and experienced teachers that focus on rigorous assessments of student outcomes that improve student learning and teacher performance.

Effective professional development programs are linked to enhanced teacher learning and student achievement. They enhance teachers' content knowledge, are aligned with standards, are school-based, are driven by student leaning data, are based on best evaluation practices, and promote collegiality and collaboration (Guskey, 2006). The American Educational Research Association's (2005) review of the literature states that in order to enhance student achievement, professional development should focus on teachers' improvement of knowledge of the subject matter they teach and on students' learning (Irvine & Fenwick, 2011).

NATIONAL CERTIFICATION

Support collaborative university and school-based programs that produce African American Board-certified teachers.

The National Board for Professional Teaching Standards (NBPTS) and its assessments complement initial teacher preparation, licensing, accreditation, and quality professional development. NBPTS is the greatest distinction for accomplished teachers in the United States, with the standards and assessments serving as a model for nations worldwide. A congressionally mandated three-year evaluation found that NBPTS exemplifies the characteristics of effective professional development and promotes student achievement and learning (Hakel, Koenig, & Elliott, 2008). Importantly, the data revealed that Board-certified teachers benefited African American and Hispanic students more than other students (Cavalluzzo, 2004). There are approximately 74,000 Board-certified teachers, of which 7,667 are African American and other teachers of color. More are needed to provide leadership in high-need schools and to contribute an important cultural lens and understanding to effective practice (Irvine & Fenwick, 2011).

CONCLUSION

The literature reveals that the recruitment, retention, and professional development of African American teachers has positive benefits for African American students and the high-need schools that many of them attend. Unfortunately, African American teachers often work in various contexts and conditions that mitigate and often neutralize their impact. These conditions make their work more difficult, constrain their efforts to teach, and impact their expectations and their students' achievement. Their presence alone cannot compensate or obliterate the effects of decades of neglect and ineffective policies and practices in schools where students of color attend. Additionally, recent data suggest that African American teacher turnover is increasing (Ingersoll & Conner, 2009). During the 2005–2006 academic year, African American teacher turnover was 20.7 percent compared to 19.4 percent for other teachers of color and 16.4 percent for White teachers. These new data suggest that the teaching profession may not be able to continue to attract effective African American teachers in high-need schools without significant resources aimed at recruiting and retaining them. This challenge should be a national educational priority. HBCUs have both a historical record of and institutional commitment to producing significant numbers of African American teachers, and with increased financial support, can produce more in the future (Irvine & Fenwick, 2011).

REFERENCES

American Association of State Colleges and Universities. (2006). Teacher induction: Trends and opportunities. *Policy Matters, 3*(10), 1–4.
American Educational Research Association. (2005). Teaching teachers: Professional development to improve student achievement. *Research Points, 3*(1), 1–4.
Carter, M., & Fenwick, L. (2001). Keeping a close watch: A cultural philosophy of school change. *National Association of Secondary School Principals (NASSP) Bulletin, 85*(15), 15–21.
Cavalluzzo, L. C. (2004, November). *Is national board certification an effective signal of teacher quality?* IRP No. 11204, Center for Naval Analysis, Arlington, VA.
Center for Educational Policy. (2006). *A public school primer.* Washington, DC.
Clewell, B. C., Puma, M. J., & McKay, S. A. (2005, April). Does it matter if my teacher looks like me? The impact of teacher race and ethnicity on student academic achievement. Paper presented at the meeting of the American Educational Research Association, Montreal, Canada.
Clewell, B. C., & Villegas, A. M. (2001). *Absence unexcused: Ending teacher shortages in high-need areas.* Washington, DC: The Urban Institute.
Couch-Maddox, S. (1999). *Teachers' perceptions of African American male students in an urban school system.* Unpublished doctoral dissertation, Clark Atlanta University.
Darling-Hammond, L., Dilworth, M., & Bullmaster, M. (1996). *Educators of color.* Washington, DC: U.S. Department of Education, Office of Educational Research and Improvement (ERIC Document Reproduction Services No. ED474898).
Ehrenberg, R. G., & Brewer, D. J. (1995). Did teacher's verbal ability and race matter in the 1960s? Coleman revisited. *Economics of Education Review, 14*(1), 1–21.
Evans, M. (1992). An estimate of race and gender role-model effects in teaching high school. *Journal of Economic Education, 23*(3), 209–217.
Farkas, G., Grobe, R. P., Sheehan, D., & Shuan, Y. (1990). Cultural resources and school success: Gender, ethnicity, and poverty groups within an urban school district. *American Sociological Review, 55,* 127–142.
Fenwick, L. T. (2001). *Patterns of excellence: Policy perspectives on diversity in teaching and school leadership.* Atlanta, GA: Southern Education Foundation.
Freeman, K. E. (2001). *Just the facts: African American teachers for the new millennium.* Fairfax, VA: The Patterson Institute.
Freeman, K. E. (2011). What works! Producing African American science and mathematics teachers at HBCUs: Evidence from the Howard University BEST study. *SOE Review, 2,* 3–5.
Gordon, J. A. (2000). *The color of teaching.* New York, NY: Routledge-Falmer.
Guskey, T. R. (2006, March). The characteristics of effective professional development. Paper presented at the Annual Meeting of the American Education Research Association, Chicago, IL.

Hakel, M. D., Koenig, J. A., & Elliott, S. W. (2008). *Assessing accomplished teaching: Advanced-level certification programs*. Washington, DC: The National Academies Press.

Hanushek, E. A. (1992). The trade-off between child quantity and quality. *Journal of Political Economy, 100*(1), 84–117.

Hess, F. M., & Leal, D. L. (1997). Minority teachers, minority students, and college matriculation. *Policy Studies Journal, 25*(2), 235–248.

Ingersoll, R. M., & Conner, R. (2009, April). What the national data tell us about minority and Black teacher turnover. Paper presented at the Annual Meeting of the American Education Research Association, San Diego, CA.

Irvine, J. J. (1990). *Black students and school failure*. Westport, CT: Praeger.

Irvine, J. J., & Fenwick, L. T. (2011). Teachers and teaching for the new millennium: The role of HBCUs. *Journal of Negro Education, 80*(3), 197–208.

Klopfenstein, K. (2005). Beyond test scores: The impact of Black teacher role models on rigorous math taking. *Contemporary Economic Policy, 23*(3), 416–428.

Lewis, C. W. (2006). African American teachers in public schools: An examination of three urban school districts. *Teachers College Record, 108*(2), 224–245.

Lynn, M. (2006). Education for the community: Exploring the culturally relevant practices of Black male teachers. *Teachers College Record, 108*(12), 2497–2522.

Meier, K. J., Stewart, J., & England, R. E. (1989). *Race, class, and education: The politics of second generation discrimination*. Madison, WI: University of Wisconsin Press.

Merisotis, J. P., & McCarthy, K. (2005). Retention and student success at minority-serving institutions. *New Directions for Institutional Research, 125*, 45–58.

Miller, R., Murnane, R., & Willett, J. (2007, August). *Do teacher absences impact student achievement? Longitudinal evidence from one urban school district*. Working paper No. W13356, National Bureau of Economic Research, Cambridge, MA.

National Association for Equal Opportunity in Higher Education. (2008). *The state of America's Black colleges*. Silver Spring, MD: Beckham Publications Group.

Recruiting New Teachers. (2002). *Tapping potential: Community colleges and America's teacher recruitment challenge*. Belmont, MA: Author.

Shulman, L. (1987). Knowledge and teaching: Foundations of the new reform. *Harvard Educational Review, 57*, 1–22.

Strong, M. (2006). *Does new teacher support affect student achievement? (Issue No. 06–01)*. Santa Cruz, CA: New Teacher Center at the University of Santa Cruz.

Teacher Education Accreditation Council [TEAC]. (2009). Retrieved from http://www.teac.org/. Accessed on May 28, 2009.

Villegas, A. M., & Irvine, J. J. (2009). Arguments for increasing the racial/ethnic diversity of the teaching force: A look at the evidence. Paper presented at the Annual Meeting of American Education Research Association, San Diego, CA.

Zeichner, K., & Conklin, H. G. (2008). Teacher education programs as sites for teacher preparation. In M. Cochran-Smith, S. Feiman-Nemser & D. J. McIntyre (Eds.), *Handbook of research on teacher education* (pp. 269–289). New York, NY: Routledge.

CHAPTER 18

EXPLORING THE RELATIONSHIP BETWEEN ACADEMIC SELF-REGULATION AND EDUCATIONAL OUTCOMES AMONG AFRICAN AMERICAN MALE EDUCATION MAJORS

Lamont A. Flowers

ABSTRACT

Spearman's rank correlation coefficients were calculated from data based on a sample of African American males pursuing education degrees who completed the National Survey of Student Engagement. The statistical results included positive correlations highlighting the relationship between academic experiences and educational outcomes. Applying student development research, implications for teacher education programs are discussed.

Data from the U.S. Department of Education (2013) indicate that African American males represent approximately 11% of the population of male

Black Male Teachers: Diversifying the United States' Teacher Workforce
Advances in Race and Ethnicity in Education, Volume 1, 251–260
Copyright © 2013 by Emerald Group Publishing Limited
All rights of reproduction in any form reserved
ISSN: 2051-2317/doi:10.1108/S2051-2317(2013)0000001022

students pursuing degrees in education. In comparison, African American females represent approximately 12% of the population of females pursuing degrees in education. Within group national data shows that of the African American college students pursuing education degrees, only 20% of these students are male and 80% of these students are female. While extensive research has highlighted the underrepresentation of African American males pursuing careers in teaching, a limited amount of studies have attempted to examine the impact of academic experiences on African American males enrolled in education programs.

Student development research has not yet fully examined the impact of African American male education students' academic engagement on achievement. Thus, while we know that many African American males are not pursuing degrees in education, we need to learn more about the effects of particular types of educational experiences on African American males in education, with regard to their academic outcomes in college. Accordingly, this study analyzes data from a sample of African American male college students to determine the extent to which academic experiences impact African American male education students' learning gains in teacher preparation programs. In light of the number of African American males in teacher education programs, the statistical results from this exploratory study may support the development of strategies and interventions designed to enhance the scholarly engagement of African American male education majors.

REVIEW OF THE LITERATURE

The influence of self-regulation on academic achievement is well documented (Perry, Hladkyj, Pekrun, Clifton, & Chipperfield, 2005; Williams & Hellman, 1998). Bandura (1986) asserts that self-regulation is a central element of social cognitive theory. He also suggests that it involves cognitive processes such as self-monitoring and self-reflection. Self-regulation also involves the use of cognitive processes to attain specific goals. Individuals who are able to skillfully self-regulate their academic behaviors possess many unique characteristics, such as the ability to (a) establish academic goals, (b) engage in scholarly pursuits, (c) cultivate academic self-efficacy, and (d) focus on performance outcomes (Zimmerman, 1998). Within the learning context, self-regulated students tend to set high academic goals (Schunk, 1996). Additionally, these students closely monitor their perceived progress toward their academic and career goals. Further, Schunk and

Ertmer (2000) suggest that academic self-regulative behaviors are influenced by students' beliefs in their ability to perform designated learning tasks.

Understanding academic self-regulation and its effects on learning and achievement is paramount. In light of the fact that academic success in education programs necessitate that African American male students work independently and function with a high degree of confidence, it is particularly important for teacher education faculty to understand the intellectual development of African American males. Because it is widely accepted that both interest and motivation are closely linked to academic self-regulation and achievement, cultivating academic self-regulation among African American male education students should become a strategic priority within teacher education programs. Research from Carlone and Johnson (2007) indirectly suggests that student achievement in education coursework may be associated with students' academic interests and identity development outcomes. Thus, as an extension of their findings, it could be hypothesized that when African American male education students achieve academically, they may be more intrinsically motivated to pursue scholarly and career goals. Several studies on the impact of academic experiences on educational outcomes in college (Pascarella & Terenzini, 1991, 2005) support this viewpoint and attest to the importance of students' self-regulation strategies and dispositions. For example, this body of research suggests that self-regulated students develop study skills that are aligned with their learning styles. Moreover, findings from a broad array of studies indicate that academically self-regulated students demonstrate higher levels of academic self-efficacy in college classrooms.

THEORETICAL AND CONCEPTUAL FOUNDATIONS

Theory of Self-Regulation

Self-regulation refers to an individual's ability to direct and pursue a course of action to achieve strategic goals (Zimmerman, 1989). The idea of self-regulation has been used in many research contexts to explain achievement outcomes and goal-oriented activities with respect to how individuals utilize thoughts and behaviors to pursue courses of action for a particular purpose (Schunk & Zimmerman, 1994). According to Schunk and Zimmerman (1994), "[s]elf-regulation refers to students' self-generated thoughts, feelings, and actions, which are systematically oriented toward attainment of their goals" (p. ix). In the context of academic experiences and outcomes in teacher education programs, research suggests that an appropriate balance of self-regulation dispositions and actions may help to increase African American male students' achievement levels and may reduce attrition rates (Pascarella & Terenzini, 2005; Schunk & Ertmer, 2000). Moreover, several studies support the notion that students who exhibit self-regulative behaviors in academic settings are more likely to understand course content, retain information, commit to their major, and graduate from college (Nota, Soresi, & Zimmerman, 2004). Confirmation for this viewpoint has been demonstrated in the scholarly literature (Nota et al., 2004; Schunk & Zimmerman, 1994). For example, in a study by Vanderstoep, Pintrich, and Fagerlin (1996) students who learned course information, adjusted to varying levels of academic rigor, and accomplished academic goals were more likely to be successful. Zimmerman (1989, 1998) suggests that the conceptual elements of academic self-regulated learning are also related to students' self-efficacy beliefs and goal orientations. Moreover, this finding suggests the need to collect and interpret data concerning the types of study strategies African American male education students use, their perceptions of their abilities to learn course information, their scholarly dispositions, as well as their academic and career goals.

Conceptual Framework of College Student Outcomes

This study is based on many research investigations on the effects of college attendance on student development (Pascarella & Terenzini, 1991, 2005). One aspect of this research suggests that student background factors and precollege characteristics influence educational outcomes (Chickering & Reisser, 1993; Flowers, Osterlind, Pascarella, & Pierson, 2001; Pascarella & Terenzini, 1991, 2005; Tinto, 1993). Research has also suggested that institutional differences impact student outcomes (Pascarella & Terenzini, 2005). Studies even indicate that students' perceptions of their institutional environments may play a role in determining academic and social development (Pascarella & Terenzini, 2005). Another line of college student development research suggests that academic experiences in college are important factors that may be used in interpreting educational outcomes (Astin, 1993; Pascarella & Terenzini, 1991, 2005; Terenzini, Springer, Pascarella, & Nora, 1995). The research regarding college student outcomes also suggests that it is important to take into account how a student spends his or her time outside of class (Chickering & Reisser, 1993;

Pascarella & Terenzini, 2005), as it relates to academic activities and experiences (e.g., preparing for class).

Data Source

The primary data source for this study was the National Survey of Student Engagement (2004a). This national survey measures students' participation in experiences in which previous studies have associated with important college student outcomes (Chickering & Reisser, 1993; Kuh, 2001, 2003). Data from the 2004 National Survey of Student Engagement data collection were analyzed for this exploratory study. The analytical sample was selected from more than 400 postsecondary institutions comprising the institutional sample (National Survey of Student Engagement, 2004a). In the current study, data from 70 African American male students majoring in education were analyzed. Of the total number, approximately 30% of the students attended historically Black colleges and universities.

Analytical Procedures

In light of the small sample size used in the study, the operational structure of the variables, and the observation that the normality assumption was not strongly supported based on the results of the a priori analysis (Hollander & Wolfe, 1999), the Pearson product–moment correlation (Jaccard & Becker, 1990) was not selected as the principal mode of analysis. To provide a more accurate assessment of the relationships among the variables for this exploratory study, Spearman rank correlation coefficients (Hollander & Wolfe, 1999) were calculated between the primary variable of interest which consisted of a proxy variable to assess a particular aspect of African American male education majors' academic self-regulation behaviors. The use of this particular nonparametric method to analyze data is preferred to the traditional Pearson product–moment correlation in the event that the data deviates from a normal distribution.

To implement the analytical procedures for this exploratory study, students' scores on a self-reported measure of the extent to which they spent time preparing for class was correlated with 16 self-reported measures of educational gains. The response scale of the primary variable consisted of eight categories ($1 = 0$ hours, $2 = 1$–5 hours, $3 = 6$–10 hours, $4 = 11$–15 hours, $5 = 16$–20 hours, $6 = 21$–25 hours, $7 = 26$–30 hours,

Table 1.   Descriptive Statistics of National Survey of Student
Engagement Variables.

Variables	Mean	Standard Deviation
Preparing for class	3.70	1.602
Acquiring a broad general education	3.25	0.775
Thinking critically and analytically	3.19	0.862
Using computing and information technology	3.09	0.981
Analyzing quantitative problems	2.77	0.957
Acquiring job or work-related knowledge and skills	3.12	0.978
Writing clearly and effectively	3.14	0.928
Speaking clearly and effectively	3.06	0.873
Voting in local, state, or national elections	2.13	1.083
Working effectively with others	3.14	0.862
Learning effectively on your own	3.20	0.759
Understanding yourself	2.90	1.100
Contributing to the welfare of your community	2.35	1.096
Developing a deepened sense of spirituality	2.23	1.214
Developing a personal code of values and ethics	2.64	1.071
Understanding people of other racial and ethnic backgrounds	2.80	1.106
Solving complex real-world problems	2.61	1.114

Note: The variable description information was obtained from the National Survey of Student
Engagement Codebook (2004b).

$8 = $ more than 30 hours). The response scale of the 16 educational gains
variables consisted of four categories ($1 = $ Very little, $2 = $ Some, $3 = $ Quite a
bit, $4 = $ Very much). As shown in Table 1, the educational gains items
included a variety of educational outcomes documented by previous
research as educationally, socially, and intellectually relevant goals of
education (Astin, 1993; Pascarella & Terenzini, 1991, 2005; Tinto, 1993).
Given the relatively small sample size, all statistical results were reported
significant at $p < 0.10$. Utilizing Spearman's rank correlation coefficients to
examine the association between the preparing for class variable and
several educational gains measures, the analysis yielded five statistically
significant and positive correlation coefficients.

RESULTS

The aim of this study was to examine academic engagement issues for
African American male college students pursuing degrees in education to

advance the research literature surrounding the representation of African American male teachers. Using theoretical perspectives and student development research to frame the exploratory study, the specific goal of this research was to assess the relationship between self-reported measures assessing the extent to which African American male education students spent time preparing for class and the educational gains they derived from this particular aspect of scholarly engagement. Employing data from a small number of African American male education majors, correlational results indicated that the amount of time students engaged in class preparation activities was positively associated with various self-reported measures of educational progress. More specifically, the statistical results showed that there were positive Spearman rank correlation coefficients between the amount of time students' spent preparing for class and the extent to which they gained with regard to using computing and information technology ($r_s = 0.245$, $p < 0.10$), analyzing quantitative problems ($r_s = 0.236$, $p < 0.10$),

Table 2. Correlation Summary for African American Male Education Majors.

Variables	r_s
Acquiring a broad general education	0.129
Thinking critically and analytically	0.064
Using computing and information technology	0.245*
Analyzing quantitative problems	0.236*
Acquiring job or work-related knowledge and skills	0.135
Writing clearly and effectively	0.102
Speaking clearly and effectively	0.158
Voting in local, state, or national elections	−0.061
Working effectively with others	0.169
Learning effectively on your own	0.350*
Understanding yourself	0.107
Contributing to the welfare of your community	0.156
Developing a deepened sense of spirituality	0.172
Developing a personal code of values and ethics	0.210*
Understanding people of other racial and ethnic backgrounds	0.067
Solving complex real-world problems	0.207*

Note: Spearman's rank correlation coefficients between the educational gains variables and the variable indicating the extent to which students spent time preparing for class (studying, reading, writing, doing homework or lab work, analyzing data, rehearsing, and other academic activities).

*$p < 0.10$.

learning effectively on their own ($r_s = 0.350$, $p < 0.10$), developing a personal code of values and ethics ($r_s = 0.210$, $p < 0.10$), and solving complex real-world problems ($r_s = 0.207$, $p < 0.10$). The results, as shown in Table 2, indicate the importance of helping African American male education majors to pursue academic self-regulation development activities while they pursue their teaching degrees. Despite the strength of the statistical results, the study's limitations included the relatively small sample of students as well as the exploratory nature of the study's research design which did not include the use of statistical control variables as proxies for demographics characteristics and college experiences.

DISCUSSION AND IMPLICATIONS

Statistical results indicate that African American male education majors should be encouraged to explore ways to prepare for class and engage in academic experiences to increase the likelihood of attaining desirable educational outcomes. The primary findings of this study, while preliminary and exploratory, highlight the importance of academic self-regulation for African American male education majors. For example, Spearman rank correlation coefficients indicated that the more time African American male education majors spent engaging in academic activities related to class preparation the more likely they were to use computing and information technology, analyze quantitative problems, and solve complex real-world problems. Also, notably, focusing on course preparation activities resulted in higher scores on a measure pertaining to the development of values and ethics. Moreover, African American students who reported higher levels of class preparation also reported higher levels of self-regulated experiences such as learning effectively on their own. Viewed collectively, the major findings reported in this chapter support the need for additional research to examine the particular characteristics of teacher education programs that promote academic engagement activities for African American male education students.

In terms of the practical implications of this research for teacher education programs, it is imperative that teacher education faculty provide African American male education students with opportunities to reflect on their academic integration experiences while also developing effective study skills, learning strategies, and academic self-efficacy. Regarding African American male education students, the data from this exploratory study reinforces this contention and highlights some potential benefits of promoting academic self-regulation behaviors among this population. The preliminary statistical findings also support the need for teacher education faculty to ensure that African American male students in education receive information about successfully navigating education courses to enable them to better understand the implications of these academic pursuits on their scholarly development in college.

Another prominent and related area of student development research has shown consistently that student effort and student engagement impacts students' academic and social integration experiences. Moreover, this line of research suggests that student involvement is an important factor in understanding how students develop in college (Astin, 1984, 1993). Because students' academic or in-class experiences play an important role in a student's personal growth and cognitive development, student involvement has been shown to be an important predictor of social and academic development in college (Astin, 1993; Pascarella & Terenzini, 1991, 2005). Astin (1993) indicates that informative student engagement experiences can positively impact students' academic and social development on college campuses. As such, teacher education faculty should also consider developing study sessions for African American male education students after class to enhance their educational outcomes in teacher preparation programs.

REFERENCES

Astin, A. W. (1984). Student involvement: A developmental theory for higher education. *Journal of College Student Personnel, 25,* 297–308.

Astin, A. W. (1993). *What matters in college? Four critical years revisited.* San Francisco, CA: Jossey-Bass.

Bandura, A. (1986). *Social foundations of thought and action: A social cognitive theory.* Englewood Cliffs, NJ: Prentice-Hall.

Carlone, H. B., & Johnson, A. (2007). Understanding the science experiences of successful women of color: Science identity as an analytic lens. *Journal of Research in Science Teaching, 44,* 1187–1218.

Chickering, A. W., & Reisser, L. (1993). *Education and identity* (2nd edn.). San Francisco, CA: Jossey-Bass.

Flowers, L., Osterlind, S. J., Pascarella, E. T., & Pierson, C. T. (2001). How much do students learn in college? Cross-sectional estimates using the college BASE. *The Journal of Higher Education, 72,* 565–583.

Hollander, M., & Wolfe, D. A. (1999). *Nonparametric statistical methods* (2nd edn.). New York, NY: Wiley.

Jaccard, J., & Becker, M. A. (1990). *Statistics for the behavioral sciences* (2nd edn.). Belmont, CA: Wadsworth.

Kuh, G. D. (2001). Assessing what really matters to student learning: Inside the National Survey of Student Engagement. *Change, 33*(3), 10–17, 66.

Kuh, G. D. (2003). What we're learning about student engagement from NSSE: Benchmarks for effective educational practices. *Change, 35*(2), 24–32.

National Survey of Student Engagement. (2004a). *Student engagement pathways to collegiate success: 2004 annual survey results.* Bloomington, IN: Indiana University, Center for Postsecondary Research.

National Survey of Student Engagement. (2004b). *The college student report: 2004 codebook.* Bloomington, IN: Indiana University Bloomington, Center for Postsecondary Research.

Nota, L., Soresi, S., & Zimmerman, B. J. (2004). Self-regulation and academic achievement and resilience: A longitudinal study. *International Journal of Educational Research, 41*, 198–215.

Pascarella, E. T., & Terenzini, P. T. (1991). *How college affects students: Findings and insights from twenty years of research.* San Francisco, CA: Jossey-Bass.

Pascarella, E. T., & Terenzini, P. T. (2005). *How college affects students: A third decade of research* (2nd edn.). San Francisco, CA: Jossey-Bass.

Perry, R. P., Hladkyj, S., Pekrun, R. H., Clifton, R. A., & Chipperfield, J. G. (2005). Perceived academic control and failure in college students: A three-year study of scholastic attainment. *Research in Higher Education, 46*, 535–569.

Schunk, D. H. (1996). *Learning theories: An educational perspective* (2nd edn.). Englewood Cliffs, NJ: Prentice-Hall.

Schunk, D. H., & Ertmer, P. A. (2000). Self-regulation and academic learning: Self-efficacy enhancing interventions. In M. Boekaerts, P. R. Pintrich & M. Zeidner (Eds.), *Handbook of self-regulation* (pp. 631–649). San Diego, CA: Academic Press.

Schunk, D. H., & Zimmerman, B. J. (Eds.). (1994). *Self-regulation of learning and performance: Issues and educational applications.* Hillsdale, NJ: Lawrence Erlbaum.

Terenzini, P. T., Springer, L., Pascarella, E. T., & Nora, A. (1995). Influences affecting the development of students' critical thinking skills. *Research in Higher Education, 36*, 23–39.

Tinto, V. (1993). *Leaving college: Rethinking the causes and cures of student attrition* (2nd edn.). Chicago, IL: University of Chicago Press.

U.S. Department of Education. (2013). *National postsecondary student aid study.* Washington, DC: National Center for Education Statistics.

Vanderstoep, S. W., Pintrich, P. R., & Fagerlin, A. (1996). Disciplinary differences in self-regulated learning in college students. *Contemporary Educational Psychology, 21*, 345–362.

Williams, J. E., & Hellman, C. M. (1998). Investigating self-regulated learning among first-generation community college students. *Journal of Applied Research in the Community College, 5*(2), 83–87.

Zimmerman, B. J. (1989). A social cognitive view of self-regulated academic learning. *Journal of Educational Psychology, 81*, 329–339.

Zimmerman, B. J. (1998). Developing self-fulfilling cycles of academic regulation: An analysis of exemplary instructional models. In D. H. Schunk & B. J. Zimmerman (Eds.), *Self-regulated learning: From teaching to self-reflective practice* (pp. 1–19). New York, NY: Guildford Press.

SECTION V
EPILOGUE FROM SERIES EDITORS

AFTERWORD: ABOUT THE BOOK SERIES

Across the United States, black male teachers are underrepresented throughout the K-12 education pipeline. The teachers of black males are frequently *white* and *female* and rarely *black* and *male*. Increasingly, school systems are expressing the need for more black male teachers in the classroom. We both are very excited that *Black Male Teachers: Diversifying the United States' Teacher Workforce* is being published as a part of our book series with Emerald Group Publishing. We believe that the edited volume sheds light on a very important education concern. We also think that the edited volume is an excellent book to launch the new series, Advances in Race and Ethnicity in Education.

The new series focus on topics that can advance our understanding of race and ethnicity in education. It is intended that the series will present answers to some of the most critical questions, discussions, and debates among education scholars, practitioners, and policymakers. A major objective of the book series is to create a substantive corpse of research and scholarship that can improve these individuals' understanding of race and ethnicity in K-12 schools and how the two may shape the schooling experiences and learning outcomes for students, delivery of instruction and services from education practitioners, and the development and efficacy of education policies.

For the book series, we are particularly interested in books (e.g., authored, coauthored, edited, or coedited) that include critical and/or new perspectives on education, race, and ethnicity. Book proposals may include theoretical, quantitative, qualitative, and mixed-methods research studies, as well as policy analysis. We also welcome book proposals that address the intersections of race and ethnicity with other identity constructs (e.g., gender, sexuality, disability, socioeconomic status, etc.).

James L. Moore III
Chance W. Lewis
Series Editors

ABOUT THE AUTHORS

Chike Akua is a doctoral student in educational policy studies at Georgia State University. A former middle school teacher, Akua taught in public schools for 15 years. During his tenure as a teacher, he was selected as a Teacher of the Year in the State of Virginia and acknowledged for exemplary teaching and service in Georgia. Akua is the author of widely disseminated instructional materials and children's literature and has led principal and teacher workshops for more than 500 U.S. schools and school districts. His book *A Treasure Within: Stories of Remembrance and Rediscovery* was nominated for the National Association for the Advancement of Colored People (NAACP) Award for Outstanding Contribution to Children's Literature.

Jamil Alhassan is a first generation college graduate of the University of Pittsburgh with a bachelor of science in biology, a minor in chemistry, and a certificate in the Conceptual Foundations of Medicine. Jamil, a 7th grade life sciences teacher, has introduced a new classroom culture model called SWAG (a term used among the youth that embodies coolness, charisma, and confidence) and has intertwined its meaning with academic excellence. In his classroom SWAG represents the acronym "Students Will Achieve Greatness," in which "greatness" pertains to their academic achievement.

Margarita Bianco is an Assistant Professor at the University of Colorado Denver. Her research interests include the underrepresentation of teachers of color and special populations of gifted learners including twice exceptional and culturally and linguistically diverse learners.

Gloria S. Boutte is the Department Chair and Yvonne and Schuyler Moore Child Advocacy Distinguished Chair in the Department of Instruction and Teacher Education at the University of South Carolina. Dr. Boutte's scholarship focuses on equity pedagogies and methodologies. She is the author of two books: and *Multicultural Education: Raising Consciousness* and *Resounding Voices: School Experiences of People from Diverse Ethnic Backgrounds*. Dr. Boutte is the founder of the Center of Excellence for the Education and Equity of African American Students (CEEEAAS).

Ed Brockenbrough is an Assistant Professor in the Warner Graduate School of Education at the University of Rochester, where he directs the Urban Teaching and Leadership Program, a Warner initiative in partnership with the Rochester City School District that prepares urban teachers with a commitment to social justice. He also teaches courses on concepts and issues in social science research, preservice teacher preparation, and diversity and social justice in American education. His research focuses on negotiations of identity, pedagogy and power in urban educational spaces, with particular attention to Black, masculinity, and queer issues in education.

Lawrence M. Clark is an Assistant Professor of mathematics education at the University of Maryland, College Park. He conducts both quantitative and qualitative research, with a focus on exploring the relationships between mathematics teachers' experiences, knowledge domains, and beliefs, particularly in the contexts of urban schools. Furthermore, a thread of his research explores the work and role of African American mathematics teachers in the U.S. education narrative. His most recent publications include "Conceptualizing the African American Mathematics Teacher as a Key Figure in the African American Education Historical Narrative" (w/ T. Jones Frank and J. Davis in *Teachers College Record*); "African American Mathematics Teachers as Agents in Their African American Students' Mathematics Identity Formation" (w/ E. M. Badertscher and C. Napp in *Teachers College Record*); "What Mathematics Education Might Learn from the Work of Well-Respected African American Mathematics Teachers in Urban Schools" (w/ D. Chazan, A. Brantlinger, A. R. Edwards in *Teachers College Record*); and "Researching African American Mathematics Teachers of African American Students: Conceptual and Methodological Considerations" (w/ W. Johnson & D. Chazan, in D. Martin (Ed.), *Mathematics Teaching, Learning, and Liberation in the Lives of Black Children*).

Erin Croke is Director of Undergraduate Educational Policy at The City University of New York. Ms. Croke holds a bachelor's degree from Vanderbilt University, master's degree in educational policy from George Washington University, and is currently pursuing her Ph.D. in Urban Education at The CUNY Graduate Center. Ms. Croke's dissertation examines the evolving nature of access to public higher education in New York City.

Candice Crowell is a doctoral student studying counseling psychology at University of Georgia. Prior to her doctoral studies, Candice taught English in rural Georgia and inner city Atlanta, at the high school and collegiate level. She is the cofounder of Washington High School's Legend Sorority, a mentoring program that focuses on developing Black female students in the areas of leadership, scholarship, sisterhood, and service. She is a graduate of Spelman College.

Travis Dale is Senior Research Associate at the John F. Kennedy, Jr. Institute for Worker Education at The City University of New York. Mr. Dale has also worked at the Mount Sinai Adolescent Health Center, and the National Center for Schools and Communities at Fordham University, where he evaluated after-school programs. He holds a bachelor's degree from Hampshire College and a master's degree in economics from Boston University.

Julius Davis is an Assistant Professor in the College of Education at Bowie State University in the Department of Teaching, Learning and Professional Development. He has two main areas of research that focus on African American students in mathematics and African American mathematics teachers. His research of African American students emanated from his dissertation research of Black middle school students' lived realities and mathematics education. He used critical race theory to examine the role of race, racism, class, and power in determining the type of education African American students received in mathematics. While working as a research assistant in the Center for Mathematics Education at the University of Maryland, College Park, he developed research exploring the historical and contemporary experiences and practices of African American mathematics teachers. He coauthored "Conceptualizing the African American Mathematics Teacher as a Key Figure in the African American Education Historical Narrative" (w/ L. M. Clark and T. Jones Frank in *Teachers College Record*) and "Racism, Assessment, and Instructional Practices: Implications for Mathematics Teachers of African American students" (with D. B. Martin in the *Journal of Urban Mathematics Education*).

William Ebenstein is University Dean for Health and Human Services and Executive Director of the John F. Kennedy, Jr. Institute at The City University of New York. For more than 20 years, Dr. Ebenstein has led efforts to develop worker education programs at many CUNY campuses. Dr. Ebenstein holds a bachelor's degree from Brandeis University and a master's and doctoral degree in psychology and literature from the University of Dallas.

Leslie T. Fenwick, Ph.D., is dean of the Howard University School of Education. An expert on education policy (particularly as it relates to urban schools and race equity), Fenwick has held administrative and faculty appointments at HBCUs for nearly 20 years and from 1999 to 2003 at Harvard University as a visiting fellow and visiting scholar in education. In recent years, she served as an appointed member of a National Academy of Sciences committee, which examined the impact of mayoral control on Washington, DC, Public Schools. Fenwick is a former urban school principal and teacher (in public and private schools) and legislative aide for the State of Ohio Senate. Additionally, she is a contributor to the bestselling book, *The Last Word: Controversy and Commentary in American Education*, which boasts essays by former President Bill Clinton and noted historian Dr. John Hope Franklin. Her published research examines the superintendency, principalship, and urban school reform. She is a member of the board of directors and national advisory board for the American Association of Colleges for Teacher Education (AACTE) and the George Lucas Education Foundation (GLEF), respectively. As the 2011 recipient of the W. E. B. DuBois Award from the National Alliance of Black School Educators (NABSE), Fenwick was recognized for her commitment to and advocacy for Black students. She earned the Ph.D. at The Ohio State University where she was a Flescher Fellow and a bachelor's degree from the Curry School of Education at the University of Virginia.

Lamont A. Flowers is the Distinguished Professor of Educational Leadership and the Executive Director of the Charles H. Houston Center for the Study of the Black Experience in Education in the Eugene T. Moore School of Education at Clemson University. Dr. Flowers has authored several scholarly publications pertaining to the factors impacting the pathways to a college degree and occupational attainment for African Americans including empirical studies regarding academic achievement, access and equity, educational policy, labor market outcomes, and student development.

Toya Jones Frank is a doctoral candidate in the Center for Mathematics Education at the University of Maryland, College Park. Her research interests include teacher beliefs about the teaching and learning of mathematics and student ability, issues of equity in mathematics education as they relate to access to opportunities to learn, and African American mathematics teachers' and students' access to mathematics from a historical perspective. She coauthored "Conceptualizing the African American

Mathematics Teacher as a Key Figure in the African American Education Historical Narrative" (w/ L. M. Clark and J. Davis in *Teachers College Record*).

Tambra O. Jackson is an Associate Professor in the Department of Instruction and Teacher Education at the University of South Carolina. Her research interests include teacher learning across the professional continuum specifically focused on culturally responsive pedagogy and teaching for social justice, the preparation and support of teachers of Color, and urban education. Her work has been published in *Teaching and Teacher Education*, *Language Arts*, and *Teaching Education*.

Khary Golden serves as the Director of the Center for College Access at the LEAP Academy University Charter High School in Camden, NJ, and has spent the majority of his life living and working in the city of Camden. Khary attended Morehouse College in Atlanta, GA prior to graduating from Rutgers University-Camden with a bachelor's degree in political science with a concentration in African-American studies. He later received his master's in public policy and administration, with a concentration in education leadership from Rutgers, the State University of NJ. Khary is the co-founder of MORE Inc. (Manifesting Opportunities for Renewal and Empowerment), a nonprofit organization dedicated to uplifting young black males through academic, pre-professional, and social development. Khary is a dedicated educator with a passion for helping urban youth make a successful transition from high school into higher education, and his efforts have been documented in a number of different publications and media outlets. Khary is happily engaged to his fiancée, Anjulie Williams, who is a third grade mathematics teacher for Mastery Charter Schools in Philadelphia, PA.

Camesha Hill-Carter is an instructor in the College of Education at Southeast Missouri State University. In addition, Dr. Hill-Carter is known as the "Education Empowerment Expert" as she speaks to school and school organizations about the importance of educating all students; especially the African American student. Her research focuses on student success in the college arena as it relates to pedagogy and matriculation. As an award winning author, Dr. Hill-Carter has written *I was Lied To: Debunking the Happily Ever After Myth*; *Proverbs 31 Woman, Live Your Destiny Now^{TM}: Understanding* and *Fire Up: 30 Strategies on Firing Up Your Potential and Living Your Destiny Now*.

Nancy Leech is an Associate Professor at the University of Colorado Denver. Her area of research is promoting new developments and better understandings in applied qualitative, quantitative, and mixed methodologies.

Randy R. Miller Sr. currently teaches Social Studies at LEAP Academy University Charter School in New Jersey. He has 6 years collective experience in both K-12 and higher education as a program coordinator, teacher, trainer, and student advisor. Randy's passion is both writing and teaching. Randy is also the Chief Executive of MORE Inc. (Manifesting Opportunities for Renewal and Empowerment), a nonprofit organization that works with African American male youth. Mr. Miller is author of The Double D's of Destruction: How Our Distracted and Desensitized Consciousness Is Destroying Our Communities And Failing Our Children. He received both his bachelor of arts degree (2005) and master's degree in public policy and administration (2008) from Rutgers, the State University of New Jersey. Mr. Miller is married and currently resides with his wife and son in Southern New Jersey.

James L. Moore III received his B.A. in English Education from Delaware State University and earned both his M.A.Ed. and Ph.D. in Counselor Education from Virginia Polytechnic Institute and State University. He is an associate provost in the Office of Diversity and Inclusion, where he also serves as the inaugural director of the Todd Anthony Bell National Resource Center on the African American Male at The Ohio State University. Additionally, Dr. Moore is a full professor in the College of Education and Human Ecology.

He has a national- and international-recognized research agenda that focuses on (a) how educational professionals, such as school counselors, influence the educational/career aspirations and school experiences of students of color (particularly African American males); (b) socio-cultural, familial, school, and community factors that support, enhance, and impede academic outcomes for preK-20 African American students (e.g., elementary, secondary, and postsecondary); (c) recruitment and retention issues of students of color, particularly African Americans, in K-12 gifted education and those high-potential college students in science, technology, engineering, and mathematics (STEM) majors; and (d) social, emotional, and psychological consequences of racial oppression for African American males and other people of color in various domains in society (e.g., education, counseling, workplace, athletics, etc.). In less than 12 years, Dr. Moore has made significant contributions in *school counseling, gifted education, urban education, higher education, multicultural education/counseling,* and *STEM education.* He recently coedited a book with Dr. Chance W. Lewis of University of North Carolina at Charlotte titled, *African American Students in Urban Schools: Critical Issues and Solutions for Achievement.* Further, Dr. Moore has published nearly 90 publications, obtained nearly $7 million in grants and contracts, and given over 150 scholarly presentations and lectures throughout the United States and other parts of the world (e.g., Canada, United Kingdom, France, India, China, Indonesia, and Spain).

As a result of Dr. Moore's professional success, he has biographies listed in Outstanding Young Men in America (1998 edition), Academic Keys Who's Who in Education (2003 edition), Manchester Who's Who among Professionals in Counseling and Development (2005/2006 edition), Prestige International Who's Who Registries of Outstanding Professionals (2007 edition), and Who's Who in Black Columbus (2008, 2009, 2010, 2011, and 2012 editions). He is also the recipient of Brothers of the Academy's National Junior Scholar Award (2003), The Ohio State University's College of Education Distinguished Scholar Award (2004), North Central Association for Counselor Education and Supervision's Research Award (2004), Ohio School Counselor Association's Research Award (2004), American Educational Research Association's Division E Early Career Award in Counseling (2005), Ohio School Counselors Association's George E. Hill Counselor Educator Award (2005), Counselors for Social Justice's Ohana Award (2006), Phi Delta Kappa's Emerging Leaders Award (2007–2008), American Educational Research Association's Distinguished Scholar Award in Counseling–Division E (2008), The Education Trust's National Center for Transforming School Counseling Trailblazer Award (2009), Institute for School-Based Family Counseling's Outstanding Contributions to School-Based Family Counseling Award (2009), National Association for Gifted Children's Early Scholar Award (2009), National Association for Multicultural Education's Carl A. Grant Multicultural Research Award (2009), National Alliance of Black School Educators' W. E. B. DuBois Higher Education Award (2010), Ohio State's Black Graduate and Professional Student Caucus' Lawrence Williamson Jr. Service Award (2011), TheBlackManCan.org's Black Man Can Award (2012), American College Personnel Association's Standing Committee on Men and Masculinities Outstanding Research Award (2013), and is an inducted member in numerous professional and honor societies, such as Alpha Kappa Mu, Phi Kappa Phi, Phi Delta Kappa, Kappa Delta Pi, and Chi Sigma Iota.

Dr. Moore was also nominated to participate in the 2012–2013 Committee on Institutional Cooperation (CIC) Academic Leadership Program (CIC-ALP) and selected as an ACE Fellow in the 2013–2014 American Council on Education Fellows Program. He is a native of Lyman, South Carolina and currently lives in Alexandria, Virginia with his beloved wife, Stephanie, and three children (i.e., James IV, Sienna Ava, and Savanna Marie-Ann).

Curtis L. Morris holds the M.S. degree in Urban Affairs from Alabama A&M University and is certified as a National Quality Assurance Review Chair for AdvanceED which provides accreditation, research, and professional services to over 65 countries, 30 states, and 23,000 public and private schools, the Navajo Nation, and the Department of Defense Schools. He serves as an education consultant specializing in strategic planning for school improvement. He has coauthored books and articles with his wife Vivian G. Morris on the education of African American Children. Published books include: *The Price They Paid: Desegregation in an African American Community* and *Creating Caring and Nurturing Educational Environments for African American Children.* Articles were published in the *Journal of Teacher Education* and the *University of Florida Journal of Law and Public Policy.*

Vivian Gunn Morris holds the Ph.D. degree in Inner City Education, Early Childhood Education Emphasis, from Peabody College, Vanderbilt University. She is a veteran P-12 teacher and is presently Professor of Education, Assistant Dean for Faculty and Staff Development in the College of Education, and Director of the New Teacher Center at the University of Memphis. Her research related to the education of African American children appears in two books she coauthored with her husband Curtis L. Morris: *The Price They Paid: Desegregation in an African American Community* and *Creating Caring and Nurturing Educational Environments for African American Children.* Related articles have been published in a variety of international and national journals such as the *British Journal of In-Service Education, Teacher and Teacher Education,* the *Journal of Teacher Education, Action in Teacher Education,* the *Journal of Home Economics, Childhood Education,* and the *University of Florida Journal of Law and Public Policy.*

Justin Newell is a 5th Grade Language Arts and Social Studies Teacher at LEAP Academy University Charter School. Justin Newell is from Glassboro, New Jersey. This 33-year-old teacher began teaching in 2002 after attending Wesley College in Dover, Delaware. Justin is a father of two boys to whom he accredits what learning to be a man means. He currently teaches 5th grade at Camden, New Jersey's LEAP Academy University Charter School.

Shafeeq Rashid is currently a Professor of English at Georgia Military College. Prior to joining GMC he worked for 6 years in the public school system as a coach, mentor, and teacher. He believes that the most important aspect of developing strong schools and learners is through building a community that is fully invested in the school's success. His ultimate goal is to further his education in the field of sociology and continue to promote reform and change in education and society as a whole.

Dawn Nicole Hicks Tafari is a native New Yorker, and is passionate about the arts, culture, education, and translating theory into practice. Her research interests include Black boys in public schools, Black male teachers, hip-hop culture's influence on identity development, critical pedagogy, critical race theory, and narrative research. She earned her bachelor's degree in psychology from Hofstra University, her master of arts in teaching from The Johns Hopkins University, a post-baccalaureate certificate in Woman's and Gender Studies from The University of North Carolina Greensboro, and is currently pursuing her Ph.D. in Educational Studies with a Specialization in Cultural Studies from The University of North Carolina Greensboro. She has served as an elementary school teacher, college professor, and currently serves as a lateral entry teacher trainer for Guilford County Schools and Developmental English Faculty at Davidson County Community College. She does educational consulting with her husband and enjoys traveling and providing interactive, research-based workshops and curricula development for institutions around the country. Dawn lives in Greensboro, North Carolina with her amazing husband, two brilliant daughters, and two spirited dogs.

Kara Mitchell Viesca is an Assistant Professor at the University of Colorado Denver. Her research interests center on advancing equity through the policy and practice of teacher preparation.

Chezare A. Warren is a postdoctoral research fellow at the Penn Graduate School of Education Center for the Study of Race & Equity in Education. He is a former teacher and administrator in the Chicago Public Schools. Dr. Warren was the founding math teacher of Urban Prep Charter

Academy for Young Men. He earned his Ph.D. in Policy Studies in Urban Education at the University of Illinois at Chicago. His research interests include the social and cultural contexts of urban education, culturally responsive curricula and pedagogies, sociology of education, and Critical Race Theory. Dr. Warren's most recent scholarship examines how teachers, particularly White women, conceive of and utilize empathy to improve student–teacher interactions with Black boys in high schools.

Brandy S. Wilson is a Visiting Assistant Professor in the Department of Leadership and Educational Studies at the Appalachian State University. Her research interests include educational equity pre-k-doctorate with a particular focus on critical theoretical perspectives of education, culturally relevant pedagogy, and diversity in teacher education.

Kamilah M. Woodson is the Director of Training, a Licensed Clinical Psychologist, and an Assistant Professor in the Howard University School of Education, Department of Human Development and Psycho-educational Studies in the Counseling Psychology Program, where she teaches courses to Ph.D. students. Dr. Woodson also serves on the Editorial Board of the *Journal of Negro Education* as the Book Review Editor. Dr. Woodson was previously Director of the Howard University Office of Nursing Research, Division of Nursing, College of Pharmacy, Nursing & Allied Health Sciences, where she taught research courses to nursing students. Dr. Woodson is a graduate of the California School of Professional Psychology, Los Angeles, where she received the Ph.D. and MA, degrees in Clinical Psychology. She earned her Baccalaureate degree in Psychology from the University of Michigan, Ann Arbor.

ABOUT THE SERIES EDITORS

Chance W. Lewis is the Carol Grotnes Belk Distinguished Full Professor and Endowed Chair of Urban Education at the University of North Carolina at Charlotte. Additionally, Dr. Lewis is the Executive Director of the University of North Carolina at Charlotte's Urban Education Collaborative, which is publishing a new generation of research on improving urban schools. Dr. Lewis received his B.S. and M.Ed. in Business Education and Education Administration/Supervision from Southern University in Baton Rouge, Louisiana. Dr. Lewis completed his doctoral studies in Educational Leadership/Teacher Education from Colorado State University in Fort Collins, Colorado.

Dr. Lewis currently teaches graduate courses in the field of Urban Education at the University of North Carolina at Charlotte. His experiences span the range of K-12 and higher education. From 2006 to 2011, Dr. Lewis served as the Houston Endowed Chair and Associate Professor of Urban Education in the College of Education at Texas A&M University. Additionally, he was the co-director of the *Center for Urban School Partnerships*. In 2001–2006, he served as an Assistant Professor of Teacher Education at Colorado State University. From 1994 to 1998, Dr. Lewis served as a Business Education teacher in East Baton Rouge Parish Schools (Baton Rouge, LA), where he earned Teacher of the Year honors in 1997.

Dr. Lewis has over 100 publications including 60 + refereed journal articles in some of the leading academic journals in the field of urban education. Additionally, he has received over $4 million in external research funds. To date, Dr. Lewis has authored/coauthored/coedited eight books: *White teachers/diverse classrooms: A guide for building inclusive schools, eliminating racism and promoting high expectations* (Stylus, 2006); *The dilemmas of being an African American male in the new millennium* (Infinity, 2008); *An educator's guide to working with African American students: Strategies for promoting academic success* (Infinity, 2009); *Transforming teacher education: What went wrong with teacher training and how we can fix it* (Stylus, 2010); *White teachers/diverse classrooms: Creating inclusive schools, building on students' diversity and providing true educational equity* [2nd edn.] (Stylus,

2011); *African Americans in urban schools: Critical issues and solutions for achievement* (Peter Lang, 2012); *Yes we can!: Improving urban schools through innovative educational reform* (Information Age, 2011); and *Black males in postsecondary education: Examining their experiences in diverse institutional contexts* (Information Age, 2012).

James L. Moore III is a full professor in Counselor Education in the College of Education and Human Ecology and coordinator of the School of Counseling Program at The Ohio State University. He also is the inaugural director of the Todd Anthony Bell National Resource Center on the African American Male.

Dr. Moore has a national- and international-recognized research agenda that focuses on the broad interrelated topical areas: *school counseling, gifted education, urban education*, and *multicultural education/counseling*. In less than eight years, Dr. Moore has made significant contributions to these fields. For example, he has published over 80 publications and has given over 150 different scholarly presentations, lectures, and keynotes around the world (e.g., United States, United Kingdom, Spain, Canada, France, China, India, etc.).

His *publications* have appeared or scheduled to appear in refereed journals, such as *Exceptional Children, Elementary School Journal, Journal of Men's Studies, Teachers College Record, Gifted Child Quarterly, Urban Education, The High School Journal, Roper Review, Theory Into Practice, Journal of Counseling & Development, Journal of Mental Health*, and *NASAPA Journal, American Behavioral Scientist*, and *Professional School Journal*. He signed book contracts with Charles C. Thomas Publishers to coedit (with Dr. Deryl F. Bailey of University of Georgia) *Survival of the fittest: Navigating your way through the counselor education graduate school experience*, with Peter Lang Publishers to coedit (with Dr. Chance W. Lewis of Texas A&M University) *Urban school contexts for African American students: Crisis and prospects for improvement*, with University Press of America, Inc. to co-edit (with Dr. Lawrence O. Flowers of Fayetteville State University and Lamont A. Flowers of Clemson University) *The evolution of learning: Science, technology, engineering, and mathematics (STEM) education at historically Black colleges and universities*, and with Sage Publishers to coauthor (with Dr. Donna Y. Ford of Vanderbilt University) *Multicultural counseling for diverse gifted learners: A guide for practice*. Additionally, he has obtained over $3.5 million in funding.

ABOUT THE BOOK EDITORS

Chance W. Lewis is the Carol Grotnes Belk Distinguished Full Professor and Endowed Chair of Urban Education at the University of North Carolina at Charlotte. Additionally, Dr. Lewis is the Executive Director of the University of North Carolina at Charlotte's Urban Education Collaborative, which is publishing a new generation of research on improving urban schools. Dr. Lewis received his B.S. and M.Ed. in Business Education and Education Administration/Supervision from Southern University in Baton Rouge, Louisiana. Dr. Lewis completed his doctoral studies in Educational Leadership/Teacher Education from Colorado State University in Fort Collins, Colorado.

Dr. Lewis currently teaches graduate courses in the field of Urban Education at the University of North Carolina at Charlotte. His experiences span the range of K-12 and higher education. From 2006 to 2011, Dr. Lewis served as the Houston Endowed Chair and Associate Professor of Urban Education in the College of Education at Texas A&M University. Additionally, he was the co-director of the *Center for Urban School Partnerships*. In 2001–2006, he served as an assistant professor of teacher education at Colorado State University. From 1994 to 1998, Dr. Lewis served as a Business Education teacher in East Baton Rouge Parish Schools (Baton Rouge, LA), where he earned Teacher of the Year honors in 1997.

Dr. Lewis has over 100 publications including 60 + refereed journal articles in some of the leading academic journals in the field of urban education. Additionally, he has received over $4 million in external research funds. To date, Dr. Lewis has authored/coauthored/coedited eight books: *White teachers/diverse classrooms: A guide for building inclusive schools, eliminating racism and promoting high expectations* (Stylus, 2006); *The dilemmas of being an African American male in the new millennium* (Infinity, 2008); *An educator's guide to working with African American students: Strategies for promoting academic success* (Infinity, 2009); *Transforming teacher education: What went wrong with teacher training and how we can fix it* (Stylus, 2010); *White teachers/diverse classrooms: Creating inclusive schools, building on students' diversity and providing true educational equity*

[2nd edn.] (Stylus, 2011); *African Americans in urban schools: Critical issues and solutions for achievement* (Peter Lang, 2012); *Yes we can!: Improving urban schools through innovative educational reform* (Information Age, 2011); and *Black Males in postsecondary education: Examining their experiences in diverse institutional contexts* (Information Age, 2012).

Ivory A. Toldson is an associate professor at Howard University, senior research analyst for the Congressional Black Caucus Foundation, and editor-in-chief of *The Journal of Negro Education*. Dr. Toldson has more than 60 publications and research presentations in 32 US states, Puerto Rico, Dominican Republic, Scotland, South Africa, Paris, and Barcelona. He has been featured on C-SPAN2 Books, NPR News, The Al Sharpton Show on XM Satellite Radio, and WKYS 93.9, and his research has been featured on *The Root*, Essence.com, BET.com, *The Griot*, and *Ebony Magazine*. He gave expert commentary in three documentaries on Black male achievement: Beyond the Bricks, Hoodwinked, and the Promise Tracker. Known as a "myth buster," Dr. Toldson has publish reports challenging the merits of popular research reports and news sources that present negative statistics about Black people, which have been widely discussed in academic and popular media. He is a contributing educational editor for *The Root* and *Empower Magazine*. Dubbed a leader "who could conceivably navigate the path to a White House" by the *Washington Post*, "a modern day Harlem Renaissance writer," by the *New African Journal*, and "Young Researcher of the Year" by Southern University, Dr. Toldson, according to Howard University's *Quest Magazine*, is "a much sought-after lecturer and researcher on a number of serious sociological and psychological issues that have implications for African Americans." According to *Capstone Magazine*, "Toldson has spent a lot of time traveling across the country talking with teachers about misleading media statistics that invariably either link Black males to crime or question their ability to learn." In 2005, Dr. Toldson won EboNetwork's Changing Faces award for outstanding literary achievement for his novel, *Black sheep: When the American dream becomes a black man's nightmare*. Dr. Toldson is also the author of "The Breaking Barriers Series," which analyzes academic success indicators from national surveys that together give voice to more than 10,000 Black male pupils from schools across the country. Through his consulting firm, CREATE, LLC, he routinely works with schools to increase their capacity to promote academic success among Black males. After completing coursework for a Ph.D. in Counseling Psychology at Temple University, Dr. Toldson became a correctional and forensic psychology resident at the United States Penitentiary. There, he completed his dissertation on Black Men in the Criminal Justice System. Upon completion, Dr. Toldson joined the faculty of Southern University and became the fourth recipient of the prestigious DuBois Fellowship from the US Department of Justice. He also served as the clinical director of the Manhood Training Village. He has received formal training in applied statistics from the University of Michigan, and held visiting research and teacher appointments at Emory, Drexel, and Morehouse School of Medicine.